NORWAY

NORTH AMERICA

EUROPE

ASIA

TSUSHIMA
May 27, 1905

ATLANTIC OCEAN

AFRICA

Emden's cruise

SOUTH AMERICA

Russian fleet's route
1904–1905

KEELING ISLAND
Emden destroyed
Nov. 9, 1914

INDIAN OCEAN

CORONEL
Nov. 1, 1914

FALKLAND ISLANDS
Dec. 8, 1914

Bergen

SKAGERRAK

Skagen

SWEDEN

BATTLE OF JUTLAND
May 31 to June 1, 1916

JUTLAND PENINSULA

DENMARK

HORNS
REEF

BALTIC SEA

RUSSIAN FLEET
October 1904

Heligoland   Bight

Rendsburg

Kiel

SEA

Kiel Canal

Rostock

helling

Lübeck

Wilhelmshaven   Bremerhaven

Hamburg

Ems Estuary

Jade Estuary

Elbe River

Berlin

HOLLAND

RUSSIAN

EMPIRE

SCALE IN MILES

0   50   100   150   200   250   300

G E R M A N Y

° E.   8° E.   10° E.   12° E.   14° E.   16° E.   18° E.   20° E.

The Seafarers THE DREADNOUGHTS

The Cover: The apogee of World War I battleship design, the superdreadnought *Queen Elizabeth* displays her might and majesty in this postwar painting by Oscar Parkes. Mounting eight immense 15-inch guns, she could fire a barrage 15 times heavier than that of Admiral Nelson's flagship *Victory* in 1805 at Trafalgar.

The Title Page: On this hand-painted porcelain bowl, a British cruiser *(center)* escorts German dreadnoughts and cruisers toward internment at Scapa Flow on November 21, 1918; in the background are dreadnoughts of the British Grand Fleet. Made by the Minton Company just after World War I, the bowl was part of a limited edition commemorating British victory.

The Seafarers

THE DREADNOUGHTS

by David Howarth
AND THE EDITORS OF TIME-LIFE BOOKS

TIME-LIFE BOOKS, ALEXANDRIA, VIRGINIA

Time-Life Books Inc.
is a wholly owned subsidiary of

TIME INCORPORATED

FOUNDER: Henry R. Luce 1898-1967

Editor-in-Chief: Henry Anatole Grunwald
President: J. Richard Munro
Chairman of the Board: Ralph P. Davidson
Executive Vice President: Clifford J. Grum
Chairman, Executive Committee: James R. Shepley
Editorial Director: Ralph Graves
Group Vice President, Books: Joan D. Manley
Vice Chairman: Arthur Temple

TIME-LIFE BOOKS INC.

MANAGING EDITOR: Jerry Korn
Executive Editor: David Maness
Assistant Managing Editors: Dale M. Brown (planning),
George Constable, Thomas H. Flaherty Jr. (acting),
Martin Mann, John Paul Porter
Art Director: Tom Suzuki
Chief of Research: David L. Harrison
Director of Photography: Robert G. Mason
Assistant Art Director: Arnold C. Holeywell
Assistant Chief of Research: Carolyn L. Sackett
Assistant Director of Photography: Dolores A. Littles

CHAIRMAN: John D. McSweeney
President: Carl G. Jaeger
Executive Vice Presidents: John Steven Maxwell,
David J. Walsh
Vice Presidents: George Artandi (comptroller);
Stephen L. Bair (legal counsel); Peter G. Barnes;
Nicholas Benton (public relations); John L. Canova;
Beatrice T. Dobie (personnel); Carol Flaumenhaft
(consumer affairs); James L. Mercer (Europe/South
Pacific); Herbert Sorkin (production);
Paul R. Stewart (marketing)

The Seafarers

Editorial Staff for *The Dreadnoughts:*
Editor: George G. Daniels
Picture Editor: Jane N. Coughran
Designer: Herbert H. Quarmby
Text Editors: Anne Horan, Sterling Seagrave
Staff Writers: William C. Banks, Michael Blumenthal,
Carol Dana, Susan Feller, Stuart Gannes, Gus Hedberg,
Mark Steele
Chief Researcher: Charlotte A. Quinn
Researchers: W. Mark Hamilton, Mindy A. Daniels,
Philip Brandt George, Barbara Levitt, Trudy W. Pearson,
Blaine McCornick Reilly, Peggy L. Sawyer
Art Assistant: Michelle René Clay
Editorial Assistants: Adrienne George, Ellen P. Keir

Special Contributors
Ezra Bowen, Champ Clark (text); Barbara Hicks,
Katie Hooper McGregor (research)

Editorial Production
Production Editor: Douglas B. Graham
Operations Manager: Gennaro C. Esposito,
Gordon E. Buck (assistant)
Assistant Production Editor: Feliciano Madrid
Quality Control: Robert L. Young (director),
James J. Cox (assistant), Daniel J. McSweeney,
Michael G. Wight (associates)
Art Coordinator: Anne B. Landry
Copy Staff: Susan B. Galloway (chief),
Sheirazada Hann, Elise D. Ritter, Celia Beattie
Picture Department: Marguerite Johnson,
Nancy Cromwell Scott
Traffic: Jeanne Potter

Correspondents: Elisabeth Kraemer (Bonn);
Margot Hapgood, Dorothy Bacon, Lesley Coleman
(London); Susan Jonas, Lucy T. Voulgaris (New York);
Maria Vincenza Aloisi, Josephine du Brusle (Paris);
Ann Natanson (Rome).
Valuable assistance was also provided by: Judy Aspinall,
Ann Usborne, Penny Newman, Karin B. Pearce (London);
Carolyn T. Chubet, Miriam Hsia, Christina Lieberman
(New York); Marie Thérèse Hirschkoff (Paris); Mimi
Murphy (Rome); Traudl Lessing (Vienna).

The Author:
David Howarth brings to his books a practical knowledge of ships and the sea. During World War II he served as a lieutenant commander in the Royal Navy and spent four years in the Shetland Islands organizing fishing boats with crews of Norwegian volunteers to land agents and arms in occupied Norway. After the War he designed and built boats, then turned to writing full time. His books include *Trafalgar,* and, in the Seafarers series, *The Men-of-War.*

The Consultants:
John Horace Parry, Professor of Oceanic History at Harvard University, was educated at Cambridge University, where he took his Ph.D. He served in the Royal Navy during World War II, rising to the rank of commander. He is the author of *The Discovery of the Sea,* and *Trade and Dominion.*

Clark G. Reynolds, curator of the museum ship, U.S.S. *Yorktown* at Patriots Point, South Carolina, has taught at the U.S. Naval Academy at Annapolis. He received his Ph.D. from Duke University. He is the author of *Command of the Sea: The History and Strategy of Maritime Empires,* and numerous articles on military history.

William Avery Baker, a naval architect and engineer, spent 30 years with the Shipbuilding Division of Bethlehem Steel Corporation, designing vessels of all sizes up to supertankers. In 1963 he became curator of the Hart Nautical Museum at the Massachusetts Institute of Technology. He is author of *The Engine Powered Vessel.*

Antony Preston, for some years on the research staff at the National Maritime Museum, is naval editor of *Defence* magazine. He is the author of *Battleships 1876-1977, Battleships of World War I,* and many other books and articles on warship design and technical aspects of naval history.

For information about any Time-Life book, please write:
Reader Information, Time-Life Books,
541 North Fairbanks Court, Chicago, Illinois 60611.

TIME-LIFE is a trademark of Time Incorporated U.S.A.

Library of Congress Cataloguing in Publication Data
Howarth, David Armine, 1912-
   The dreadnoughts.
   (The Seafarers)
   Bibliography: p.
   Includes index.
   1. Battleships—History. 2. Great Britain. Navy—
History. 3. Navies—History. I. Time-Life Books. II.
Title. III. Series.
V800.H87   359.3'2'520941   78-27881
ISBN 0-8094-2713-3
ISBN 0-8094-2712-5 lib. bdg.
ISBN 0-8094-2711-7 ret. ed.

Contents

Chapter 1

A Teutonic challenge to Britannia's rule

Awesome in its majesty, the British fleet is reviewed by the royal yacht (right) at Spithead in 1897. But dreadnoughts soon made the fleet obsolete.

n the afternoon of June 26, 1897, a sun-warmed day of the rare sort the Victorian English liked to call "Queen's weather," 165 British warships lay imposingly at anchor at Spithead, an arm of the sea lying between Portsmouth and the Isle of Wight. Strung out in five arrow-straight columns—their freshly painted raven hulls gleaming darkly against bright red water lines, their white upper works sporting ocher-yellow smokestacks—the warships stretched on for five miles toward the sea: 21 battleships, 42 cruisers of various classes, 30 long, lean destroyers, 20 torpedo boats and another 52 miscellaneous craft. The gathering was the most formidable ever assembled at a single anchorage. And, to the tens of thousands of exhilarated spectators who lined the shore and bobbed about the water in small craft, the fleet was all the more impressive for the fact that it represented only one half of the Royal Navy. Some 165 other vessels were guarding British interests in Bombay and Hong Kong, Sydney and Kingston, and dozens of other ports scattered across the Seven Seas.

The occasion for this Naval display was the Diamond Jubilee of Queen Victoria, during whose reign the British Empire had expanded until it encompassed a staggering 11 million square miles, one quarter of the globe. And of all the proud symbols of that vast, abounding and dynamic empire, none could equal the Royal Navy. More than 330 ships strong, with 92,000 officers and men, it was by far the largest and most powerful navy in the world. Government policy mandated that it be maintained equal in size to the navies of any two world powers that might seek to challenge it—a circumstance that had not arisen for nearly a century, since Admiral Horatio Nelson had destroyed the Combined Fleet of France and Spain at Trafalgar in 1805. The Royal Navy was the true bond of the Empire, observed the London *Times*; without it the Empire would be "merely a loose aggregate of States." And so it was appropriate that, on this final day of a week-long gala in honor of the Queen and her Empire, the culminating ceremony should be a review of Her Majesty's fleet at Spithead.

At precisely 2 o'clock the royal yacht *Victoria and Albert* edged her gilded prow out from the shore to be saluted by the waiting ships. Standing conspicuously on the quarter-deck was the portly figure of the Prince of Wales, wearing the uniform of an Admiral of the Fleet and representing his 78-year-old mother (who was watching through a telescope from a castle on the Isle of Wight). Behind the royal yacht in stately procession came a train of magnificent private and Naval vessels that carried rank upon rank of assorted dignitaries: the *Enchantress* with the Lords of the Admiralty on board; the *Wildfire* with a panoply of colonial premiers; the *Eldorado* with a delegation of foreign ambassadors; the *Danube* with virtually the entire House of Lords; and the Cunard liner *Campania* with the members of the House of Commons as well as a horde of journalists.

Up and down the ranks of warships the reviewing flotilla passed, while the guns thundered, the shipboard bands played "God Save the Queen," and the seamen lining the rails raised their caps to the Prince of Wales and roared deep-throated cheers. Coming to a halt alongside the flagship *Renown*—a 12,350-ton behemoth bearing four 10-inch guns, ten 6-inchers, a dozen 12-pounders and 22 others of various sizes—the royal visitor received the fleet's flag officers aboard his yacht for congratulations and expressions of mutual esteem. Then the *Victoria and Albert* steamed back to Portsmouth, while the anchorage once again resounded with 165 ships' companies roaring cheers in unison. The men were cheering not only the Queen and her son, the future monarch; they were cheering the Royal Navy itself—and their cheers were joyously answered by the spectators in the harbor. Observed *The Times* with satisfaction: "Truly a marvelous pageant and one which Britons may take pride in knowing to be such as could be exhibited by no other nation, nor indeed by all of them put together."

Hardly anyone present at Spithead or reading *The Times* suspected it, but that proud and magnificent fleet, for all its pomp and glory, represented the end of an era. Incredibly, within a single decade it would be ordered scrapped by an acerbic admiral named John Arbuthnot Fisher, who at the time of the Spithead celebration was preparing to assume command of the North American and West Indies Station, the least significant of the Navy's five divisions and the one that watched benignly over the friendly North Atlantic and Caribbean.

The cold fact—which scarcely anyone realized—was that the Royal Navy, smugly basking in agelong memories of invincibility, was obsolescent and vulnerable. It had not kept pace with the Industrial Revolution that fueled the very empire the Navy was charged with protecting. The Navy's last innovation had been to discard sail for the reciprocating steam engine 25 years before. Since then, battleship design had remained virtually unchanged—despite the fact that new developments in machinery, weapons and explosives had proceeded apace. The fleet was a hodgepodge of vessels of such varying size, speed and armament that coordinated fleet action—had the Navy been called upon for such—would have been difficult if not impossible.

To begin with, the machinery that moved the Royal Navy was ancient. All the ships were powered by the piston-driven reciprocating steam engine. That device, a marvel when invented more than a century before, had long since reached the virtual limit of its development. It was clumsy, heavy and subject to frequent breakdown. In its most modern models, it could drive a ship at a speed of 18 knots—but 11 knots was the best that could be expected from most of the ships at Spithead.

The reciprocating engine was also incredibly messy. "When steaming at full speed in a man-of-war fitted with reciprocating engines," remembered Sir Reginald H. Bacon, then a Royal Navy captain, "the engine room was always a glorified snipe marsh; water lay on the floor plates and was splashed about everywhere; the officers often were clad in oilskins to avoid being wetted to the skin. The water was necessary to keep the bearings cool. Further, the noise was deafening; so much so that telephones were useless and even voice pipes of doubtful value." An answer to its problems was available: an eccentric tinkerer named Charles Parsons had already invented the turbine engine, which provided direct rotary power from fanlike vanes turned by steam, had fewer parts and was therefore more dependable. It was also quiet and dry. But the Navy had been paying no heed.

Armament presented other problems. British ships had for nearly a century been collecting guns like barnacles, with the result that the strengths and virtues of one kind often canceled out those of another. The newest of the vessels at Spithead carried four modern 12-inch guns, mounted on the broadside; but they also carried a dozen 6-, 8- and 10-inch guns, and a number of 3-, 6- and 12-pound cannon. The 12-inch guns could be accurately fired only 2,000 yards, scarcely more than the smoothbore cannon used in Nelson's time; the rest had such varying ranges and different rates of fire that they could not be used effectively at the same time. Two of the vessels at Spithead, both more than 20 years old, actually carried no armament more modern than muzzle-loading cannon firing shells that would bounce harmlessly off all but the thinnest plate of armor.

Meanwhile, munitions-makers had already developed artillery pieces that could hurl projectiles 4,000 yards and more with accuracy, and powerful new explosives that could punch through armor like the eight-inch plate of the flagship *Renown* as if it were paper.

Some of this technological advance was taking place in England, the home of the Industrial Revolution. But—as was becoming increasingly evident—a new industrial genius was stirring across the North Sea in Germany, a late-comer to imperial and maritime circles alike. With Germany's growing technological prowess came increasing trade, and an appetite for the worldwide power that such prowess bestowed. And soon that growing might was to thrust upon England a challenge of the first magnitude. "In the coming century," German Foreign Minister Bernhard von Bülow was shortly to assert in a public address, "the German people must be either the hammer or the anvil." And there was no doubt as to which function he expected them to serve. Germany's ruler, Kaiser Wilhelm II, expressed the point even more bluntly: "The trident must be in our fist."

Wilhelm's allusion to the trident—the three-pronged spear that, as the traditional symbol of sea power, had long been firmly grasped in Britannia's right hand—was no casual bit of imagery. At the moment, although Germany could boast a superb army, she possessed only a mediocre navy. With a paltry 68 vessels to Britain's 330, Germany ranked a lowly fourth among the world's naval powers, behind France (with 95 warships) and Russia (with 86). But this poor standing the Kaiser was determined to rectify.

His instrument would be a brilliant admiral named Alfred von Tirpitz, who believed no less than Wilhelm in Germany's claim to the trident. Together they would mount the first serious threat to British naval supremacy in a century. The threat was to provoke a naval upheaval in Britain. Under the impetus of "Jacky" Fisher—who in 1904 was to become Tirpitz' opposite number in London—the British Admiralty would unveil a totally new warship in 1906. That ship was the H.M.S. *Dreadnought*, bigger, faster and more powerfully armed than any other ship in history. So many and so effective were her innovations—in propulsion, in armor, in her huge guns that could hurl shells with great

Splendidly attired in full-dress military uniform, Kaiser Wilhelm II in this 1903 portrait appears the very image of Germany's "Supreme War Lord," as he titled himself. A lifelong Navy buff, he brought all his weight to bear in the drive to forge a powerful High Seas Fleet, which he unabashedly—and with some justification—called "my creation."

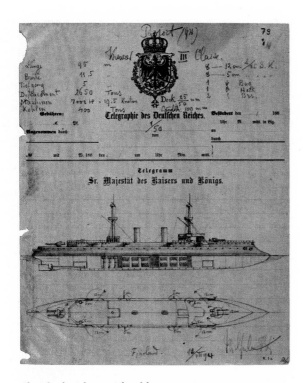

Sketched with considerably greater detail than might be expected for something drawn on a telegram form, this 1894 design of the Kaiser's for a medium cruiser was greeted with polite condescension by professional naval architects. "Very very lovely," one German official wrote privately about the Kaiser's warship sketches, "only they could not float."

accuracy farther than the eye could see—that with her launching every other warship instantly became obsolete.

The H.M.S. *Dreadnought* represented such a quantum leap in war at sea that she gave her name to a whole new class of ship and triggered the greatest naval arms race the world had ever known. Beginning in 1906, dreadnoughts came down the ways of British and German shipyards in ever-increasing numbers, with greater tonnage and higher speed, more and more guns of larger and larger caliber. And when war erupted in 1914, the new dreadnoughts overturned sea-war tactics that had been in use for some 200 years.

Kaiser Wilhelm, who with Tirpitz was principally responsible for the German Navy's sudden efflorescence, was a man of quick intelligence but erratic whims and poor judgment. He had no grasp of the human forces at work in his nation. In a day of rising demands everywhere for social equality, and a widening prosperity among the working classes to make it possible, he was capable of proclaiming, without any sense of anachronism: "The soldier and the army, not parliamentary majorities and decisions, have welded the German Empire together," and "We Hohenzollerns derive our crowns from heaven alone and are answerable only to Heaven."

As a grandson of Queen Victoria (whose eldest daughter, Victoria, had married Crown Prince Friedrich of Prussia), Wilhelm was a nephew of the Prince of Wales, later to become King Edward VII. The two men were bitter rivals. Wilhelm was known to refer to Edward as "an old peacock" and "a Satan"; Edward denounced Willie, as the family called him, as an *"enfant terrible,"* saying that his "pleasure seems to be to set every country by the ears." And it sometimes appeared that Wilhelm lusted after a navy for no better reason than that his rich and powerful uncle had one.

There were deep veins of psychological pressure underlying the Kaiser's personal pique. As the offspring of an English princess and a Prussian prince he had had the ideals of two cultures drummed into him with bewildering contradiction beginning in babyhood, providing a legacy of conflict and confusion that were to beleaguer him throughout his life. "Bring him up simply, plainly," Queen Victoria counseled her daughter in 1865, when Willie was a boy of six, "not with that terrible Prussian pride and ambition." But at seven the child was turned over to a stern Prussian tutor, George Hinzpeter, who from then until the Prince was 20 imposed on his charge a regimen that would have exhausted a weaker boy than the resilient Willie.

Lessons began at 6 or 7 a.m. and might go on till after sunset. Besides schoolbooks, the instruction included visits to museums, factories and mines, and plenty of fresh air and exercise. An injury to a nerve at birth had left Wilhelm with a permanently shrunken and lifeless arm, a fact that in later years he could disguise by hiding his hand in his pocket or resting it on the hilt of his sword. But it also left him with a lack of balance, which was not so easy to camouflage. The tutor drove his young pupil to overcome that defect by force of will, seating him without stirrups on a pony and doggedly remounting the child every time he fell off.

Willie learned to ride. He also learned to hold himself as erect as any Prussian soldier, and—with only one good arm—to swim, play tennis and shoot. The compulsion for physical exercise remained with him all his life. As Kaiser he kept a rowing machine in his bedroom, and on his yacht, so went the tale, he led guests in compulsory early-morning calisthenics on deck. The yacht was one of his first purchases on coming to the Crown in 1888 on the death of his father.

Kaiser Wilhelm's strong attraction to the sea owed itself at least in part to his maternal connections. As a boy—and indeed as Kaiser—he attended many a naval review in England as the guest of his grandmother. Clearly, these events made a profound impression. Once in a flight of poetic fancy he composed a "Song to Aegir," the Teutonic god of the sea. As Kaiser he painted a picture of a squadron of torpedo boats attacking a fleet of ironclad warships, and had it exhibited at the Berlin Academy of Art.

If Wilhelm's love of things naval was romantic, he also had compelling practical reasons for finding a navy essential to his imperial equipage. When he came to the throne, the world was viewing the rosy dawn of an unparalleled burst of economic productivity. In Germany, per capita income was to soar from 417 marks a year in 1890 to 716 in 1911 in a period of very little price inflation. As farm boys eager to share in the industrial boom left the countryside to work in the factories turning out steel, chemicals, optical instruments and all manner of manufactured goods, the percentage of the German population living in towns rose from 47 in 1890 to 60 in 1910. The shift brought a corresponding rise in urban representation in the Reichstag, Germany's lower house of parliament, and a counterweight against members of the older landed and military aristocracy who, with their minds on the frontiers with France, the Low Countries, Poland, Austria and Switzerland, had never looked out to sea.

World trade trebled in the years between 1880 and 1913—and Germany was one of the principal beneficiaries. British exports during that period, while maintaining an absolute lead, dropped proportionately from almost 40 per cent of the world total to around 27 per cent. But Germany's exports during the same interval rose by a spectacular 240 per cent, and her share of the world total swelled from 17 per cent to 22 per cent.

One of the reasons for Germany's sudden increase in trade was the Kiel Canal, the cornerstone of which was laid just one year before Wilhelm's accession to the throne. That marvel of industrial progress cut right through the base of the Jutland peninsula south of Denmark and reduced the voyage between Germany's Baltic and North Sea coasts from about 700 miles to 61. The canal had the effect of doubling German naval strength. The fleet, which previously had to be divided between the Baltic and the North Sea, could now be completely assembled in one sea or the other on short notice.

Another factor crucial to Wilhelm's thinking was the phenomenal growth of Germany's most important industry, steel. In 1888 Germany was still importing steel plate from England. Shortly thereafter, the great Krupp steelworks—already grown rich by providing Germany with

With the flag-bedecked German fleet in the background, government officials and their guests gather along the gigantic locks of the Kiel Canal for the gala dedication of the waterway in 1895. The 61-mile canal across Jutland was crucial to German ambitions, allowing the High Seas Fleet to move rapidly between the Baltic and the North Sea.

A Baltic mermaid (lower right) and a sister enchantress from the North Sea clasp hands, heralding the opening of the Kiel Canal in this 1895 commemorative postcard. Constructed between the reigns of Wilhelm I (center, left) and Wilhelm II (center, right), the canal, which cut days from the passage around Jutland, conferred commercial benefits as well as strategic advantages.

ever-lengthening miles of railroad track, mounting numbers of railroad cars and guns—added facilities for manufacturing steel plate. By 1897 German steel-plate production was double that of England. And steel plate was a *sine qua non* of warships.

For German statesmen and merchants, no less than the impulsive Kaiser Wilhelm himself, it was easy in the flush of quickening success to leap to the conclusion that their vigorous nation was overtaking an older rival whose star was setting. And as they were gaining on the English economically, it did not seem unreasonable that their country should challenge the bulwark on which British supremacy rested—the hallowed Royal Navy.

The man who made it possible to bring that bright hope within an ace of realization was Alfred von Tirpitz. The son of a Prussian civil servant, he was born in Brandenburg in 1848. At 16 he enlisted in the Prussian Navy as a midshipman. Quickly displaying a genius for engineering and for tactical principles, he rose through the ranks, becoming a rear admiral in 1895. He left Germany the following year to command a squadron of cruisers in the Far East, where German commercial interests were rapidly growing.

Tirpitz was a suave and seemingly amiable person who could effect a touch of the modesty that the Kaiser conspicuously lacked. "As a scholar

I was very mediocre," he wrote of himself; but in executing the job with which the Kaiser charged him he revealed a penetrating intellect. His comments on his own countrymen were shrewd, sometimes amusing and often critical. The Prussians, he said, "looked as if they had swallowed their ramrods." The typical German was "an incorrigible political illusionist; he wavered between two extremes, the fear of power and the intoxication of power." The German view of world politics was ill informed and prone to unrealistic hopes and fears.

Any one of those observations would have described the Kaiser himself, and in fact it was by fanning just such hopes and fears that Tirpitz first came to the monarch's notice. In the early 1890s, Tirpitz began writing memorandums for the Prussian Navy on the importance of sea power. He took his cue—as, for that matter, did most naval thinkers of the day—from a book called *The Influence of Sea Power upon History* by Alfred Thayer Mahan, an American Naval officer and historian who was one of the first writers to document the correlation between economic and political power on the one hand and prowess on the sea on the other (*pages 24-25*).

Mahan ascribed the rise of the British Empire to that island nation's domination of the sea. In Tirpitz' lucid mind, the inverse of Mahan's thesis presented itself: without sea power, there could be no political power for Germany in the modern world. In becoming an industrial nation, Germany had made herself dependent on rubber, oil and cotton imported from afar, Tirpitz pointed out. "If we intend to go out into the world and strengthen ourselves commercially by means of the sea," he wrote, "then if we do not provide ourselves simultaneously with a certain measure of sea power, we shall be erecting a perfectly hollow structure." Stated baldly, that meant Germany must build a navy to guard against imperial predators.

To the Kaiser, with his streak of megalomania, such a theory naturally struck a responsive chord. Before long he had plucked the author from his outpost in the Far East and installed him in Berlin in the new post of Secretary of State of the Imperial Naval Office, and charged him with building a navy to challenge the British.

Tirpitz settled into his new post in early June, 1897, just before England's gala review at Spithead. At his desk by seven every morning, he swiftly raised a staff, appointed committees and set them to work— exploring the latest in ship design, gunnery and shells; examining training programs; studying docks and shipyards.

One of his shrewdest moves was to enlist public support for building a large, modern navy. "We organized meetings and lectures and made special efforts to get in touch with the press on a large scale," Tirpitz recalled in his memoirs. "We instituted tours to the waterside and exhibited the ships and the wharves; we turned our attention to the schools and called upon authors to write for us; stacks of novels and pamphlets were the result."

The drive paid off. In December 1897, when Tirpitz went before the Reichstag, his proposals for a brand new fleet were swiftly voted into law. The new Navy Bill, a document of astonishing aspirations, called

Symbolizing France's fear of the emerging German Naval power, two cockade-wearing women turn their backs in despair as an international fleet, including French warships, inaugurates the new Kiel Canal in this cover for an 1895 Paris magazine supplement. The French agreed to participate only out of diplomatic politeness; said one officer, "The peaceful intentions that Emperor Wilhelm has manifested make it our duty to take part in the celebration."

for the construction of no fewer than 69 vessels. Among them were to be 19 battleships of 13,000 tons, and a dozen armored cruisers ranging from 9,000 to 11,000 tons. The ships would double the size of the German fleet—all in the short space of seven years, and at a phenomenal cost to the public of 408 million marks.

Construction got under way immediately. In two years' time, the keels for five new battleships were laid down. In general design they were much the same as the most advanced ships the British had shown at Spithead in 1897, having reciprocating engines of 16,000 horsepower and mixed armament, ranging from 6.7- to 11-inch guns and 24-pounders for antitorpedo cannon.

The first ships were no sooner launched than Tirpitz was ready with another, and even more ambitious, plan—and the assiduously courted Reichstag was ready to listen. In January 1900 he put before it a second Navy Bill. This one not only called for building three new ships a year, it also included plans for enlarging harbors and docks to contain them. And it called for recruiting more officers and men, and establishing new schools for training them.

The bill passed the Reichstag with a two-thirds majority. Ironically, it was among the middle classes in the Reichstag—the representatives Wilhelm so bitterly scorned—that his enthusiasm for the Navy won its readiest support.

Notwithstanding the pains he took to educate the German public on the desirability of having a navy, Tirpitz remained close mouthed about any details that would give away too much information. But he was unable to restrain the ebullient Kaiser from flaunting the nation's burgeoning might. Wilhelm invited his English uncle, now King Edward VII, to pay a state visit in June 1904, for the express purpose of showing off the Navy at Kiel.

Edward accepted, and with him came a retinue that included the Earl of Selborne, First Lord of the Admiralty, and a number of other high-ranking Naval officers. To Tirpitz' chagrin, the Kaiser insisted on parading almost the whole available strength of the German fleet before the anxious English eyes. The fleet now included an astonishing 25 battleships commissioned just since the beginning of the Tirpitz program, some of them displacing 13,000 tons and carrying batteries of four 11-inch guns, fourteen 6.7-inchers and another 16 miscellaneous smaller weapons. As the reviewing yacht traced its path back and forth between the lines of warships, King Edward "exchanged many meaningful looks and words with Selborne," Tirpitz noticed, "which impressed me unpleasantly."

A British warship commander with the royal party noted in his official report: "The Germans are straining every nerve to perfect their Navy as a fighting machine." And indeed it was not necessary to visit Kiel for Englishmen to feel a growing sense of alarm. The German Ambassador, reporting from London to Berlin later during the summer, related a rising stridency in the English press. Even the moderate *Spectator* pronounced Germany to be "the mischief-maker of the world." The Ambassador concluded: "Most of the papers regard every step in the progress of

our fleet as a menace to England." So did virtually the whole English population. England was clearly being challenged.

The challenge was not being ignored by the British government. Naval budgets had already risen from £21,823,000 in 1897 to £34,457,000 in 1904. In that period England had laid down 28 new battleships, with the undisguised aim of staying ahead of Germany's mounting numbers. But something more complex than numbers was now at stake. A fundamental change in the essence of naval strategy was slowly evolving, forced by the technological changes wrought by machine power and weaponry. It would take someone of surpassing genius to discern that fact in the din of the moment, and to seize the initiative and resolve matters.

The genius arose in the person of John Arbuthnot Fisher, whose brilliance enabled him to see in a flash the virtues of untested hypotheses. He was, as well, an utterly ruthless man, who forged single-mindedly ahead toward his goals, irrespective of whose views he might call into question or whose prerogatives he overrode. "His was not the method of leading smoothly but of driving relentlessly and remorselessly," remembered Admiral Alfred Ernle Montacute Chatfield, who would one day succeed Fisher as First Sea Lord—the top-ranking Naval officer. Fisher served as Britain's counterweight to Germany's Tirpitz, while at the same time facing quite a different problem. Tirpitz had created a navy where none existed; Fisher pitted himself against a venerable institution of hidebound tradition and no inclination to change in a world that demanded change for survival.

Fisher came to the Admiralty as First Sea Lord in 1904, at the age of 63, with a string of impressive achievements already behind him—and a reputation for rasping eccentricity preceding him. "Heaven only knows what he may not attempt to run," said a rueful Admiral Sir Reginald Custance, a commander stationed in the Mediterranean. "Any wild cat scheme finds a supporter in him."

A more favorably inclined observer would have called Fisher's schemes foresighted. The fact was that Fisher was the first among his colleagues in the Navy to seize on virtually every innovation of the era. In the 1860s, the electrically detonated torpedo (then a stationary mine, not the self-propelled missile of later years) had no sooner appeared than he proposed the Navy should adopt it—though, as he later recalled, the Navy's attitude to the newfangled device was summed up by a First Sea Lord who "told me that there were no torpedoes when he came to sea and he didn't see why there should be any of the beastly things now."

As Director of Naval Ordnance in 1886 he had ordered the muzzle-loading guns still in use at the Navy's gunnery school discarded. He then installed the newer, quick-firing, breech-loading weapons already in use in the fleet. Just after the turn of the century, given charge of officer training at Dartmouth and the Isle of Wight, he required all officers to "stoop to oil their fingers"—i.e., to acquaint themselves with the working of steam engines—though many officers of the day thought they were meant to pace the deck like Lord Nelson, not sully themselves with the work of their social inferiors belowdecks. Such were among the harebrained schemes that Fisher had espoused.

Rear Admiral Alfred von Tirpitz, Germany's top-ranking Naval officer and a relentless advocate of dreadnoughts, brusquely declared in a secret 1897 memorandum: "The military situation against England demands battleships, in as great a number as possible."

This tin German medallion was issued in 1897 as part of a nationwide campaign to promote popular support for the Kaiser and his all-out drive for naval power. The medal shamelessly flatters Wilhelm II as a "bold warrior," as well as Germany's "savior in distress."

Seamen and young officers regarded this irregular fellow with a mixture of terror and affection—terror because he was pitiless when conducting drills, affection because of his humor and his concern for the men's well-being. "He prowled around with the steady rhythmical tread of a panther," recalled one junior officer who served under him. "The quarterdeck shook and all hands shook with it. The word was quickly passed from mouth to mouth when he came on deck. 'Look out, here comes Jack.' "

But the same man also remembered Fisher's attention to living conditions. The admiral introduced the first knives and forks to the seamen's mess (previously seamen had been expected to make do with spoons and their fingers) and the first bakeries to supply fresh bread daily. And he had been known to clamber into the colliers to coax weary seamen through the thankless task of coaling.

They also remembered the hilarious parties he gave off duty, where he could seldom restrain the impulse to dance, whether or not there were ladies present to serve as partners. "He pulled me out, off we went, faster and faster, dashing about, whirling and whirling," one junior officer recalled. "We caught our legs in another pair and rolled over and over in the scupperway of the quarterdeck. Everyone was convulsed with laughter, including the Admiral."

For an admiral to be so free from pomposity before his men was extraordinary, and that was what seamen and young officers loved about Jacky Fisher. If older and stodgier officers looked askance at such antics, they could not deny that Fisher had a galvanizing effect on the Navy. As Commander in Chief of the Mediterranean Fleet between 1899 and 1902 he had replaced routine cruises with tactical and strategic exercises, experimented with new fire-control techniques that increased the accurate range of big guns to as much as 7,000 yards, staged gunnery contests between ships with prizes for the winners and in general made the Mediterranean Fleet the most effective in the entire Navy. When the post of First Sea Lord became vacant in 1904, Fisher was the natural candidate. As a matter of courtesy and shrewd politics, Fisher's name was first submitted to King Edward VII, who wielded a considerable influence on naval affairs. And that forward-looking monarch quickly approved the nomination.

Fisher chose to take office on a suitably dramatic day—the 99th anniversary of Admiral Nelson's historic victory at Trafalgar. "I join the Admiralty on 21st October," he wrote a friend, "a good fighting day to begin work."

He already had a plan for what he meant to do—a plan that, several weeks in advance of taking office, he had thrust upon the Earl of Selborne, the First Lord of the Admiralty (who, as the Cabinet minister in charge of the Navy, was Fisher's boss). "I sat him in an armchair in my office," Fisher recalled, "and shook my fist in his face for two and a quarter hours without a check; then he read 120 pages of foolscap, and afterwards collapsed."

Whenever Fisher was excited about anything—which was most of the time—he wrote in the tone of a tabloid newspaper, with headlines, capital letters, exclamation points, underscorings and epigrammatic

"Fighting made me what I am"

The man who revolutionized the Royal Navy enjoyed none of the family wealth or position that helped so many of his contemporaries rise to exalted rank. John Arbuthnot Fisher, born in 1841 in Ceylon, was the son of a coffee planter so impecunious that he had to ship his seven children back to England to live on the charity of relatives. Many a youngster would have been blighted by such a fate. But it made Fisher a scrapper. "I had to fight like hell for everything," he later recalled, "and fighting made me what I am."

At the age of 13, Fisher joined the Navy as a cadet and immediately applied his pugnacious nature to the task of shaping his destiny. He worked "like a young elephant," as he put it, to learn seamanship and mathematics. At 20 he turned to gunnery and mastered all the newest techniques so rapidly that within six months he became an instructor aboard the three-decker *Excellent*, which was the Navy's principal gunnery school.

Fisher's ability left an indelible impression on his superiors, and at age 28 he was promoted to commander and assigned to the flagship *Ocean* on the China Station. He chafed at spit-and-polish routine and groused about devoting "severe thought to the cleaning of paintwork."

Off duty, he turned to analyzing flaws in the Navy and to penning treatises on gunnery, ammunition, battle tactics and naval administration. "My heart is full," he once wrote, "of things in the Service which appear to want capsizing." It proved a prophetic statement. For in the end, Fisher did virtually capsize the old Royal Navy in order to build the most fearsome fighting fleet the world had ever seen.

As First Sea Lord in 1905, Jacky Fisher shows the bulldog determination that first won him an admiral's flag in 1890 at the relatively young age of 49. Fisher said his formula for success was tackling any assignment with "the earnestness, if need be the fanaticism, of a missionary."

As a young lieutenant, 24-year-old Jacky (right) joins his siblings, brother-in-law (seated) and two nieces for a portrait in 1865, the only time all the Fisher children gathered together. Fisher's own children, said a biographer, were raised in almost "complete ignorance of their father's brothers and sisters."

At 19, when this picture was made, Fisher served briefly as acting master of his admiral's sloop Coromandel. This early taste of command was a reward from the admiral, who found Jacky "sharp, well-conducted and anxious to do his duty."

At 42 and captain of the gunnery training ship Excellent, Fisher was known as an inspiring and exacting officer who, wrote a colleague, "electrified the men and made them work as if for their lives."

Commanding the Mediterranean Fleet, 59-
year-old Vice Admiral Fisher relaxes on
the Renown in 1900. Even in friendly waters
he kept each ship at combat readiness.

Clustered around his son, Cecil, on his
graduation from Oxford, Fisher, his wife and
their daughters share a rare close moment:
for him the Navy was "in first place."

phrases. The 120-page memorandum with which he assailed Lord Selborne was no exception. In it were wrapped up his exuberance over his own ideas, his impatience to get on with the work, and his penetrating foresight. "The whole scheme must emerge next Christmas morning from the Board of the Admiralty," he exclaimed in the preamble, "like Minerva from the head of Jupiter." Because the scheme he proposed would make the Navy more economical in the long run, he went on, "the country will acclaim it! the income-tax payer will worship it! the Navy will growl at first! (they always do growl at first!) BUT WE SHALL BE THIRTY PER CENT MORE FIT TO FIGHT AND WE SHALL BE READY FOR INSTANT WAR!"

In spite of the hyperbole of his language, the scheme that Fisher proposed was a model of plain sense. It called for four sweeping reforms. The first was the introduction of a so-called nucleus crew system, by which reserve ships were to be manned at all times with at least two fifths of their full complement (instead of idling virtually empty, as was the custom) and thus be ready much more quickly for service. The second was for a redeployment of the Navy's five fleets, thinning out the forces in trouble-free spots such as the Caribbean and the Indian Ocean, and concentrating the greatest strength closer to home. The third was perhaps the most dramatic of all: across a list of 154 outmoded British warships he scrawled the bold prescription, "Scrap the lot!" And the fourth proposal was for a massive building program that would modernize the Navy's fleet of battleships, cruisers, destroyers and submarines. Most particularly he wanted to concentrate on a new kind of super-battleship that would be the greatest fighting machine ever built. "The first duty of the Navy is to be instantly ready to strike the enemy," he wrote, "and this can only be accomplished by concentrating our strength into ships of undoubted fighting value."

About the only one of Fisher's proposals to go unchallenged was the one for the nucleus crew; nobody argued with the wisdom of keeping ships at the ready. The other proposals were hotly contested. Imperialists predicted the doom of the Empire in the shifting of the fleets. Fisher countered with logical reasoning. He pointed out that the Navy's far-flung stations harked back to the days of sail. "The wind formerly determined the course of action," he wrote. "Fleets and ships were formerly days coming into action. Now only minutes." The fact was that it had formerly taken three months to sail to India; in 1904 an 18-knot steamer took less than a month.

Not surprisingly, the scrapping policy drew the loudest cries of outrage from those who insisted that the size of the Royal Navy was its greatest asset. To such reasoning Fisher retorted: "Millions of ants can do nothing against one armadillo!" To the milder protest of Lord Selborne, who said that "a reserve of old battleships would be of great value after Armageddon," Fisher rejoined that the old battleships in question made the fleet nothing but "a floating museum from bygone ages." The scrapping order held, and by the end of 1905 ninety ships had been condemned to the wrecker's yards at a saving of tens of thousands of pounds in maintenance costs.

By Christmas, Fisher had appointed a Committee on Designs, with

Applauding Admiral Fisher's plan to remove obsolete ships from the British fleet, a 1904 London newspaper illustration catalogues their defects: "unarmoured and slow," "small gun power," "wasteful of coal." Fisher (center) "cultivated the Press unblushingly," noted a contemporary journalist, "and we rewarded him with such an advertisement of himself and his ideas as no seaman ever received from the newspapers."

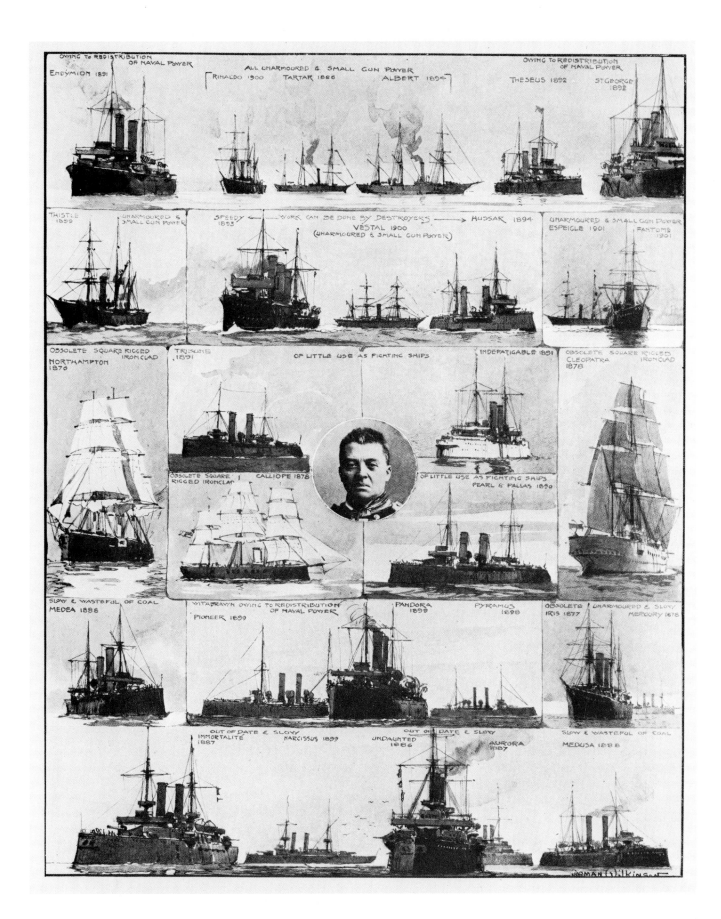

OWING TO REDISTRIBUTION OF NAVAL POWER

ENDYMION 1891

ALL UNARMOURED & SMALL GUN POWER

RINALDO 1900   TARTAR 1886   ALBERT 1894

OWING TO REDISTRIBUTION OF NAVAL POWER

THESEUS 1892   ST GEORGE 1892

THISTLE 1899   UNARMOURED & SMALL GUN POWER

SPEEDY 1893   WORK CAN BE DONE BY DESTROYERS   HUSSAR 1894

VESTAL 1900
(UNARMOURED & SMALL GUN POWER)

UNARMOURED & SMALL GUN POWER

ESPEIGLE 1901   FANTOME 1901

OSSOLETE SQUARE RIGGED IRONCLAD

NORTHAMPTON 1876

TRIBUNE 1891

OF LITTLE USE AS FIGHTING SHIPS

INDEFATIGABLE 1891

OBSOLETE SQUARE RIGGED IRONCLAD

CLEOPATRA 1878

OBSOLETE SQUARE RIGGED IRONCLAD   CALLIOPE 1878

OF LITTLE USE AS FIGHTING SHIPS

PEARL & PALLAS 1890

SLOW & WASTEFUL OF COAL

MEDEA 1888

WITHDRAWN OWING TO REDISTRIBUTION OF NAVAL POWER

PIONEER 1899

PANDORA 1899   PYRAMUS 1898

OBSOLETE

IRIS 1877   UNARMOURED & SLOW   MERCURY 1878

OUT OF DATE & SLOW

IMMORTALITE 1887   NARCISSUS 1899

OUT OF DATE & SLOW

UNDAUNTED 1886   AURORA 1887

SLOW & WASTEFUL OF COAL

MEDUSA 1888

NORMAN WILKINSON

himself as chairman, to implement his fourth proposal, the building of a whole new fleet centered around a new kind of battleship. Two questions were at issue in the design of this fleet. One was speed. Some tacticians saw speed as valuable only to a weaker fleet, one that must run from danger. Throughout British Naval history, speed had been secondary to stout hulls and overwhelming firepower; battles were fought broadside to broadside with the opposing lines moving along at a snail's pace. But to Fisher, alert to the prospects offered by modern technology, speed was "the first desideratum in every class of fighting vessel," for "then, and only then, we can choose our distance for fighting."

The other question at issue had to do with armament, and the answer to that one followed from the first. "If we can choose our distance for fighting, then we can choose our armament for fighting! But how in the past has the armament been chosen?" he asked rhetorically. "Doesn't it sometimes look like so many of each sort as if you were peopling the Ark, and wanted representatives of all calibers?"

Before the matter was settled, there occurred an event on the far side of the world that briefly diverted attention from Anglo-German rivalry, and at the same time gave the Admiralty a chance to check some hypotheses at no cost to the British.

In February 1904, eight months before Fisher's arrival at the Admiralty, Japan and Russia came to blows in the Far East, where both had imperial designs on Manchuria and Korea. Japan proved to have an unexpectedly efficient navy and, in a series of engagements that culminated off Port Arthur in August 1904, had wiped out the full complement of Russia's Pacific Fleet of 40-odd ships. Doggedly determined to carry on the war, Czar Nicholas II renamed his Baltic Fleet the Second Pacific Squadron and ordered it to steam to Vladivostok. From its station at Kronstadt on the west coast of Russia there was only one way to get there: a tortuous voyage of 18,000 miles by way of the Atlantic, the Indian Ocean and the South China Sea, then through the strait that separated Korea and Japan, and past the Japanese island of Tsushima.

It was a fool's errand, for any number of reasons. The war on land was already lost; with the Russian Pacific Fleet out of action, Japan had landed expeditionary forces in Manchuria and was laying siege to the Russian enclave of Port Arthur. That port city would capitulate four months before the Baltic Fleet could reach the area. Moreover, since the Russian Pacific Fleet had shown itself incapable of dealing with the surprising Japanese, what reason was there to think that the Baltic Fleet, completely inexperienced in Far Eastern waters, would have any greater success?

"Ten thousand Russian men led not into battle but to the sacrificial altar," wrote Captain Vladimir Semenov, one of the few ranking officers to have survived the earlier debacle at Port Arthur. Semenov had made his way back to western Russia, and now was with the hastily assembled fleet that steamed out of the Baltic on October 16, 1904. Semenov alone seems to have understood fully the melancholy fate that awaited the Russian Navy in Japanese waters.

The Commander in Chief of the Imperial Japanese Navy was Admiral

The American oracle of sea power

ALFRED THAYER MAHAN

"The due use and control of the sea is but one link in the chain of exchange by which wealth accumulates; but it is the central link." So asserted an obscure American Navy captain named Alfred Thayer Mahan in his 1890 treatise: *The Influence of Sea Power upon History*. Mahan was stating what the British had understood for centuries, but he developed the thesis with such cogent reasoning and applied it so effectively to international politics that his work soon circulated among government leaders and naval officers the world over. Indeed, both the Germans and the British quoted Mahan in rationalizing their great race for naval supremacy.

The man who was to become the oracle of sea power graduated from Annapolis in 1859 and saw action aboard several Union warships during the Civil War. Yet Mahan was more a historian than line officer and soon turned to a study of naval battles for their effect on history. By 1886, he was President of the Naval War College and preaching that "control of the sea was a factor which had never been systematically appreciated." Examining the history of Europe and America, Mahan concluded that in one struggle after another, victory went to those with mastery of the sea. Moreover, naval power far more than army strength was the decisive factor in "the control over distant regions." Finally, wrote Mahan, strong fleets of capital ships, even when not engaged in battle, exerted a sort of "noiseless pressure, whose silence is the most striking and awful mark of its working."

Within a few years of publication, Mahan's book had been translated into Russian, French, Italian, Spanish, Japanese and German. Kaiser Wilhelm II confessed, "I am now not just reading it, but devouring Captain Mahan's book. It is on board all my ships." In England, which won Mahan's admiration for "firm maintenance of sea power and the haughty determination to make it felt," Prime Minister William Gladstone proclaimed Mahan's work "the book of the age." And when Mahan visited London in 1894, he was accorded the signal honor of becoming the first foreigner ever invited to dine at the Royal Navy Club—where he was given three rousing cheers by an assembled throng of 100 admirals and other high-ranking officers.

Heihachiro Togo, who combined a stout impassivity with a fondness for British tradition. As a young Naval cadet in the 1870s, Togo was selected by his commanders to take special training in England. He served two years aboard the 52-gun sailing man-of-war *Worcester*, and studied mathematics at Cambridge, naval engineering at Greenwich and gunnery at Portsmouth. Returning to Japan in 1878, he fulfilled the expectations of his patrons, rising rapidly to take command of the Japanese main fleet by 1900.

The fleet was not large—but it was as well prepared as he was himself. It consisted of four battleships, eight heavily armored cruisers and a number of smaller cruisers and torpedo boats, which brought the total to about 60. The battleships were armed like the newest British ships, with four 12-inch guns and a miscellaneous array of smaller guns. The 12-inch guns were supplied with a newly perfected hypersensitive shell that exploded much more readily than older models. The slightest contact—even against a wireless aerial—would send a shower of steel and flame down on the target. Moreover, the shells were packed with a new Japanese explosive called shimose, which reached hotter temperatures more quickly than other powders. And along with that fearsome armament went speed. Virtually every unit of the fleet could steam at a respectable 18 knots.

Above all, the men—Togo's comrades and pupils during eight years of his command—were supremely well trained, with a discipline that Togo never let slacken. After dealing the final *coup de grâce* to the Russian fleet at Port Arthur, Togo had taken his own fleet back to Japan, where he set his men to target practice with the new shells while the ships underwent repairs. He wasted not a moment during the lull before the next confrontation.

Against this powerful and tightly knit force the Russians sent from the Baltic a makeshift fleet that was plagued from the start with mishaps, delays, demoralized men and poor command.

The Baltic Fleet had 12 major warships—the same number as the Japanese—but only five were new, and each of these had failings. The flagship *Suvorov* was designed for a displacement of 13,500 tons and a speed of 18 knots, but she had had so much equipment hastily added as an afterthought—mostly in the form of extravagant fittings in the officers' quarters—that she now displaced well over 15,000 tons; she was top-heavy and unstable, and could manage only 16 knots. The *Alexander III* was a knot slower than that. The *Borodino*'s engines overheated at only 12 knots and had to be shut down to cool off, or the vessel held to a lower speed. The *Orel* was so new that she had not even finished her trials, and she broke down twice during the voyage to the Far East. The fifth new ship was the *Svetlana*, with an impressive speed of 20 knots, but she was only a lightly armed cruiser.

The remaining seven major warships were so inadequate that Captain Semenov ruefully likened them to "old flatirons and galoshes." Some were almost 40 years old, and a number mounted hopelessly obsolete muzzle-loading cannon. Altogether, including a hodgepodge of destroyers and supply craft, the fleet numbered 38 vessels. Its speed was that of the slowest unit—11 knots.

The man in command of the ill-fated mission was to prove no more promising than the ships. He was Admiral Zinovy Rozhestvensky, who had never commanded a fleet in combat in his life but who had the great good fortune to have served as a favored aide to the Czar. He was a large man, tall and strong, with an imposing presence; in uniform with his full beard and all his military decorations on his chest he looked every inch the fighting admiral.

Alas, his behavior did not live up to his looks. Although most of the men he commanded were raw recruits hastily brought into service since the Port Arthur debacle, he appears to have given no attention to training during the voyage. Neither did he convey to his officers any plan of battle against the enemy that lay in wait at the end of the journey. Instead, Rozhestvensky spent the voyage seated on his bridge, watching to make sure that the ships stayed in line and kept the prescribed distance from one another, and filling everyone from officers to seamen with terror, recalled a sailor who made the voyage, "as though he had been a 15-inch shell about to burst." And burst he did, if a ship dared to fall out of position. Then, the sailor continued, "after a volley of oaths directed at the offending vessel the order would come: 'Signal that idiot a reprimand!' "

The fleet's overriding problem was coal. Half a million tons were needed to fuel the fleet around the world, but most coaling stations everywhere were in the hands of the British, who had been allied since 1902 with Japan and had closed their stations to the Russians. So the Russians had to carry as much coal as possible, packing every ship until she was grossly overloaded. The flagship *Suvorov* had bunkers for 1,100 tons; she had to carry twice that load. Coal was everywhere, recalled Semenov, "not only up to the neck but over the ears." There was coal in bags on deck; and coal dust in the heads, coal dust in the boats, coal dust in the food lockers. When the original supply ran out, the ships had to coal at sea, from colliers fetched from whatever friendly ports the Russians could find along the way. Coaling in any circumstances was messy and arduous, but it was especially nightmarish in the tropics, as at Dakar in French West Africa. Inside the bunkers the temperature was 115°, and the strongest and healthiest men could stand the job for only 20 minutes at a time.

Between a bearish commander, the stifling heat, the choking coal and the snail's pace of the voyage, Russian morale was at rock bottom when on May 27, 1905, the fleet finally reached the Strait of Korea—seven months after leaving home. But the Russians were now entering on the last 600-mile leg of the journey. The weather was misty. They had not yet been sighted, and hope rose that they might reach Vladivostok—and supplies—before having to face the Japanese. "How can they find us in weather like this?" the commander of the *Suvorov* asked Semenov. "Look! You can't even see the rear of the fleet! It's two hundred thousand to one against anyone running into us accidentally."

But Togo, unlike Rozhestvensky in his bridge-top armchair, had left nothing to accident. He had stationed scouts along the route, while he himself waited in perfect calm aboard his flagship, the *Mikasa*, in Chinnae Bay, Korea, 90 miles to the north. At dawn on May 27, the Japanese

auxiliary cruiser *Shinano Maru* sighted the first of the Russian ships, and relayed the information to Togo by wireless. "All the conditions of the enemy were as clear to us," wrote Togo, "as though they had been under our very eyes." The Russians steamed on, unaware of the approaching catastrophe.

On board the Japanese warships, Togo reported, "the whole crews of our fleet leaped to their posts. Our ships weighed at once, and each squadron, proceeding in order to its appointed place, made its dispositions to receive the enemy." Moving at more than half again the speed of the Russians, the Japanese fleet reached the Strait of Tsushima shortly after noon on that day. At 1:45 p.m. the Russians for the first time made out the Japanese battleships approaching in line ahead—but only dimly, for the Japanese ships were cleverly shrouded in gray-green paint that faded into the gray-green ocean mist.

The biggest naval confrontation since Trafalgar was about to begin. At 1:55 Togo hoisted a flag signal reminiscent of the one Nelson had conveyed to the British fleet before that historic battle 100 years earlier: "The fate of the Empire depends upon today's event. Let every man do his utmost!"

To the uneasy Russians, who were steaming in two parallel but staggered columns, Togo's first maneuver was mystifying. He turned to starboard and swept across the path of the Russian line. This was a maneuver, called crossing the "T," that had been much debated by naval strategists in recent years. Theoretically it enabled the crossing fleet to concentrate its broadside fire on the leading vessel of the enemy line, while the enemy, in line-ahead formation, was unable to fire, except for the bow turrets of the lead ship. But Togo made the move while still seven or eight miles away, and out of range, so that it brought him no immediate advantage; he was aiming to reach a position opposite the Russians' port column, which his scouts had reported to be the weaker of the two lines. His next move was even more perplexing. He led the fleet in a great U-turn, moving the ships so that they pivoted, one after the other, until they lined up on a parallel course on the Russians' port side. The maneuver involved a daring risk, because at the moment of the pivot, the Russians had a perfect chance to hit each ship as she was taking her turn in the maneuver. Semenov saw the chance. "My heart beat furiously," he recalled. "If we could only put one out of action! The first success—was it possible?"

With a well-drilled crew it should have been possible—but not with the inexperienced recruits under Rozhestvensky's uncertain leadership. He finally summoned up a few ranging shots at 9,000 yards, a lucky one of which struck the *Mikasa*, the Japanese flagship, knocking down her bridge ladder and nicking Togo in the thigh. But the *Mikasa* moved on without further damage, and Togo stoically held his post. Then the Russians fell into confusion, firing wildly but with little effect. In 15 minutes Togo's ships had all come through the perilous turn with no disabling damage, and the two fleets were broadside to broadside, about 7,000 yards apart. Only then did Togo send the new Japanese shells howling over the water at the Russians—concentrating on the flagship *Suvorov* and the *Oslyabaya*, an elderly hulk nearby.

Under an officer's watchful eye, the crew of a Russian warship shovels coal into wicker baskets, which were then carried from dockside bins into the ship's bunkers. This exhausting process, which afflicted all navies, could keep fully 25 per cent of a fleet in harbor at any one time and was one of the evils Jacky Fisher sought to correct in the Royal Navy; he regarded it as "criminal folly" and in 1912 led a drive to convert British ships from coal to infinitely more efficient oil fuel.

The effect of the new shells devastated the Russians. "They burst as soon as they touched anything," wrote Semenov aboard the *Suvorov*. "Handrails were quite sufficient to cause a thoroughly efficient burst. Iron ladders were crumpled up into rings, and guns were literally hurled from their mountings." The heat of explosion made everything combustible burst instantly into flames. Fires broke out everywhere, flying splinters tore the hoses to shreds; the air was filled with flame and blood and flying metal.

The *Suvorov*'s bridge was hit; inside it Rozhestvensky suffered wounds in his head and his legs. Crippled and only half-conscious, he was transferred to the destroyer *Buiny*. Other shells disabled the flagship's steering and communications gear. Nearby, the *Oslyabaya*, having been pierced at the water line, suddenly upended and sank bow first, taking with her hundreds of sailors who were trapped in the blazing engine room below.

The battle was decided within the hour, as one after another of the Russian ships became an inferno. Togo relentlessly kept up a barrage until seven that evening, and as darkness fell he ordered his torpedo boats to finish off the remaining Russian ships, while he retired his battle fleet. The next day a Russian junior admiral surrendered what wreckage was still afloat, and what men were still alive, including the comatose Admiral Rozhestvensky.

The toll was fearsomely one-sided. In half a day and a night, 20 Russian ships had been sunk—among them four of the new warships. Another seven struck their flags and surrendered; two foundered and sank after the battle. Six ships escaped the Japanese and made for the neutral ports of Shanghai and Manila, where they were interned. One was unaccounted for and presumably lost. Of the 38 ships that had begun the awful voyage from Kronstadt nearly eight months before, only two slipped through the inferno to reach Vladivostok. Some 6,000 men were taken prisoner; more than 4,000 were killed or drowned. In the Japanese fleet, by contrast, only three torpedo boats were lost. Japan's casualties totaled 116 killed and 538 wounded.

Every other navy in the world examined the Battle of Tsushima with rapt attention, and out of the Russian disaster two facts emerged. One was that speed was crucial. Togo's fast-moving battleships had determined the nature and the arena of the fight, cornering their Russian prey before the latter could counter. Even without the added handicap of Rozhestvensky's deficiencies as a commander, the sluggish Russian ships were deathtraps. A few slow ships jeopardized not only the unlucky men aboard them, but the whole fleet, which was held to the pace of its most laggard member.

The other fact, less readily seen, was the overriding importance of the big long-range 12-inch guns. The smaller guns and the torpedo boats had played a role, to be sure, but they came onstage only for the finale, delivering the death blow to ships already mortally wounded. The issue had been decided within the first hour of battle, when the big guns hit their targets from 7,000 yards off. As would later come to light, there were a number of virtues to all-big-gun armaments beyond their power-

Admiral Zinovy Rozhestvensky, whose Russian fleet was destroyed at Tsushima, led such panicky crews that en route to the Pacific they fired on British trawlers, thinking them to be Japanese warships.

Admiral Heihachiro Togo, the victor at Tsushima, was a master at training and tactics. He recommended that all naval officers learn to play chess because "it teaches much about the study of war."

Under smoke-smudged twilight skies, Russian sailors abandon a pair of sinking ships and take to their boats in this somewhat overwrought scene from the Battle of Tsushima by a Japanese artist. The fight was so one-sided that within an hour, wrote an observer, the movements of the Russian ships "could no longer be dignified by the name of tactics; they became nothing more than the efforts of a defeated fleet to escape."

ful size and long range; for the moment it was enough to note that the lesser guns of 10 and 8 inches with their short range were excess baggage on battleships.

All of this, of course, had been foreseen by Britain's Jacky Fisher. The First Sea Lord called for an immediate analysis after the annihilation of the Russian fleet at Tsushima. "If, as seems probable, the lesson is equally appreciated and acted on by other maritime powers," said the report in part, "it is evident that all existing battleships will shortly become obsolescent, and our preponderance of vessels in that class will be of little use."

Actually, Fisher had already started the process of scrapping useless ships, and replacing them with modern ones. In his fidgety hand, Fisher scribbled in the margin alongside that passage: "How glad we ought to be that we dropped out the battleships and armored cruisers last year! Why, they are now as obsolete as the Ark!"

But the mighty Royal Navy would not be obsolete much longer. Fisher had already given orders to lay down the keel of the ship that was to be the H.M.S. *Dreadnought.* With her advent, a new round of the naval arms race was set to begin.

Training for a new era of ships without sails

One of Jacky Fisher's firmest beliefs was that the men of a navy were every bit as important to its effectiveness as were warships. In 1902, he became Britain's Second Sea Lord, responsible for all Naval training, and although he held the position for only 15 months, in that time he boldly launched the most ambitious and farsighted educational reform in Royal Navy history.

Fisher felt the old system of instructing officer-cadets for only 18 months aboard moored training vessels before sending them off to sea was in effect offering them no training·at all; on the hulks they learned Naval routine but very little of the complexities of modern warfare. Fisher sharply reduced the role of the old ships, and instead established two Naval colleges ashore: one at Osborne on the Isle of Wight and the other at Dartmouth on the south coast of Devon. Cadets spent two years at Osborne studying basic skills and general academic subjects, then went on for two more years at Dartmouth, where they specialized in advanced naval science and mechanics. "The education of all

our officers, without distinction," insisted Fisher, "must be remodelled to cope with machinery instead of sails."

To provide their education and still send midshipmen to sea at the age of 16, Fisher lowered the entry age from 14 to 12 years old. He also tried to push through a scholarship system so that all qualified boys could enter the corps, "irrespective of the depth of their parents' purse." Traditionally students paid a £75 yearly tuition fee, except for the sons of Army, Navy and Marine officers, who were admitted for a £40 annual fee. Fisher's scholarship proposal failed at first, but was instituted almost a decade later.

At the same time, Fisher moved to reform the training of seamen. He built schools for ratings in several major ports, with technical programs for gunners, signalmen and boy artificers—the lads who would become the Navy's engine-room specialists. Inevitably these reforms brought howls of protest from the Navy's old guard, but Fisher held fast. "The Naval Rip Van Winkles have dubbed it a d----d revolutionary scheme," he wrote. "So it is!"

Officer-cadets practice with semaphore flags at Dartmouth College. Since wireless was in its infancy, flags were still the preferred method of communication between ships, and Fisher insisted upon "greater celerity and simplicity" in their use.

On a hillside overlooking the River Dart the Royal Naval College at Dartmouth looms above the old school for officer training—the two 19th Century wooden warships moored at right. Completed ' in 1905, Dartmouth had facilities for about 400 cadets, almost 150 more than the dank, vermin-infested hulks.

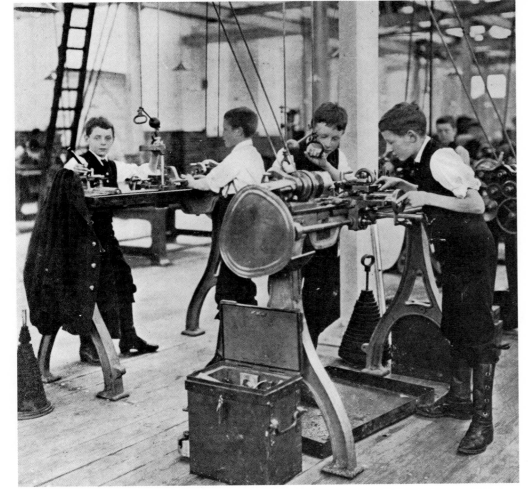

Coatless and with their shirt sleeves rolled up, young cadets gingerly learn to operate lathes and other machine tools in the shop at Osborne College in 1903. Related Fisher: "The Naval Officer of the future will think no more of handling machinery of any sort than the ordinary mortal does of riding a bicycle."

Easing the wheel onto a new compass heading, an apprentice seaman practices his helmsmanship on a simulator at Shotley Barracks, one of the schools for ratings founded by Fisher. "When we went to sea," a graduate recalled, "we knew as much as the Ordinary Seaman, though of course we hadn't put it into practice."

Mustered for a lecture about the inner workings of a steam engine, boy artificers—candidates for engine-room duty—study a diagram of a steam piston, and compare it with a cutaway model. "These boys," Fisher boasted, "are suckled on the marine engine."

START   1   2   3

Balancing on their stomachs, seamen at Portsmouth learn the breast stroke on dry land before venturing into the water. Vital for survival, and valued as healthy exercise, swimming was considered by the Admiralty to be a part of the training of every seaman.

At dockside in 1910 a young sailor puts swimming theory to the test. Until the instructors were certain the candidate could float, the seaman practiced with life lines secured around his waist. As a final test, all seamen were required to swim 100 yards with their clothes on.

Armed with stiff brushes, apprentice seamen scrub down a spread of canvas on the training ship St. Vincent in Portsmouth Harbor. Fisher abolished training cruises in sailing ships in 1903, but the youngsters still gained a sense of tradition by living for a while at dockside on board an old man-of-war.

Bent double as they strain at a line, trainees at Portsmouth struggle past a small mountain of washtubs, encouraged by the barracks band. It was customary in the British Navy for a ship's band to cheer the men with a tune during especially onerous tasks.

Morning prayers over, seamen at the Portsmouth Naval barracks emerge from chapel on the double as petty officers jog alongside. Fisher, a deeply religious person who once sat through four sermons in a single day, considered religion an integral part of training.

Chapter 2

The fabulous fleet that Jacky built

hile the Russian fleet was still steaming blindly toward its doom off the coast of Japan in early 1905, First Sea Lord John Arbuthnot Fisher's Committee on Designs in London was already thrashing out the plans that would overhaul the Royal Navy from stem to stern. "I'll alter it all," Fisher had vowed as he embarked on his new assignment, "and those who get in my way had better look out. I'll ruin anyone who tries to stop me." In a memorandum circulated among his colleagues at the Admiralty, Fisher wrote: "The new Navy is to be absolutely restricted to four types of vessels, being all that modern fighting necessitates." He listed the four: battleships of 15,900 tons, capable of making 21 knots; armored cruisers of 15,900 tons, 25½ knots; destroyers of 900 tons, 36 knots; and submarines of 350 tons, 13 knots.

The committee that Fisher assembled to bring the radical new fleet into being was a distinguished body of seasoned Naval officers and eminent civilian scientists and industrialists. Together they shared an awesome pool of knowledge about guns and armor, fire control and torpedoes, propulsion, fuel, and communications. Among the civilians were such luminaries as Sir Philip Watts, a naval architect who had left private enterprise to become Director of Naval Construction at the royal shipyards at Portsmouth, and Lord Kelvin, an Irish mathematician and physicist at the University of Glasgow who was famous for devising the Kelvin temperature scale and who had invented an underwater cable that made international telegraphy a reality. The Naval officers included Rear Admiral Prince Louis of Battenberg, Director of Naval Intelligence, who was a nephew by marriage of Edward VII, and 46-year-old Captain John R. Jellicoe who, like Fisher, was a crack practitioner and teacher of gunnery. Unknown outside Naval circles at the time, Jellicoe was destined to command the new fleet when its fateful hour came.

The committee's first order of business was the battleship. For Fisher, the opportunity to put his hand to such a creation represented a dream come true. While overseeing gunnery exercises afloat, one of his favorite commands had been an axiom of Napoleon's, *Frappez vite et frappez fort* ("Hit fast and hit hard"), and Fisher had long wished for ships that would strike harder and steam faster than any yet known. Five years before, in 1900, he had induced his friend W. H. Gard, then Chief Constructor at the British dockyards at Malta, to work up sketches for a battleship that would achieve his ideal. Fisher called his imaginary battleship the *Untakeable,* and that was the working name by which the committee called their aborning project in early 1905. Nobody knows how the epochal and aptly symbolic name *Dreadnought*—meaning "fearless"—was eventually chosen. But the name was an old one that had been used seven times before for Royal Navy vessels (the first *Dread-*

The immense steel hull of H.M.S. Dreadnought lies in dry dock at Portsmouth in April 1906, preparatory to being fitted with her superstructure and her enormous 12-inch guns. Built at a cost of £1,783,883, half again the amount spent on earlier battleships, she was labeled "a piece of wanton and profligate ostentation" by her critics. But the British Admiralty considered her firepower the equal of almost three existing warships.

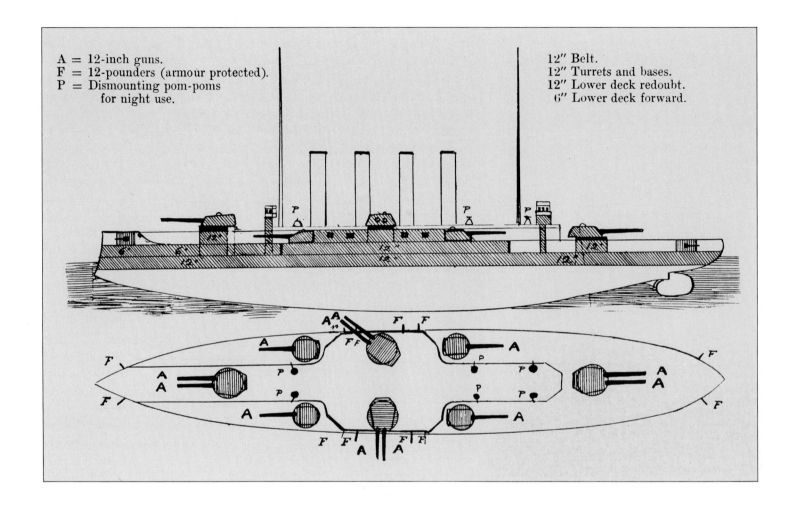

A = 12-inch guns.
F = 12-pounders (armour protected).
P = Dismounting pom-poms
      for night use.

12″ Belt.
12″ Turrets and bases.
12″ Lower deck redoubt.
6″ Lower deck forward.

nought had been among the ships that fought the Spanish Armada in 1588) and reflected an old British tradition of investing ships with spirit by giving them awe-inspiring names.

By any name the ship now under consideration represented a daring venture in seafaring—and yet, for all her novelty, she was a vessel whose time had come. Though Fisher was later generally credited with having invented the *Dreadnought,* he did not in fact originate the idea of her definitive features, the all-big-gun armament and the dazzling speed. As advances in gunnery had made it possible to fire from greater and greater distances, and as ships became increasingly cluttered with miscellaneous ordnance, naval opinion throughout the world had for some years been drifting in the direction of combing out the superfluous and settling on a heavy, uniform armament.

Aside from bringing the heaviest firepower to bear at the longest possible range, uniform armament would greatly simplify the problems of range finding, ascertaining the distance of the target. Historically, range finding and fire control had been a haphazard affair, and they would continue to be so until the advent of Admiral Sir Percy Scott's electrically powered director firing in 1912 (*pages 114-117*). However, in the meantime range finding would remain not much more advanced than in Horatio Nelson's time. Officially it was known as "spotting" or

This 1903 plan by Italian naval architect Vittorio Cuniberti was the first formal design for a fast, heavily armored capital ship that concentrated on a single type of big gun rather than on many and various smaller weapons. Such a ship, wrote Cuniberti, could "get in at least one fatal shot from a great distance before her enemy has a chance of getting a similar fortunate stroke." Cuniberti's ship was never built, but his ideas were later used in dreadnoughts.

"bracketing"; unofficially it was wryly referred to as "go as you please."

At the onset of combat a range-finding officer posted in the conning tower would order the guns to fire a series of salvos, and "spot" the splashes by peering through a telescope to see where they landed. Then he would shout corrections through a voice pipe connected to the gun turrets, and hope for the best. Only when the splashes "bracketed" the target, half of them landing short of it and half beyond, had the correct range been found. At that the process was a prodigal one, for the bracketed area could cover an expanse as big as an acre or more. Even Admiral Togo and his superbly drilled gunners scored less than 50 per cent at Tsushima; for every 42 heavy shells that struck the Russians from 7,000 yards away, another 58 plunged futilely into the sea.

Obviously, the small guns aboard ship lay idle throughout the long-range stage of the drama. But when combat closed to a range that all the guns could reach, the difficulties of the crude spotting method were compounded. For the officer charged with the spotting, it was often difficult to discern the small-gun splashes through the more conspicuous geysers thrown up by the large ones. And even when he could determine them correctly, his task had only just begun. The 6-, 9- and 12-inch guns, having different trajectories, all required different elevations if they were to hit the same target. Thus the range-finding officer had to add to the pandemonium of battle by shouting into his voice pipe not one set of orders, but as many as there were gun sizes aboard.

The first-known blueprint for a ship able to carry a large number of big guns came from a distinguished man attached to a minor navy: Vittorio Cuniberti, architect to the Italian fleet. Cuniberti had already given Italian warships the first electrically powered gun platforms and ammunition hoists. In 1902 he proffered his government a plan for a 17,000-ton battleship armed with a dozen 12-inch guns and 12-inch armor to protect them. But Italy had neither the funds nor the facilities for building such a ship, and declined to act on his plan. Cuniberti next broached his idea to Fred T. Jane, proprietor of an annual British publication called *Fighting Ships*. Jane, whose volume was both a registry of warships in commission and a forum of current opinion, leaped at the plan and in the 1903 issue published Cuniberti's sketch, together with an article by the architect entitled "An Ideal Battleship for the British Fleet."

Aside from her big guns, the ideal ship would have an unheard-of speed of 24 knots, six knots faster than the standard of the day. "The bull in the vast ring of the amphitheater deludes himself with the idea that because he is more powerful than the agile toreador he therefore has absolute command of the scene of the combat," Cuniberti declared in a burst of Latin imagery, "but he is too slow in following up his adversaries, and these almost always succeed in eluding his terrible horns."

When Cuniberti's architectural plan appeared in Jane's publication, it got mixed reactions that reflected the mixed state of contemporary naval opinion. Conservative naval experts in England reacted to Cuniberti's ideas with attitudes that ranged from indignation to polite skepticism. Sir William White, former Director of Naval Construction, thought the elimination of secondary armament outrageous. The magazine *Engineer* took an equivocal view and hedged its bets, remarking: "Some such vessel is bound to come in the end, but we hardly think that the day has yet arrived." But the day *had* arrived. In Washington, President Theodore Roosevelt, a naval buff of more than average knowledge, proposed the building of all-big-gun ships for the U.S. Navy, and by early 1904 Congress was debating a bill that would eventually authorize the construction of two such vessels. And in Japan the Imperial Navy dockyards already had a pair laid down. However, it took Jacky Fisher, with his demonic alacrity and goading tongue, to induce the reluctant Royal Navy to get the jump on the rest of the world.

To the men whom Fisher had assembled on his committee, the problems of hodgepodge armament were by now self-evident, and at issue was not whether to opt for uniformity—that was a foregone conclusion—but how many big guns to mount, and where to locate them. The committee finally settled on 10—two fewer than in Cuniberti's design; the decrease was dictated by the fact that the committee had agreed to hold the tonnage to less than 18,000.

The arrangement the group chose called for one pair of guns in the bow; two more pairs forward of amidships, one of them on the port side and the other to starboard; and another two pairs abaft of amidships on the center line so that both could fire simultaneously on either broadside, or astern. All told, six guns could be fired simultaneously ahead or astern, or eight could be fired simultaneously on one broadside or the other. As the best of the predreadnought battleships, with their four 12-inch guns, could fire only two ahead and astern, and four on the broadside, the *Dreadnought* had power equal to three earlier battleships firing ahead, or two firing broadside. The great increase of power for forward shooting particularly pleased the aggressive Fisher, who fondly imagined that any enemy would always be "flying" from British pursuit, and therefore found end-on fire vastly more exciting than broadside action.

The design was worked out by May 1905. The blueprints went to the royal shipyards at Portsmouth; the keel was laid down on October 2. From that day forward, the building proceeded at breakneck speed. So relentlessly did Fisher hustle along everyone concerned with the construction that his insistent phrase, "Get on or get out," became a byword among the dockyard workers.

But he did more than browbeat; he introduced novel procedures that saved time at every step of the way. One of his innovations was the introduction of standard parts. The 16,500-ton battleship *King Edward VII*, undergoing completion just as Fisher's committee was working out the design for the *Dreadnought*, had thousands of steel plates girding her massive hull, and these had to be cut into uncounted different shapes and sizes from the large sheets that arrived from the steel mills, and then fitted together jigsaw-puzzle fashion, which took months. Fisher had the hull of the *Dreadnought* designed to consist mostly of interchangeable rectangles. As the loads came in from the steel mills, one ready-cut plate was usually as good as another and could be riveted into place wherever needed just at that moment; little time was lost waiting for special pieces to fit sections of the hull. By the introduction of that simple expedient, Fisher shaved nearly a year off construction time. The average turn-of-

One of the most confusing bits of nautical terminology is the use of the word ton as a measure of size. Both warships and merchantmen are rated by tonnage, but the word has a very different meaning in each case.

Since warships are nearly always fully loaded and ready for battle, naval tonnage is a measure of the vessel's weight. It is calculated by means of the Archimedean principle that a floating body pushes aside, or displaces, its weight in water. The cubic footage of a ship's hull below water at combat load corresponds to the volume of water displaced; each 35 cubic feet of sea water weighs a long ton, or 2,240 pounds.

Therefore a warship that displaces 35,000 cubic feet of sea water has a weight, or displacement, of 1,000 long tons. A typical dreadnought displaced at least 700,000 cubic feet of sea water, which translates into 20,000 tons.

In merchant shipping, tonnage has always been a measure of capacity rather than displacement. It is reckoned by dividing the usable interior volume in cubic feet by 100—an arbitrary figure. Thus a vessel that has 100,000 cubic feet of capacity is rated at 1,000 tons. This measure has nothing to do with the weight of the vessel. Indeed, the word ton itself derives from the 16th Century English practice of taxing merchant ships according to the number of wine casks—or tuns—that a ship could carry in her hold.

the-century ship was 16 months a-building from the laying of her keel to launching; the *Dreadnought*'s 527-foot hull took shape before the astonished eyes of the workmen in an unprecedented 18 weeks and was ready for launching on February 10, 1906.

Once she was launched, the fitting-out was equally rapid. Gun foundries of 1905 ordinarily required 22 months to cast 12-inch guns and their mountings. To get the 10 big guns for the *Dreadnought* would have taken a couple of years by conventional means. But Fisher, never one to be hamstrung by convention, conjured up eight of the 10 instantly; he summarily seized the guns intended for the *Lord Nelson* and the *Agamemnon*, two predreadnought battleships midway through their construction. By that action many more months were lopped off the schedule.

By such measures the *Dreadnought* was fitted out and ready to go to sea for her trials on October 3, 1906. Instead of the customary three to three and a half years required by her immediate predecessors, the mighty *Dreadnought* had sprung into being in a year and a day, a mere wink of time that seemed nothing short of providential. If Fisher did not invent the ship with all her revolutionary features, no one disputed the unprecedented rapidity with which he got her built, or the wizardry with which he orchestrated the Gargantuan undertaking.

The *Dreadnought*'s performance on sea trials was nothing short of sensational. From Portsmouth she steamed south to the Mediterranean, then shaped a course across the Atlantic to Trinidad, and back again. With her turbines she proved fully capable of steaming at her promised top speed of 21 knots; even more remarkable, she made the return trip from the West Indies, a total of nearly 7,000 miles on a round-about course, at an average speed of 17.5 knots, with no mechanical breakdown—an achievement no ship with reciprocating engines had ever equaled.

The most suspenseful moment of the trials came when it was time to fire her 12-inch guns, eight to the broadside. It was a moment that Sir Philip Watts, as director of the Portsmouth shipyards that had turned her out, awaited with trepidation. "He looked very grave and serious," wrote one officer who was present, "and I am quite sure that he fully expected the decks to come down wholesale. Presently there was a muffled roar and a bit of a kick on the ship. The eight guns had been fired and scores of men between decks had no idea what had happened." That "bit of a kick" had hurled a total of 21,250 pounds of shell 8,000 yards.

Throughout the whole voyage the *Dreadnought* showed only one flaw and encountered only one mishap; both were minor and easily remedied. The flaw was a skittish tendency to spin like a saucer when making a turn. Sir Reginald H. Bacon, who served as the *Dreadnought*'s first captain, recalled that "if the ship was given more than 10 degrees of helm when going over 15 knots, the steering engine was not powerful enough to bring the rudder central again; the ship therefore continued to turn in a circle until her speed had fallen below 15 knots." The remedy was to strengthen the steering engine, a matter easily done when the ship returned from her trials. The single mishap was that on the return trip across the Atlantic the speed mysteriously fell by a knot and then after two days just as mysteriously picked up again. It turned out that the

An "act of poetry" that brought a naval revolution

"There are few acts more poetical," wrote the London *Times* on February 10, 1906, "than that of launching a great ship, few spectacles more moving." And so it was on that wintry, overcast morning in Portsmouth as a crowd too enormous for *The Times* even to estimate jammed the dockyard quays and put out in small boats to witness the birth of H.M.S. *Dreadnought*.

Atop a bunting-bedecked platform next to the immense hull, King Edward VII stood before a distinguished gathering that included the naval attachés of 10 nations, the bulk of the Houses of Commons and Lords, Cabinet members and the Board of Admiralty. Because Britain was in mourning for Edward's father-in-law, King Christian IX of Denmark, the festivities were accented with only the most important flags and bunting, and music was almost entirely lacking. But the sense of history was so keen, noted *The Times*, "as to be quite independent of any artificial enhancement."

At the appointed time, the Bishop of Winchester blessed the ship. Then the King swung the baptismal bottle of Australian wine against the *Dreadnought*'s towering prow. Alas, the bottle failed to break. But no matter. A second, heftier swing succeeded. As the colonial wine streamed down the steel plates, the monarch used a mallet and chisel to sever a cord, releasing heavy weights that knocked away the last timbers holding the ship in place.

Amid cries of "She's moving!" the *Dreadnought* slid backward, faster and faster, smoke issuing from the friction of her wooden launching cradle moving against the ways, until she splashed into the harbor.

"In a few moments," said *The Times* account, "the event of the day was over." The *Dreadnought* was ready to receive her superstructure and armament, and join the fleet as "the latest expression of thought and experience in the domain of naval architecture."

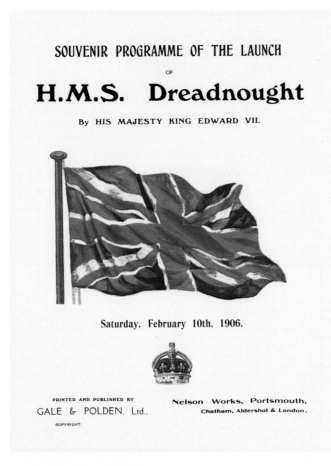

Distributed to spectators at the launching, this program contained a history of the construction of the Dreadnought, a list of her specifications and a painting of the ship as she would look under steam.

Arrayed in the bicorn hat and full-dress uniform of an Admiral of the Fleet, King Edward VII christens the mighty battleship by shattering a garland-draped bottle of wine against her stem.

Carved of oak from Nelson's Victory, a box called a launch casket, presented to Edward VII, held the mallet and chisel used to cut the Dreadnought's last ties to land. On sale to the public were handkerchiefs (right), on which the ship was pictured with one more funnel and two more turrets than it was to have.

Without superstructure or guns, the Dreadnought rides easily, flags flying, in Portsmouth Harbor after her auspicious launching in 1906.

plating had peeled off one of the rudders; it must have acted as a brake until it fell off altogether. But the rudder plating was easily replaced. Otherwise the *Dreadnought* was an unqualified success, and when she returned home in December 1906, Fisher was ecstatic with the reports. "A new name for the *Dreadnought*," he crowed. " 'The Hard-boiled Egg!' Why? Because she can't be beat!"

Like all great revolutionary departures, the *Dreadnought* provoked her share of naysayers. Sir George Clarke, Secretary to the Committee of Imperial Defense, complained that to make such an untested leap in technology was foolhardy, and pontificated: "It should be an axiom of our policy never to lead in ship construction but always to follow with something better." Sir William White, who had been Director of Naval Construction at Portsmouth prior to the advent of Fisher and Sir Philip Watts and may have been tasting sour grapes, railed against the folly of putting "all one's naval eggs into one or two vast, costly, majestic but vulnerable baskets." And the acid-tongued Admiral Lord Charles Beresford, a colleague and rival of Fisher's, snarled, "We start at scratch with that type of ship."

As a fleet commander answering directly to the abrasive First Sea Lord, Beresford had a profound dislike for Fisher and was nursing a growing grudge that colored his view of the *Dreadnought*. Nevertheless, that particular objection was widely held and had some merit. Like all such quantum leaps in weaponry, the *Dreadnought* had created a worrisome paradox for its inventors. By rendering every extant battleship obsolete, it had at a stroke made meaningless the Royal Navy's vaunted numerical superiority. What could a fleet of the old, slow, under-gunned and lightly armored battleships do against a squadron of the fearsome new dreadnoughts? The Germans could be expected to seize on the *Dreadnought* as a means of closing the naval gap—and the British would have to engage in a whole new arms race in order to maintain their historic supremacy at sea.

The *Dreadnought* was only the first of Jacky Fisher's disturbing brainstorms. Five days before the *Dreadnought* was launched in February 1906, the British dockyard at Clydebank, near Glasgow, had laid down the first of a trio of Fisher's new class of armored cruisers. They were to be the *Invincible,* the *Indomitable* and the *Inflexible*. Like the dreadnought, the new armored cruiser was the result of Fisher's fierce desire for speed and hitting power. Four years before, when he was ruminating over the mythical *Untakeable,* which was eventually to materialize as the *Dreadnought,* Fisher was also scheming for an ideal cruiser that he fancifully called the *Unapproachable*.

Initially she was to be a scouting vessel that would serve the modern battleship in the same way the frigate had served Lord Nelson's ships of the line, as the "eyes of the fleet." In Nelson's time the eye could see farther than a gun could shoot and, as Fisher pointed out, a frigate, being swifter than a man-of-war, "could sail round a fleet and count their numbers without danger." But, Fisher went on, whereas "the range of eyesight has remained constant, that of gunfire has increased." Now, to reconnoiter an enemy fleet, a scout would have to approach within gun

The "Dreadnought": key to the future

H.M.S. *Dreadnought*'s claim to a place in history was not based on what she did. She never fired her great guns in anger, and her only battle action in World War I was to ram and sink a German U-boat in the North Sea in March 1915. Rather, her fame rested on what she was: a ship so far advanced when she was commissioned in 1906 that every battleship that came after embodied her basic concept. Her badge was a golden key clasped in an iron gauntlet, representing, no doubt, what the Admiralty hoped would be the key to absolute control of the seas.

The *Dreadnought*'s great breakthrough, of course, was the mounting of 10 heavy 12-inch guns on a single ship. But there were many other inspired innovations in her design in addition to that of her armament.

An unusually long forecastle and a 28-foot freeboard at the bows kept her deck dry in bad weather, greatly enhancing the accuracy of her gunlaying. The bow itself was shaped with a bulbous forefoot below the water line, which also improved her sea-keeping qualities. At midships her hull squared off into boxlike sections to inhibit rolling. And along each side below the water line, long triangular bilge keels jutted downward to add resistance to turbulence.

Among her defensive arrangements was a row of hull-mounted diagonal booms that could be hauled out to support wire nets intended to intercept torpedoes. A second defense against torpedo-boat attack was provided by 27 hand-operated 12-pound guns mounted at various points on her superstructure, some atop the turrets.

The *Dreadnought*'s unique tripod mainmast was designed to give steady support for the maintop, from which fire-control information was relayed to the turrets. The idea proved eminently sound. But the mast's position between the funnels was the one real blunder in the ship's design. Not only did the smoke from the forward funnel often obscure the view from the top, it also threw so much heat on the tripod tubing—inside of which was the ladder leading aloft—that it was impossible to climb to the maintop while steaming into a head wind.

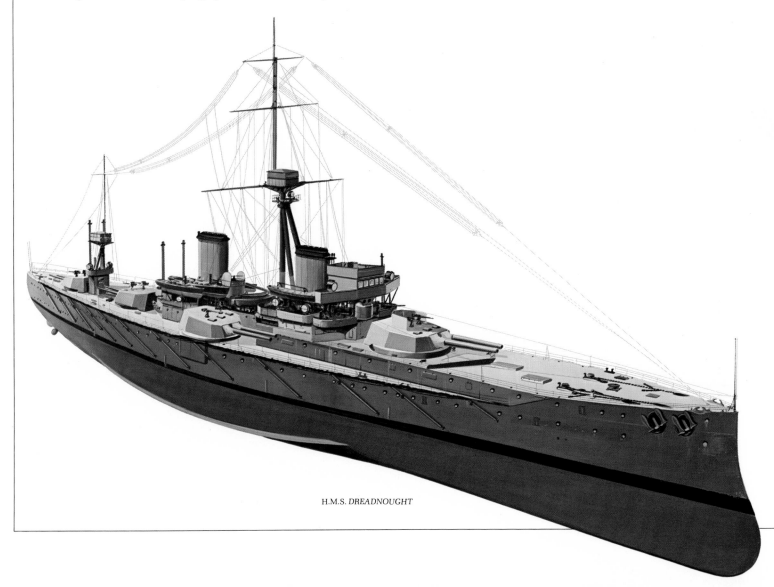

H.M.S. DREADNOUGHT

By any measure the *Dreadnought* was the most complex piece of machinery devised up to that time. She was longer (527 feet), wider (82 feet) and deeper in her draft (26.5 feet) than any earlier battleship. At 17,900 tons, her displacement was 750 tons greater than that of her nearest rival.

Each of her enormous turrets weighed 500 tons; each one of the big guns exceeded the weight of the entire armament of Horatio Nelson's *Victory*. The turrets rode atop stationary circular barbettes reinforced with vertical steel beams (*see forward turret*) and protected by drums of 11-inch armor plate (*see stern turret*). To protect the magazines and other vitals, belts of 11-inch armor sheathed the hull amidships along the water line. Just inside the armor, wedge-shaped wing bunkers holding much of the *Dreadnought*'s 2,900 tons of coal formed another bulwark.

In addition, watertight transverse bulkheads reached from the keel to a point nine feet above the water line and divided the hull into 18 sealed sections. So thoroughly compartmentalized was the *Dreadnought* that engineers believed she could absorb two torpedo hits without serious trouble. (The *Dreadnought*, incidentally, could deliver her own torpedo sting with five underwater tubes.)

The power plant that drove all this bulk was a radical departure from the usual reciprocating engines with their roaring, banging pistons. The *Dreadnought* was the first major warship to run on steam turbines. She carried eight Parsons turbines linked to 18 Babcock and Wilson boilers. Generating a total force of 23,000 horsepower to turn her four screws, the turbines enabled the *Dreadnought* to cruise at an amazing 17.5 knots over a range of 6,620 miles. And at flank speed she could get up to 21 knots.

The *Dreadnought*'s twin counterbalanced rudders were controlled from a wheel on the bridge or from any of four other auxiliary positions around the ship. Two of these—in battle stations on either mast—could be entered only by ladders running up communications tubes located behind the heaviest armor belowdecks.

It took a crew of 773 to operate this floating fortress. And their disposition was another of the *Dreadnought*'s departures. By tradition, crews had been confined to cramped fo'c's'les, while officers lorded it aft in more spacious stern quarters. But on the *Dreadnought* the crew was quartered in the stern, where they would be closest to the engines, while the officers lived amidships so as to be nearest the bridge.

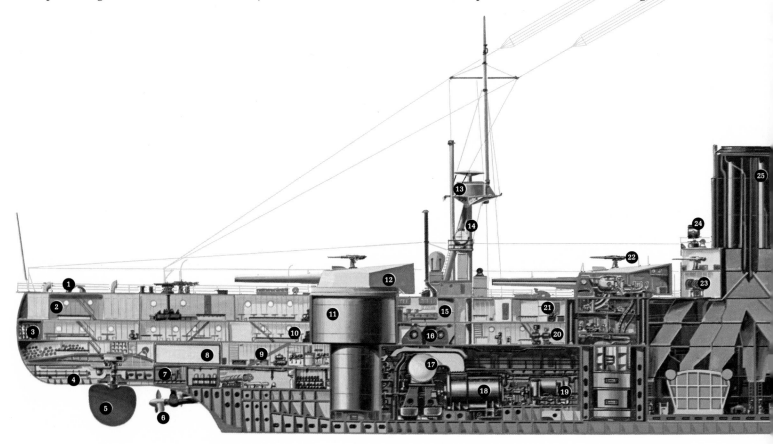

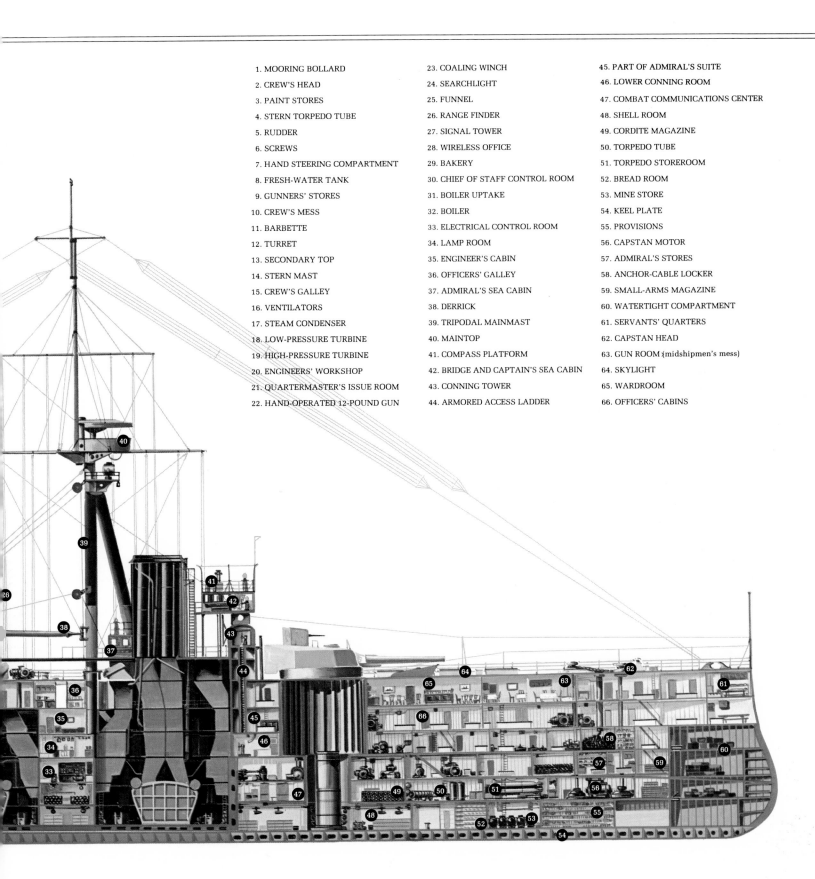

1. MOORING BOLLARD
2. CREW'S HEAD
3. PAINT STORES
4. STERN TORPEDO TUBE
5. RUDDER
6. SCREWS
7. HAND STEERING COMPARTMENT
8. FRESH-WATER TANK
9. GUNNERS' STORES
10. CREW'S MESS
11. BARBETTE
12. TURRET
13. SECONDARY TOP
14. STERN MAST
15. CREW'S GALLEY
16. VENTILATORS
17. STEAM CONDENSER
18. LOW-PRESSURE TURBINE
19. HIGH-PRESSURE TURBINE
20. ENGINEERS' WORKSHOP
21. QUARTERMASTER'S ISSUE ROOM
22. HAND-OPERATED 12-POUND GUN

23. COALING WINCH
24. SEARCHLIGHT
25. FUNNEL
26. RANGE FINDER
27. SIGNAL TOWER
28. WIRELESS OFFICE
29. BAKERY
30. CHIEF OF STAFF CONTROL ROOM
31. BOILER UPTAKE
32. BOILER
33. ELECTRICAL CONTROL ROOM
34. LAMP ROOM
35. ENGINEER'S CABIN
36. OFFICERS' GALLEY
37. ADMIRAL'S SEA CABIN
38. DERRICK
39. TRIPODAL MAINMAST
40. MAINTOP
41. COMPASS PLATFORM
42. BRIDGE AND CAPTAIN'S SEA CABIN
43. CONNING TOWER
44. ARMORED ACCESS LADDER

45. PART OF ADMIRAL'S SUITE
46. LOWER CONNING ROOM
47. COMBAT COMMUNICATIONS CENTER
48. SHELL ROOM
49. CORDITE MAGAZINE
50. TORPEDO TUBE
51. TORPEDO STOREROOM
52. BREAD ROOM
53. MINE STORE
54. KEEL PLATE
55. PROVISIONS
56. CAPSTAN MOTOR
57. ADMIRAL'S STORES
58. ANCHOR-CABLE LOCKER
59. SMALL-ARMS MAGAZINE
60. WATERTIGHT COMPARTMENT
61. SERVANTS' QUARTERS
62. CAPSTAN HEAD
63. GUN ROOM (midshipmen's mess)
64. SKYLIGHT
65. WARDROOM
66. OFFICERS' CABINS

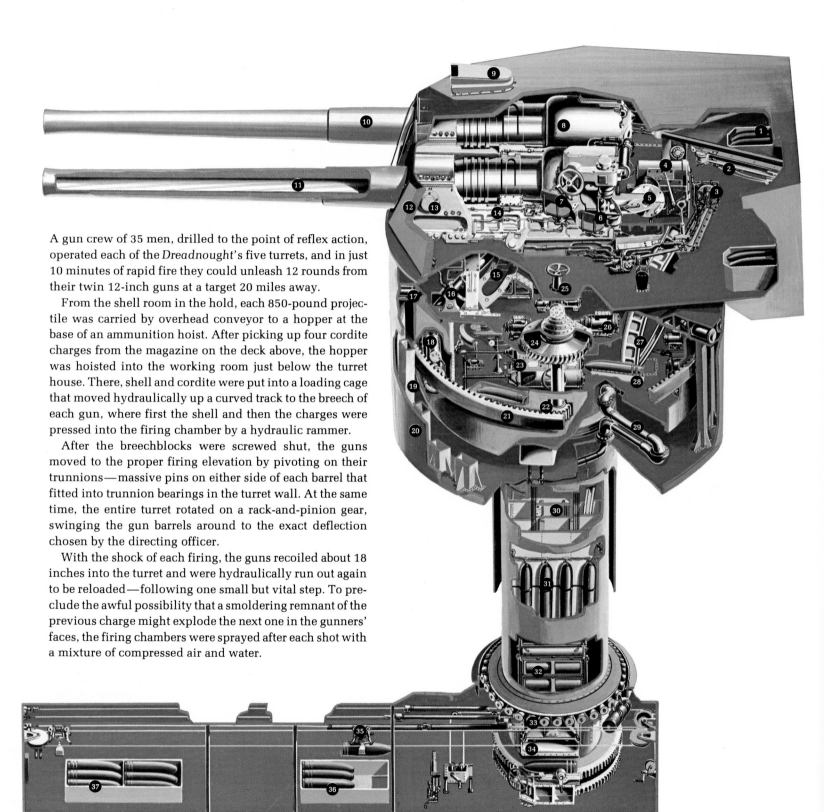

A gun crew of 35 men, drilled to the point of reflex action, operated each of the *Dreadnought*'s five turrets, and in just 10 minutes of rapid fire they could unleash 12 rounds from their twin 12-inch guns at a target 20 miles away.

From the shell room in the hold, each 850-pound projectile was carried by overhead conveyor to a hopper at the base of an ammunition hoist. After picking up four cordite charges from the magazine on the deck above, the hopper was hoisted into the working room just below the turret house. There, shell and cordite were put into a loading cage that moved hydraulically up a curved track to the breech of each gun, where first the shell and then the charges were pressed into the firing chamber by a hydraulic rammer.

After the breechblocks were screwed shut, the guns moved to the proper firing elevation by pivoting on their trunnions—massive pins on either side of each barrel that fitted into trunnion bearings in the turret wall. At the same time, the entire turret rotated on a rack-and-pinion gear, swinging the gun barrels around to the exact deflection chosen by the directing officer.

With the shock of each firing, the guns recoiled about 18 inches into the turret and were hydraulically run out again to be reloaded—following one small but vital step. To preclude the awful possibility that a smoldering remnant of the previous charge might explode the next one in the gunners' faces, the firing chambers were sprayed after each shot with a mixture of compressed air and water.

1. EMERGENCY SHELL BIN

2. CRANE FOR LOADING EMERGENCY SHELLS

3. HYDRAULIC RAMMER

4. HOUSING FOR LOADING CAGE

5. BREECHBLOCK

6. SEAT FOR LOADER

7. SEAT FOR BREECH OPERATOR

8. FIRING CHAMBER

9. OBSERVATION HOOD

10. BARREL JACKET

11. RIFLING IN BARREL

12. 11-INCH TURRET ARMOR

13. TRUNNION BEARING

14. CARRIAGE

15. ELEVATING TRACK

16. ELEVATING CYLINDER

17. ROLLER BEARING

18. EMERGENCY GENERATOR

19. REINFORCING BEAM

20. BARBETTE SHEATHING

21. RACK

22. PINION

23. CAGE-LOADING MECHANISM

24. TRAINING GEAR

25. CLUTCH FOR TRAINING GEAR

26. TRAINING ENGINE

27. TRACK FOR LOADING CAGE

28. LOADING CAGE (cutaway)

29. HYDRAULIC PIPES

30. HOIST SHAFT

31. COMPRESSED AIR TANKS

32. CORDITE CHARGES IN HOPPER

33. SHELL PICKUP

34. HOPPER PORT

35. OVERHEAD TRACK

36. SHRAPNEL SHELLS READY FOR FUSES

37. ARMOR-PIERCING SHELLS

range. That being the case, she would need extra speed to elude pursuit. But Fisher also wanted her to have guns to match those of her quarry. And therein lay a tale of woeful portents.

The ship that finally emerged from the drawing board was a variant on the *Dreadnought*, of similar displacement (17,250 tons) and comparable length (567 feet). But she incorporated a number of innovations— among them telescopic funnels that could be retracted on a moment's notice so as not to be visible on the enemy's horizon—and was in some respects an even more astonishing ship than the *Dreadnought*.

The greatest advance of all was in her machinery: turbine engines with a staggering 41,000 horsepower, almost twice that of the *Dreadnought*. And this enormous power worked even better than expected. She was planned for 25 knots, and proved capable of an even more astonishing 28 knots when put into service—seven knots more than the *Dreadnought*.

After speed, the second great innovation for a cruiser was the armament: eight 12-inch guns, only two fewer than the *Dreadnought*. Armored cruisers of the previous class had carried mixed armament, of which the most formidable were generally a half dozen 9.2-inch guns. The 12-inchers on the new cruisers were disposed two at the bow, two at the stern and four amidships. The guns amidships were situated to port and to starboard, but one was located a few feet aft of the other so that if one turret were disabled, the other could fire on either broadside. In sum, the cruiser had an artillery one and one half times the primary armament of any existing warship, save the *Dreadnought*.

Speed and hitting power, the two great virtues of these gigantic cruisers, appealed to Fisher more than anything else. In his aggressive mind the cruisers came nearer than the *Dreadnought* herself to an ideal ship, and throughout the long controversy that was to rage over the new shipbuilding programs, the cruisers remained his favorites. He called them "ocean greyhounds," for their nimble swiftness, and often exclaimed, "Speed equals protection."

That was one of his rare instances of clouded vision. The great speed of the cruisers, which could be had only by keeping the weight down, was obtained by the hazardous expedient of skimping on armor. The cruisers had a niggardly belt of armor that was six inches at the waist (compared with the *Dreadnought*'s 11 inches), and even that diminished to a precarious four inches on the bow; there was no armor whatever aft of the afterturret, and none on the deck.

The cruiser's manifold strengths—obscuring her manifest frailty— suggested manifold uses. The ship was hardly off the drawing board before, in addition to scouting duties, she was proposed for intercepting commerce raiders, for finishing off crippled battleships, even for opening fleet action by encircling the enemy. Meanwhile her name had shifted from armored cruiser to dreadnought cruiser to battle cruiser— underscoring a certain fuzziness of purpose.

Fisher himself was less than clear about the nature of the new ships. Although he viewed them as scouting vessels, he also maintained that an "armored cruiser of the first class is a swift battleship in disguise." And he felt that "no one can draw the line where the armored cruiser becomes a battleship any more than when a kitten becomes a cat!"

Alas, the growing cat was to be thrust into a jungle of water-borne lions and tigers. Baron Brassey of Bulkely, an avid yachtsman, Member of Parliament and editor of a distinguished publication called the *Naval Annual*, foresaw as much, writing prophetically that "an admiral having *Invincibles* in his fleet will be certain to put them in the line of battle, where their comparatively light protection would be a disadvantage." That was grossly understating the case. When war came, commanders were to find the cruisers' big guns altogether too tempting not to use them—and they would learn to their sorrow that the thin coat of armor made the vessels catastrophically vulnerable.

But in the heady and fast-paced days of Fisher's term at the Admiralty, such tragedy was not foreseen. All three of the initial battle cruisers were rushed afloat right in the wake of the *Dreadnought* herself, and reached completion in March, June and October of 1908—before Germany had come near completing her first dreadnought or even laid the keel for a comparable cruiser. Thus, for better or worse, England was four up on the rest of the world in the naval arms race before any other nation had even entered the track.

Meanwhile, both dreadnought and cruiser had to be protected against torpedo attack, a menace that Germany was known to be perfecting. This was to be the job of the third member of Fisher's modernized battle fleet, the oceangoing destroyer.

The destroyer was essentially two boats in one: a vessel designed to destroy an enemy's torpedo boats, and a carrier of torpedoes herself. Such a dual-purpose vessel had existed for a decade or so, and the Navy had about a dozen and a half on hand in the fleet when Fisher arrived at the Admiralty in 1904. The typical destroyer of the day carried a 12-pound gun and five quick-firing 6-pounders that could knock out an enemy torpedo boat at close range, and two tubes for debouching torpedoes at enemy battleships and cruisers. But these early destroyers were small (335 to 550 tons), averaged only about 25½ to 30 knots and carried from 80 to 130 tons of coal, which limited most of them to coastal areas.

Fisher demanded something seaworthy enough to accompany the dreadnoughts wherever they might go. By 1905, his second year in office, British shipyards were furiously working to turn out six new destroyers averaging nearly 900 tons. These ships burned oil, which made fueling offshore quicker and cleaner, and which gave them a speed of 36 knots. Together with a pair of 18-inch torpedo tubes (not significantly changed from those of earlier models), each of these vessels carried two 4-inch guns that fired 25-pound shells. By 1914 Britain would have 125 new destroyers in service—nearly a sevenfold increase over the 1905 flotilla.

With dreadnoughts, battle cruisers and destroyers under way, there remained only the submarine to fill out the ideal fleet that Fisher envisioned. And that was the only vessel not to come to life according to his own prescription. The fact was that the submarine had few fans among the British. Admiral A. K. Wilson, respected senior officer and a cordial friend of Fisher's, spoke for most of his countrymen when he avowed that the submarine was "underhand, unfair and damned un-English."

The day the "Emperor" came to call

A bearded Virginia Woolf (left) joins her cohorts for a portrait following their visit to the H.M.S. Dreadnought.

One glance at the telegram, from the permanent head of the Foreign Office on February 10, 1910, was enough to galvanize the Commander in Chief of the British Channel Fleet into action. He urgently ordered his staff to roll out the red carpet, the Royal Marines to line up for review and the bandmaster to find the appropriate anthem—for within three hours the Emperor of Abyssinia would arrive to inspect the pride of the Channel Fleet, H.M.S. *Dreadnought*.

At the appointed time, a swarthy, imperious figure in embroidered robes and turban appeared, along with bearded retainers and an interpreter. After solemnly inspecting the honor guard, the party toured the ship, listening with rapt attention as an escorting officer—through the interpreter—explained the wonders of the warship's gun turrets, range finders and wireless installations. As the visitors were leaving, they tried vainly to bestow the Order of Abyssinia on the shy officer who had accompanied them.

Shortly thereafter, London papers gleefully reported that the whole thing had been a hoax. The "Emperor" and his party were a group of prankish London literati, including the soon-to-be-famous novelist and essayist Virginia Woolf (as one of the bearded retainers). The "interpreter" had spoken not Abyssinian, but a sonorously mispronounced mixture of Latin and Greek, with a touch of Swahili.

The incident, when England stopped laughing, pointed up the appalling security aboard Britain's warships. After questions in Parliament, rules were tightened—which led Woolf to remark, "I am glad to think that I too have been of help to my country."

By 1914 the British had built 74 submarines. But the number was more impressive than the vessels themselves. No more than a handful of them could go far out to sea. The remainder were little advanced beyond those of a decade and a half before. Their underwater range was limited to about 100 miles, and they could do no more than guard British harbors.

Across the North Sea, Jacky Fisher's opposite number, Germany's Tirpitz, greeted the great new *Dreadnought* and her consorts with mixed emotions. "On the one hand, England's Naval measure contained the admission that our fleet building was being taken seriously," he wrote, full of pride in Germany's growing influence. On the other hand, Tirpitz could not escape the conclusion that "at the bottom of it all there was the clear intention of making us afraid."

In July 1906, as the *Dreadnought* was being fitted out, the Germans were laying down the keel for what was to be their biggest battleship yet, the 18,900-ton *Nassau*, named after the Rhenish duchy. But then, as the implications of the *Dreadnought* began to sink in, the Germans found themselves so concerned that they abruptly halted work on the *Nassau* within the year. "Germany has been paralysed by the *Dreadnought!*" Fisher gloated in a letter to King Edward VII in October 1907.

But now it was the British turn to wonder what was up. Unlike the British, whose security was so lax that almost any hoax would serve to give the curious a look at a new warship, the Germans jealously guarded their Naval secrets. The British did make one ingenious but fruitless effort to get information. Captain Reginald Hall, a future Director of Naval Intelligence, borrowed a yacht from the Duke of Westminster and outfitted two officers in workmen's overalls. They sailed the princely yacht right into the Kiel harbor and feigned engine trouble just as they came alongside the Krupp slips. While Hall caused a stir on deck, loudly commanding his overalled officers to hurry along with the engines, the officers hastily took photographs from the concealed recesses of the bridge. Alas, they could see nothing more than armed sentries pacing back and forth before tall, locked gates. So the British had to wait with everyone else to learn the results of what was a-building at Kiel.

The ship that finally emerged from the Kiel dockyards in July 1909, three full years after the *Dreadnought* was launched, showed the effects of makeshift and uncertain imitation. She had 12 big guns—two more than the *Dreadnought*. But these were only 11 inches in diameter, and the supposed inferiority of this armament evoked reproaches in the German press. Tirpitz, who would one day discover how fickle were his public and his monarch, wrote ruefully: "An opportunity was afforded, and eagerly grasped by faultfinders in Germany, to complain that our heavy guns were of a smaller caliber than the English guns." Actually, the one-inch difference between the *Nassau*'s and the British guns was not significant, as the German shells had greater penetrating power. But the *Nassau*'s armament had other limitations. Two of the three turrets, instead of being on the center line and able to swing to either side as were the *Dreadnought*'s, were placed in port and starboard wings that blocked each other's broadside fire. The net result was that the *Nassau*'s 12 guns had no more broadside firing than the *Dreadnought*'s 10.

Even more telling, the *Nassau* carried a cumbersome mixed armament of a dozen 5.9-inch guns and another sixteen 3.4-inchers. In their zeal to exceed the *Dreadnought*'s firepower, the Germans had evidently missed the all-important significance of uniformity.

The amount of armament gave the *Nassau* another shortcoming: to man all those guns, she needed a complement of 963 men against the 773 the *Dreadnought* would require, and her accommodations were accordingly cramped. Although the Royal Navy was never conspicuous for attention to the comforts of the British tar, the seamen's quarters aboard the *Dreadnought* were generous compared with those on the *Nassau*.

Finally, the *Nassau* was powered by old-fashioned reciprocating engines, which, besides being as subject as ever to breakdowns, kept the top speed to 19 knots and contributed to the ship's displacement of 19,000 tons—1,000 more than the *Dreadnought*.

In short, the *Nassau* was overgunned, overweight and underpowered.

This hybrid ship did have, however, some well-designed and peculiarly German strengths. Being in the vanguard of steelworks and explosives, the Germans gave particular attention to the ship's protection. The *Nassau* had an armor belt of 11¾ inches (three quarters of an inch thicker than the *Dreadnought*'s) and deck armor that was uniformly four inches thick (considerably more generous than that of the *Dreadnought*, which was nowhere more than three inches and in some areas thinned out to a mere inch and a half). In addition, the Germans constructed the *Nassau* with a "torpedo bulkhead," an interior steel wall that ran without interruption the whole length of the vital parts of the ship on both sides; it formed a hull within a hull. Together with coal bunkers running the length of both sides of the ship, those long bulkheads acted as stunningly effective shock absorbers when the German ships met enemy fire. And for the crews, the Germans provided one useful amenity that eluded the British: individual life jackets in case the community lifeboats should fail.

The *Nassau* dominated the German public's attention, but Tirpitz no less than Fisher kept a watchful eye on other ships for his fleet as well. Next on his list was a battle cruiser to reply to Britain's *Invincible,* and accordingly the German shipbuilders laid down their first vessel of that class—the *Von der Tann*—in March 1908. With this ship the German builders put on their swiftest performance, turning her out in a rapid two years, and showed their best talents for construction, producing a ship that would actually prove better than the British model. The *Von der Tann* had eight guns, disposed like those of the *Invincible,* but she had a main armor belt three and three quarters inches thicker than the *Invincible*'s and she had the inner protection of a torpedo bulkhead like that of the *Nassau*. Two more battle cruisers quickly followed—the *Moltke* and the *Goeben,* laid down in the spring of 1909—and with these Germany caught up with the turbine engine. Still another four battle cruisers followed those, so that seven had been laid down by 1912.

When they turned to destroyers, the Germans were not so innovative; their destroyers were somewhat smaller than the British ones, only a few exceeding 680 tons and all having an average speed of 32.5 knots. The building program called for about a dozen a year, and between 1906 and

As her twin-turreted 11-inch guns sweep
the horizon, the first German dreadnought,
the Nassau, plows through the seas in this
photo shot from a newfangled Zeppelin.
Hastily completed in 1909, the Nassau
had an outmoded reciprocating engine,
and some of her armament lay so near the
water as to be useless in high seas.

1913 the Germans were to build 107 of these useful if modest little ships.

In submarine construction the Germans were to be phenomenally successful—devising long-range and powerfully armed craft that would cause the British untold grief in the later days of the War. But those lethal and nearly invisible monsters would play virtually no role in the arms race, or in the monumental fleet action at Jutland that ultimately decided the war at sea.

Meanwhile all of Germany's technological inventiveness was more than canceled out by Britain's overwhelming advances in numbers. By the spring of 1909, when Germany's *Nassau* was finally commissioned, the Royal Navy not only had the *Dreadnought* and the three battle cruisers in service, but was well along in a building program that would add another six dreadnoughts to the fleet by 1910. And yet another 10 dreadnoughts were proposed, which would bring the fleet to 18 by 1913. Against another 10 British battle cruisers and 18 destroyers in the same years, the Germans, try as they would, would never catch up.

After four and one half years as First Sea Lord, Jacky Fisher had achieved three of his four objectives for reforming the Royal Navy. He had established the nucleus crew system, so that every ship stood ready for service at all times. He had honed down the fleet, scrapping the obsolete vessels and retaining only those with modern guns and high speed. And the building program had replaced the scrapped vessels, not in numbers, but with fewer ships of such revolutionary proportions that they outgunned and outsteamed all other ships afloat. All that remained was completion of his fourth aim: redeploying the Navy to get the right ships in the right places. Meanwhile every navy in the world was paying him the sincerest form of flattery, imitating his mighty creation and scrambling to catch up *(page 58)*.

Alas, success and power had made Fisher increasingly sarcastic, rude, intolerant and spiteful. His friend Viscount Esher, a confidant of the King's, had early on genially counseled him: "In a country like ours, governed by discussion, a great man is never hanged. He hangs himself. Therefore pray be Machiavellian, and play upon the delicate instrument of public opinion with your fingers and not with your feet." But such advice ran counter to Fisher's pugilistic nature. "I am going to kick other people's shins if they kick mine!" he growled—and marched forth to hang himself.

As he went about implementing the fourth objective, redeploying the fleets, Jacky Fisher finally fell afoul of his enemies and paid dearly for his highhandedness. Redeployment, while a tangential issue, was to provide the match that set ablaze a scandal that brought chagrin to the unassailable Navy, and bitter defeat to Jacky Fisher.

Redeployment had been under way for some time. Starting as early as 1904, Fisher had begun to redistribute the overseas fleets, thinning out the squadrons on friendly foreign stations by decommissioning the outmoded vessels and not replacing them. Next, he reshuffled the ships lying closer to home, assigning most of the newest and best ships to a newly named Home Fleet, which was euphemistically described as a reserve fleet. The proclaimed object was to strengthen the defenses around the British Isles, but one real effect was to downgrade

Channel Fleet Commander Lord Charles Beresford, shown here on board the predreadnought King Edward VII with his bulldog, Kora, led a large anti-Fisher faction in the Navy. His animosity dated to a trivial incident in 1901 when Beresford's vessel botched a mooring at Malta, and Fisher, then Mediterranean commander, ordered Beresford to repeat the maneuver "in a seamanlike manner."

the Channel Fleet—hitherto the major combat arm of the Royal Navy.

For one man in particular, this redistribution came as a terrible personal blow. He was Admiral Lord Charles Beresford, who was next in line for command of the Channel Fleet. For many years Beresford had been one of Fisher's bitterest foes in the entire Navy; he was the man who had first greeted the *Dreadnought* with a conservative's criticism. A blue-blooded member of the Irish gentry, Beresford was the darling of London society; to friends and admirers he was a dashing figure of charm and social grace, blessed with a blend of elegant manners and high spirits that the English expected of their Naval officers. To his enemies he was a popinjay and short on brains. The journalist J. L. Garvin, editor of the liberal newspaper *The Observer* and a Fisher fan, dubbed Beresford "the great dirigible," explaining that he was "the biggest of all recorded gasbags."

Beresford and Fisher had a personal enmity that grew out of their irreconcilable natures and went back to 1901, when Beresford had served as second-in-command to Fisher during the latter's stint as Commander in Chief in the Mediterranean. Fisher from the outset had appeared determined to make Beresford toe the line. Every move his second-in-command made was scrutinized, and Fisher lost no opportunity to criticize Beresford's actions. Beresford naturally smarted under such treatment, but as a subordinate he had little means of redress. Once he made a misguided attempt to get even by huffily declining to serve on one of Fisher's multitude of committees. Then it was Fisher's turn to be angry. "I shall be surprised if Fisher does not play some trick on him and pay him out in some way or other," one observer noted after witnessing the heated argument between Fisher and his subordinate.

Beresford succeeded to command in the Mediterranean when his superior moved on to become First Sea Lord, and he lost no time in seeking to discredit Fisher. At officers' dinners he railed against "the rotters their Lordships expect me to work with," and he made so bold as to canvass the captains under his command for written opinions on decisions emanating from the Admiralty. To a navy grown strong on unquestioning obedience to orders and unwavering loyalty to fellow officers, such behavior was not only indiscreet; it smacked of insubordination and subversion. Fisher took no official cognizance of Beresford's actions at the time, but there were those who thought the First Sea Lord found his means of getting back at Beresford in the redistribution of the fleets.

Beresford's next command after the Mediterranean was to be the Channel Fleet, and he looked forward with great anticipation to flying his flag over the greatest of all Royal Navy fleets; in fact, he believed it to be the stepping stone to the supreme position of First Sea Lord—once Fisher was out of the way. But by the time Beresford took command of the Channel Fleet in March 1907, it had been depleted by Fisher to one third its earlier strength and had been relegated to a secondary role as a backup for the new Home Fleet. Beresford, who had expected to take command of a force of 67 warships, found himself instead with only 21.

Bitterly disappointed and fiercely angry, Beresford had no sooner hoisted his flag aboard the *King Edward VII* in the Channel than he began rallying sympathizers, whom Fisher took to calling the "Syndicate of

Their heavy armament giving them a far more formidable appearance than the aging Victorian vessels at the 1897 review (pages 6-7), the battle-gray

dreadnoughts and other units of the new British fleet are arrayed at Spithead in 1911 to mark the coronation of King George V.

Discontent." Beresford wrote to Lord Knollys, Secretary to the King and a friend to Fisher, that the Admiralty was in a state of "chaos and pandemonium." He campaigned through London society, taking jibes at Fisher and his "Fishpond," meaning the men who supported Fisher. And he wrote a petulant letter to Lord Tweedmouth, who had succeeded Selborne at the Admiralty, complaining that the Home Fleet "is a fraud and a danger to the Empire." Beresford did not offer any evidence for his charge; he merely trumpeted it.

Beresford's insubordination was now so flagrant that Tweedmouth would have been justified in ordering the angry admiral to strike his flag forthwith. Instead Tweedmouth invited the wayward Beresford to the Admiralty and offered to hear him out. The meeting took place in July 1907. Present were Beresford, Tweedmouth, Fisher (as creator of the new Home Fleet) and a stenographer to record the proceedings.

"I think so serious a charge against the Home Fleet ought to be substantiated," Tweedmouth told Beresford; "you ought to say how it is a fraud, and how it is a danger to the State." Given his chance, Beresford could do no better than protest that he had been using only a "term." He added: "That I had any notion of insubordination I absolutely deny."

Fisher, resolutely on his good behavior, asked Beresford what might be done to improve matters. "Shall you be satisfied if we make your armored cruisers up to six?" Again Beresford was flummoxed. "I cannot see the thing straight off," he temporized. "I will write to you."

"You must have thought about it," Fisher rejoined. "You have been writing about it for months."

After several hours of fencing, the meeting ended with formal expressions of cordiality all around—and no one any better off than before. Beresford, retaining his command of the Channel Fleet, went forth into London society, calling Fisher "a dangerous lunatic" and adding to his charges a new one, that the Navy had no war plans. Again the Admiralty might have taken steps to silence Beresford but, fearing to open a Pandora's box, held a posture of forbearance.

For the first several months the feud between Beresford and the Admiralty, though gathering momentum, was confined to Naval circles and to society gossip. It took a more serious turn when the newspapers got wind of a sublimely ridiculous bit of trivia that came to be known as "the paint-work incident." Suddenly the hallowed Royal Navy found itself the subject of a public scandal.

King Edward, still maintaining civil if cooling relations with his nephew the Kaiser, had invited the latter to a Naval review at Spithead in November 1907. In anticipation of the state occasion, Beresford issued an order calling all ships of the Channel Fleet to port to be painted for the edification of the imperial eyes. Most of the officers in the fleet responded with mute obedience. But Rear Admiral Sir Percy Scott, a member of the Fishpond and the future hero of the development of director firing, was at the moment conducting gunnery exercises with the 1st Cruiser Squadron somewhere offshore. Puckishly—but rashly—he signaled the captain of one of his ships: "Paintwork appears to be more in demand than gunnery, so you had better come in, in time to make yourself look pretty by the 8th inst."

A status symbol for the world

The launching of H.M.S. *Dreadnought* in 1906 set off an epidemic of dreadnought fever that soon infected most of the world. The warship was such a symbol of might that every nation with pretensions to power had to have at least one in its navy.

Joining Britain and Germany in the frenzied naval race, France boasted four dreadnoughts by the time war erupted in 1914. Italy built two, Austria-Hungary three, and Russia laid down four. Not to be outdone, the Japanese built three dreadnoughts in 10 years, and the United States had 14 superships when it entered the War in 1917. Among them was the 31,400-ton *Arizona (below)*, with twelve 14-inch guns and such heavy armor plate (up to 18 inches) that it was one of the world's most awesome warships.

Even lesser powers, which could not build their own dreadnoughts, drained their treasuries to buy foreign ships. Brazil paid a British firm £3,642,800 to build the 19,200-ton *Minas Gerais* and *São Paulo*, each with a dozen 12-inch guns. Meanwhile, neighboring Argentina signed a $21,330,600 contract with American shipbuilders for the 27,720-ton *Rivadavia* and *Moreno*, also with a dozen 12-inch guns each.

Brazil countered by ordering, for £2.9 million, a third British-built dreadnought—the 27,500-ton *Rio de Janeiro*, with 14 of the 12-inchers. But alas, the Brazilian treasury was empty. And so in 1916 Brazil's folly, renamed the *Agincourt*, went to the Battle of Jutland as part of the British Grand Fleet.

Distinctive for her sturdy lattice masts, the U.S. dreadnought *Arizona* is seen here in New York in 1916.

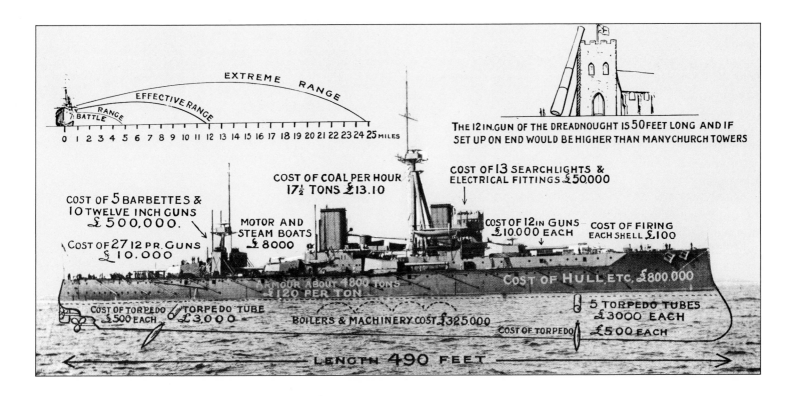

The imposing size and range of a dreadnought's 12-inch guns, as well as the enormous cost of the great warship's various components, are detailed in this illustration from a souvenir booklet from the 1911 Spithead Review of the Grand Fleet. For the £2 million needed to build one dreadnought, the government could equip and maintain for a year 18 battalions of infantry—18,000 men. The 490-foot length indicated here is for the main deck; the hull was 37 feet longer.

The signal doubtless sent smiles rolling over the faces of Scott's captain and a good many others; but the grapevine carried it to Beresford, and it threw that vain and self-important officer into a rage. He—who had so shortly before been inciting his fellow officers against the Admiralty—now lashed out savagely at a subordinate's whimsy. He summoned Scott aboard the flagship and, in the presence of some of Scott's fellow officers, rebuked him for having been "contemptuous in tone" and "insubordinate in character." Not content with this face-to-face scolding, Beresford ran up a flag signal before the eyes of the entire fleet, making public his censure of Scott.

Such a spectacle before such an audience was too much to ignore; the press seized upon it at once. Newspapers of all complexions, from the old gray *Times* to the flamboyant *Daily Express*, promptly sprouted banner headlines. "A NAVAL SENSATION!" and "FLEET ASTOUNDED!" they cried. And the stories below the headlines quickly snowballed, giving the curious public juicy accounts of the Fisher-Beresford feud that lay behind the incident. Partisans in and out of the Navy separated into two camps, those who championed Fisher and those who championed Beresford.

Inevitably, the cause célèbre ceased to be a matter for drawing-room snickering, and seemed to threaten the nation's very security. Such grave disharmony at the Admiralty raised questions about the officers' fitness to do their jobs. Some people began to call for the dismissal of Beresford, some for the ouster of Fisher; others demanded that both should go. Many of those on the sidelines became as venomous as the participants themselves. Sir Frederick Richards, a Beresford partisan who was lusting for Fisher's dismissal, wrote to a friend: "May you be on the spot with the other good and true men when the time comes for the removal of the cancer which is eating into the heart of the Navy." But Fisher, at any rate, still seemed secure; as Lord Goschen, a former First Lord, had written: "Fisher has the whole press at his back, and the King is in his pocket." And indeed, the King's confidant Lord Esher published a letter in the *Times* saying: "There is not a man in Germany from the Emperor downwards who would not welcome the fall of Sir John Fisher." That prompted even the Kaiser to jump into the fray. "People over here would be very thankful if at least Germany was left out of the discussion," he wrote Lord Tweedmouth.

The arrival of a new First Lord of the Admiralty to replace Tweedmouth, Reginald McKenna, opened a new act of the drama. McKenna announced the last phase of Fisher's redeployment plan, absorbing the old Channel Fleet into the new Home Fleet. That move relieved Beresford of his command without actually firing him. Far from hushing up the truculent Beresford, the removal merely impelled him to carry his grievance to Prime Minister Herbert Asquith, who appointed a Cabinet committee in a belated effort to get at the root of the trouble.

The committee charged with the inquiry sat for 15 sessions from April till July of 1909. In the end it came to the equivocal conclusion that "no danger to the country resulted from the Admiralty's arrangements for war." In other words, the redistribution of the fleet was justified, and Lord Charles's allegations were unfounded. The report went on, however, to give a mild rebuke to both warring adversaries, saying: "The Board of Admiralty do not appear to have taken Lord Charles Beresford sufficiently into their confidence" and that "Lord Charles Beresford, on the other hand, appears to have failed to appreciate and carry out the instructions of the Board, and to recognize their paramount authority." To Fisher and his supporters, that was an unfair piece of sophistry that amounted to condoning insubordination. "It was a dirty trick to say the Admiralty had not given their confidence to Beresford," Fisher wrote to a friend, "when Beresford had abused that confidence within 24 hours of hoisting his flag!"

For Fisher there was a more stinging blow to come. The report concluded that the members of the committee "look forward with much confidence to the further development of a Naval War Staff"—in other words, a body that would take precedence over the First Sea Lord, Fisher himself—in the disposition of the fleet and in the making of war plans.

Nothing could have made Fisher more furious. A Naval War Staff, he grumbled to a friend, would be "a very excellent organization for cutting out and arranging foreign newspaper clippings."

Sulk as he might—and, with some cause, considering how much he had done and how little thanks he was getting—not even Jacky Fisher could defy a Cabinet decision. Though he and his supporters argued that war plans had to be kept secret, it was too much to expect, in a day of such lethal weapons, that one man carry in his head the plans for sending those weapons into action if and when war demanded. The War Staff had to come—and Jacky Fisher would have to go. His years of power had made him quite unable to work with any committee. And so, while he stayed on in his Admiralty office for four more months, he was eventual-

In Portsmouth in October 1912, for the launching of the Iron Duke—first of a class of 25,000-ton superdreadnoughts—a jubilant Winston Churchill is accompanied by his fur-wrapped wife, Clementine, and an escorting officer. As First Lord of the Admiralty, Churchill wanted to be more than the Navy's titular head. He often visited the yards to study dreadnought construction and spent weeks at sea with the fleet—at times annoying admirals with his attempts to direct maneuvers.

ly awarded with a peerage on the King's birthday, November 9, 1909, and on his own 69th birthday two months later he was retired from the Navy. Winston Churchill was soon to note that destiny had not done with him yet. True enough, but for now, Jacky Fisher disappeared from public life. "So, Jacky is growing roses, is he?" one officer said. "Well, all I've got to say is that those roses will damned well have to grow."

Fisher's departure from the Admiralty did nothing to slow the Naval race. On both sides of the North Sea, dreadnoughts and battle cruisers continued to be built in ever-increasing size and at an ever-accelerating pace. At the close of Fisher's term in January 1910, Britain had four dreadnoughts completed, three more due for trials and another six laid down; she also had five new battle cruisers laid down, in addition to the three already finished. That made a total of 21 capital ships undertaken in little more than five years, a phenomenal rate never before attempted.

In the same month of January 1910, Germany had four dreadnoughts due for trials, nine laid down and three battle cruisers under construction, for a total of 16 capital ships undertaken in four years. In the coming four years Britain would complete 10 more dreadnoughts and another battle cruiser; Germany would strain to keep up the fantastic pace with four dreadnoughts and one battle cruiser.

During the hectic years of Fisher's regime, Britain had kept the lead in numbers, and was usually first with innovations. In 1909 Fisher had ordered an increase from 12-inch to 13.5-inch guns on eight dreadnoughts, with all guns disposed on the center line for maximum efficiency. These ships had gone to sea in 1912. Germany had followed with 13.5-inch guns and centerline disposition in the ships she laid down in 1911 and put to trial in 1915. After bringing the first generation of dreadnoughts to a peak in the *Iron Duke* and three sister ships laid down in 1911 and ready in 1914 *(pages 104-105)*, the British Admiralty made still another leap with the *Queen Elizabeth* and four other superdreadnoughts laid down in 1912 and rushed to completion by 1915; they went to 15-inch guns and 27,500 tons, nearly 10,000 more than the original *Dreadnought*. That massive tonnage was propelled at 25 knots by 24 boilers, generating a staggering 75,000 horsepower.

An equally novel feature was the introduction of something Fisher, though he was now gone, had long championed—oil fuel. That move was made possible because in 1914 the British government entered into agreement with the Anglo-Persian Oil Company, paying a bargain £2 million to guarantee herself vast quantities of oil. Besides being cleaner and easier to load, oil had the great advantage of giving no telltale cloud of black coal smoke to precede the ship over the horizon.

The *Queen Elizabeth* and her sister ships were the last of the dreadnoughts to be ready for the approaching War. And they represented the culmination of every effort to combine speed, power, grace and balance.

By the summer of 1914 the British Grand Fleet—a new name for the combined Home and Channel Fleets—based at Scapa Flow in the Orkney Islands, had 20 dreadnoughts and four battle cruisers, supported by eight predreadnought battleships and 42 destroyers. Across the few hundred miles of shallow, stormy sea separating Britain from her rival, the German High Seas Fleet, based in Wilhelmshaven on the North Sea coast, had 13 dreadnoughts, three battle cruisers and 88 destroyers. Together the two fleets had some 560 guns that fired shells weighing as much as three quarters of a ton a distance of 10 miles. They marked the biggest change in sea power since gunpowder was introduced to Europe in the 14th Century—and the change had taken less than 10 years.

Throughout the decade of their building, there had been little question in anyone's mind that they were being built to go to war. "The great nations of Europe are raising enormous revenues," British Foreign Secretary Sir Edward Grey had mused in 1909, "to kill each other."

So they were. But in a last gasp of the old era's formal etiquette, the two fleets met once more in peace. At last the Kaiser had a navy he could review with a pride equal to that his uncle had shown at Spithead in 1897. In June of 1914 he held a grand regatta at Kiel on the Baltic coast. It is not known whether Wilhelm invited the British King—now George V, son of Edward VII, who had died in May 1910—but King George did not

Firing a ceremonial salute, a British squadron enters the German harbor of Kiel in June 1914, in the last meeting of the rival naval powers before the War. The occasion, significantly, was the enlarging of the Kiel Canal, a shortcut between the Baltic and the North Sea. The route now accommodated the biggest vessels, specifically the new German dreadnoughts.

come. The British did send three dreadnoughts and three battle cruisers.

The Kaiser paraded some of the best new German warships before the British. For four and a half days, British and German seamen and officers competed in sailing races, and after sundown they attended banquets and dances on each other's ships. They shared a certain comradeship of the sea, but that amity showed a strain; everyone felt that when they met again it would be in battle. "England is ready to strike," said one German officer sourly to another; "the object of this visit is only spying. They want to see how prepared we are."

The rupture came even sooner than they expected. On June 28 news was brought aboard the *Meteor*, the Kaiser's personal racing yacht, where Wilhelm was entertaining the British Ambassador, that Archduke Ferdinand of Austria had been assassinated in Sarajevo. The news was to set Europe on fire. The Kaiser departed abruptly for Berlin with the enigmatic words, "Now I shall have to start all over again."

The ships of the Royal Navy steamed out of German waters to take up their stations for war.

Artful appeals to a nation at war

DESIGNED BY LT. GEN. SIR R.S.S. BADEN POWELL

Are **YOU** in this?

PUBLISHED BY THE PARLIAMENTARY RECRUITING COMMITTEE, LONDON. POSTER NR.112.

PRINTED BY JOHNSON, RIDDLE & CO., LTD., LONDON, S.E.

Dedicated sailors and soldiers and industrious civilians busily make their contributions to the war effort in this British poster. In sharp contrast to the heroic crew, a shirker (right) stands idly to the side, giving a double edge to the poster's question: "Are you in this?"

While the Admiralty's low-key recruiting efforts and Parliament's annual appropriation kept the Royal Navy well enough supplied with men and money during peacetime, the wartime demands of the new dreadnought fleet called for more aggressive tactics. Launching an all-out drive for public support, the government enlisted the aid of newspapers, printed hundreds of leaflets, sponsored slide shows and drafted famous personalities to promote the Navy. But the best instrument of all in this campaign was the poster.

Well established by 1900 as an advertising medium, the poster was uniquely suited to mass persuasion. While the audience for newspapers and leaflets was limited, the poster, through an arresting combination of image and word, could bring the government's appeals to virtually everyone. And so it did. The government assembled lithographers and slogan writers, typographers and printers under the command of the propaganda bureau and a bipartisan Parliamentary Recruiting Committee. Together the two agencies produced hundreds of different posters, which were plastered by the millions across Britain.

Appealing to glory and patriotism, the posters featured waving flags and gleaming ships, knights in armor, even saints on horseback. Wartime camaraderie and a sense of destiny *(right)* were favorite themes, and many were calls to conscience *(left)*. Such methods had their critics. An observer complained that some of the posters demonstrated "a low notion of the British public" (one invited sailors to roll up their sleeves for a "good fight"). But the campaign was instrumental in raising a million recruits by 1916.

A second, equally effective program was aimed at the nation's pocketbook and living habits. The poster makers turned out a series of appeals for war-bond and savings programs to build ever more ships. Posters also spurred the populace to work harder, eat less, even donate their wine and tobacco to the services. But perhaps the greatest success of Britain's poster campaign was intangible. By rallying the nation behind the War, posters gave to Britain's fighting men a morale boost of incalculable proportions.

Ignoring wartime realities, the Naval recruitment poster at left suggests that sailors whiled away their days in light duties and companionable conversation —under blue skies and equally clement officers. The dramatic stance of the uniformed figure in the poster above suggests that women could find a future in the Naval Auxiliary.

Poster appeals used compelling pictures of ships and guns to remind citizens that buying war bonds and savings certificates was an investment — as one poster explained — in "earlier victory." Although these bond and savings programs provided the funds Britain desperately needed to pay sailors, provision ships and buy raw materials, the nation mortgaged her future to pay the costs of the War: while it lasted the national debt multiplied 11 times.

Chapter 3

The long wait for Armageddon

The last of Scharnhorst and Gneisenau

W.L. Wyllie

hen the men of His Majesty's Royal Navy and the Imperial German Fleet awoke on the morning of August 5, 1914, to learn that their two countries were at war, they rejoiced. On Germany's Jade River estuary in Heligoland Bight, where the new dreadnoughts and their consorts of the High Seas Fleet rode at anchor, the news rang through vessel after vessel with a reverberating cheer. "For the first time in German history," exulted a chauvinistic and highly promising battle-squadron commander named Reinhard Scheer, "sea power will play a mighty part in the great fight for existence with which our nation is now faced."

Indeed, virtually every man in Germany concerned with naval affairs was proudly aware of the fatherland's new strength on the seas—though every man surely did not agree on how to use it. Small wonder. "We had no personal experiences," admitted Scheer, "of commanding and handling in battle the big ships that had recently come into existence." Nevertheless, he reported that all hands on those big ships felt "a burning enthusiasm and lust for battle."

On the British side of the North Sea, the officers of the Royal Navy swelled with the pride and anticipation of a nation whose fighting ships had not lost a single battle since the War of 1812. To Winston Churchill, the 40-year-old First Lord of the Admiralty, the magnificent dreadnoughts and their supporting craft represented "the culminating manifestation of naval force in the history of the world." That force could scarcely have been more ready for battle. The entire service had been pulled into fighting trim for July maneuvers, and then held on alert by an Admiralty order issued on July 29.

Such was the power of these two fleets that the War itself might conceivably be settled in the wake of a single great sea battle. Yet paradoxically, with the stage now more perfectly set for a cataclysmic naval clash than at any other time in history, most of the principal actors on both sides were seized by a stage fright that all but paralyzed the two fleets while the War dragged on for four years. The fact was that the dreadnought fleets, because of their awesome strength, had suddenly become too valuable to risk. Both belligerents had invested enormous treasure and a full decade of work to create these leviathans. When the reality of war forced each side to face the fact that the other had dreadnoughts too—and in large numbers—then the advantage of possession was all but canceled. There remained the fear of loss, and with it came an overwhelming reflex to go on the defensive. Thus the two naval giants stood glaring at each other for months on end across a strip of dirty gray ocean, at times lashing out with flickers of their lethal power to do

As her sister ship, the Gneisenau, fights hopelessly on, the German armored cruiser Scharnhorst rolls over and sinks after encountering British battle cruisers in the South Atlantic. The British destroyed both ships by scoring with more than sixty 12-inch shells while suffering only 25 hits in return.

horrifying damage, but not really coming to grips. Meanwhile the naval war went on by other means and, in some measure, in other seas.

This temporary stalemate between the dreadnought fleets was no fault of the man who had brought the modern German Navy into being. Admiral Alfred von Tirpitz, the 65-year-old architect of Germany's new capital ships, knew exactly how his beloved dreadnoughts should be used. In short order he fired off a nine-point manifesto whose principal message was that the German Navy must get up steam and slug it out with the British Grand Fleet: "The aim of all our work for 20 years or more has been battle. Accordingly, we have our best chance in battle."

Tirpitz' rationale for combat had the ring of Götterdämmerung. "In a battle," he wrote, "the English fleet will suffer as many losses as we do." To combative minds such as his, a ship-sinking contest made excellent sense. For if the Imperial German Navy could lure the British Grand Fleet into the North Sea for a pyrrhic clash, the relative effect on Germany, with its superb land army and interior communications, would be far less severe than on Britain, a sea power that could not afford to lose its capital ships. And if the whims of North Sea weather, or the human blunders upon which so many battles turn, or some other stroke of fortune gave victory to Germany, then the War would be all but over. Neutral trade, free of British high-seas control, could fill Germany with fresh matériel for the Imperial Army to use in the systematic crushing of France, Russia and the marooned remnants of any British expeditionary forces. And England herself would lie wide open to invasion.

Fortunately for the Allies, Tirpitz' advice fell on the wrong ears— those of Kaiser Wilhelm II. During the years immediately leading up to war, Tirpitz had been fenced ever more tightly into his prestigious but increasingly impotent position as Secretary of State of the Imperial Naval Office, until he was in charge of little more than administration and supply. That was just where the Kaiser—and a coterie of advisers led mainly by Army men—wanted the aging firebrand. The de facto head of the Imperial Navy was the Kaiser. "I need no chief," he said; "I can do this for myself." The top admirals reported directly to him. And Kaiser Wilhelm made it abundantly clear that while—or because—he was intensely proud of his fine new ships, he did not want them risked as expendable weapons of war.

Naval officers might regard the Kaiser as more of a navy buff than a true commander in chief, and might scorn his amateurism. But there was no questioning his power. Any man who coveted high office in the Imperial Navy would do well to heed the instructions of His Majesty: "For the present," advised the Kaiser, "I have ordered a defensive attitude on the part of the High Seas Fleet." And his admirals surely heeded by formulating a protective strategy for the dreadnoughts, in fact for all major units of the Imperial Navy. The ships' principal duty would be as guardians—of their own safety and that of Germany's shoreline.

This cautious policy was warmly applauded by the Army. The General Staff wanted Germany's flank and rear protected for the Army's thrust through France. This the Navy could do simply by sitting at the ready inside Heligoland Bight. The High Seas Fleet would be shielded by shore guns and a thick field of mines, to be laid from Terschelling on the

Dutch coast to Horns Reef off Denmark. Thus ensconced, the fleet would guarantee that the Allies could not hit Germany from behind with a Baltic or North Sea landing supported by England's dreadnoughts.

Furthermore, went the reasoning of the Kaiser and his advisers, the British would surely blockade Germany. Every page of British Naval history showed that the blockade would be an aggressive one in which British men-of-war would steam close to the enemy's coastline. When they did, the High Seas Fleet must be on hand at peak strength, ready to strike if the proper opportunity presented itself. Tirpitz disagreed: he waggled his forked white beard and complained in his incongruously high, reedy voice that it was "simply nonsense to pack the fleet in cotton wool." But the Kaiser paid him no attention.

The man delegated to preserve the German fleet in being was Vice Admiral Friedrich von Ingenohl, freshly minted Commander in Chief of the High Seas Fleet. Ingenohl's Order of the Day for August 14 set the pattern for German Naval operations for the next two years: "Our immediate task is to cause our enemy losses by all the methods of guerrilla warfare. This task will fall primarily to our light forces (U-boats, destroyers, minelayers and cruisers). The duty of those of us in the battleships of the fleet is to keep this, our main weapon, sharp and bright for the decisive battle." And he included the thought that every good German sailor held in his heart: "They must, and will, come to us someday or other. And then will be the day of reckoning."

The very first day of the war at sea brought an incident that seemed to confirm the promise of at least part of the German position. Cheating a little on the midnight declaration of war, the auxiliary minelayer *Königin Luise* had slid out from Heligoland during the early night of August 4 to sow her deadly seeds around the Thames estuary. Next morning the new British 3,500-ton light cruiser *Amphion*, leading a hornet swarm of attackers against the *Königin Luise*, hit a mine and went down with 131 men. And though the German minelayer was caught and sunk too, Britain's loss of a genuine ship of war was a far greater blow.

Nevertheless, the Royal Navy remained supremely confident, even contemptuous of the Germans. At Scapa Flow the men were in splendid spirits. On liberty days and in the long summer evenings, they played football on shore. They also held boxing matches, regattas and concerts, and went fishing, picnicking and even to the movies. In the camaraderie of the first days of war, the court-martial of a seaman who was late coming back from leave was adjourned when the man testified he had missed the liberty boat because his sleeping girl friend had been wearing his flannel shirt and he did not want to wake her. "Thank God the Age of Chivalry is not past," declared the court's presiding officer.

This easy manner came straight down from the Grand Fleet's personable Commander in Chief, Admiral Sir John Jellicoe. A smallish man, scarcely five feet six inches tall, with gentle eyes, a large nose and an engaging smile, he was described by future Prime Minister Stanley Baldwin as "a man of wonderful understanding of the human heart. He was kindly and thoughtful to every one in every rank."

More to the wartime point, other admirers, such as his colleague Ad-

Seabags over their shoulders, men of the Royal Naval Reserves march briskly through Portsmouth en route to active service soon after the Admiralty's mobilization order of August 2, 1914. So efficient was the Navy's recall system that virtually every vessel of the British Grand Fleet was fully manned and ready for duty within 12 hours of the directive.

miral Sir William James, said that Jellicoe had the "eye for battle," the ability "in a minute to make up his mind on the deployment of an entire fleet for combat." Jacky Fisher went much further. "Sir John Jellicoe is the future Nelson!" he trumpeted. "He is incomparably the ablest Sea Admiral we have."

Jellicoe may well have been England's best sea admiral, but he was no future Horatio Nelson. Britain had been searching for another Nelson ever since the original had died on his quarter-deck at Trafalgar more than a century before. And there was a tendency to see in any outstanding officer the so-called "four aces" that made up the Nelsonian character: leadership, imagination, openness to the ideas of subordinates, and offensive spirit.

Though Jellicoe probably did possess the first three aces, he lacked the all-important fourth. Perhaps the strongest card he had held during his rise through the Navy had been the support of Admiral of the Fleet Jacky Fisher. As a young lieutenant, Jellicoe had caught Fisher's eye because he was an outstanding student at the Royal Naval College, where Fisher taught gunnery. Jellicoe had continued to impress his mentor, first as an able deck officer and later as a brilliant captain of various vessels under Fisher's command in the Mediterranean and elsewhere. Jellicoe, in turn, made himself so agreeable in backing Fisher's fleet-building plans that he soon became known to opponents as one of "Fisher's jackals." Fisher had put him on the committee that designed the *Dreadnought*, and had shared his innermost thoughts with the man he came to call "my beloved Jellicoe." Even after leaving office in 1910, Fisher had connived, mainly with Churchill, in private meetings and passionate letters, many of them marked "burn" (but somehow never burned), to keep moving Jellicoe ahead until the protégé was in the slot to become "admiralissimo when the Battle of Armageddon comes along."

When Armageddon actually loomed in August of 1914, Fisher, much like Tirpitz, found himself still off stage in retirement. His furious doctrine ("Hit your enemy in the belly and kick him when he is down") erupted, unheeded, from his rose garden.

As for Fisher's future Nelson, he quickly showed himself to be about as pugnacious as Germany's reluctant dragon, Ingenohl. Jellicoe believed the place for the Grand Fleet was at Scapa Flow, where its very existence would pin down the German High Seas Fleet, while keeping the shores of England safe from attack. There would not be the close blockade the Germans expected. Let patrolling destroyers and cruisers deny the North Sea to any neutral freighter trying to reach Germany. "It is suicidal," Jellicoe wrote to Churchill soon after hostilities began, "to forego our advantageous position in the big ships by risking them in waters infested with submarines. The result might seriously jeopardise the future of the country by giving over to the Germans command of the Seas."

Such caution would, in time, cause Fisher to complain that Jellicoe lacked Nelson's "divine spark of disobedience." But the controlling voices in Britain's Naval establishment, principally those of Churchill and the First Sea Lord, Prince Louis of Battenberg, concurred—in unwitting duplication of the Kaiser's cautious strategy.

The Grand Fleet would stay where it was. So would the Channel Fleet,

In the first major naval action of the War, a massive British raiding force of 52 vessels routs a 38-ship German squadron in Heligoland Bight, sinking three light cruisers and a destroyer. Along the horizon in this composite, which shows the action of several hours, five heavy British battle cruisers depart in triumph as the surviving Germans (background, far right) race for the protection of their minefields off Heligoland Island.

whose 19 predreadnoughts with their flotilla of escorts and support ships lay well to the south in Portland Harbor; there they could prevent any freighters from reaching Germany through the Strait of Dover, at the same time assuring safe passage to France for British troopships.

Meanwhile out on the sea-lanes of the world, a thin but effective scattering of older vessels and a few new ships protected merchantmen bearing food and weapons for Great Britain, and chased about looking for German raiders. In all, the balance of all large warships lay 177 to 87 in England's favor, enough to provide King George V's subjects with a comfortable conviction that Britannia still ruled the waves.

On the night of August 26, a heavy fog lay over the Gulf of Finland, and in that dark haze there occurred a stroke of chance that, as much as any other event of the War, served to keep the advantage in British hands. The German light cruiser *Magdeburg* ran aground, to be battered to bits by Britain's Russian allies. On the body of a drowned signalman, the Russians found the German Navy's secret codes and position grid charts for both Heligoland Bight and the North Sea. Stained by sea water but still legible, these invaluable books were sent to Britain.

The Germans, unaware that their closest Naval secrets had fallen into enemy hands, were deeply distressed by the careless loss of the *Magdeburg*. But they had little time for regrets before much worse news broke over them. At 7:00 a.m. on the foggy morning of August 28, the regular dawn patrol of half a dozen or so German destroyers that poked out of Heligoland Bight to look for British submarines heard the boom of guns and suddenly found itself amid a fire storm of shells from a flotilla of enemy raiders. The British had raced over during the night with eight light cruisers (half of them spanking new and all but one with 6-inch guns), 31 destroyers and eight submarines. Their dual purpose was to ambush the methodical destroyer patrol—and anything that might come out to help it—and to draw German attention from a landing of Allied troops at Ostend, Belgium. Behind the raiders, in case anything went wrong, bristled the 12- and 13.5-inch rifles of five battle cruisers under the command of a handsome young admiral, Sir David Beatty.

Things quickly went wrong for both sides. At the first salvos two badly overmatched 4.1-inch-gun German light cruisers rushed out from Heligoland to join the fray. They were later joined by another six cruisers, but four heavy German battle cruisers with steam up were held inside the bight by the timorous Ingenohl. The action over the next several hours was frightening, confused, and further muddled by fog and by the terrible British communications system, which failed to inform the various British units where their sister squadrons were. In the melee the British cruiser *Arethusa* started to take a pasting from the more accurate light German guns. Then, at the critical point of battle, just after noon, the fog lifted momentarily, and there stood Admiral Beatty's British battle cruisers with their turrets at the ready. In 40 minutes three German cruisers were on the bottom, 712 German sailors were dead and the remnants of the German force had fled back into Heligoland. The British had but 35 dead, all aboard the damaged *Arethusa* and three destroyers.

"A fine feat of arms," crowed Churchill, while Germany's one unabashedly bellicose sea commander, Admiral Franz von Hipper, leader of the High Seas Fleet's battle-cruiser squadron, fumed at his do-nothing superiors. Almost too bitter for Hipper to bear, in the aftermath, was the Kaiser's approval of Ingenohl's orders to hold back—and a follow-up imperial edict that henceforth "fleet sallies and any greater undertakings must be approved by His Majesty in advance."

The shocking loss of ships—plus the reaffirmation of Germany's doctrine of great caution—was soon matched on the other side of the North Sea. For in this moment of apparent triumph the British fleet had entered into the gravest period of danger it had faced since Trafalgar. A tight-fisted prewar Cabinet had refused the money to make Britain's North Sea bases at Scapa Flow, Cromarty and the Firth of Forth secure against submarines. Thus all of the Grand Fleet's grand ships, when at anchor, lay wide open to sneak attack—as plump a collection of sitting ducks as any skulking poacher could ever wish to find.

On August 9 one bold German submarine, the U-15, penetrated right into Scapa Flow before she was rammed and sunk by an alert cruiser captain. Soon thereafter, on the clear morning of September 22, the elderly German submarine U-9 spotted three British armored cruisers, the Hogue, the Aboukir and the Cressy, steaming off the Hook of Holland at a slow 10 knots with no escorts. The U-9's very first torpedo hit the Aboukir's magazine and blew her in two. The Hogue turned to help her stricken sister, took a torpedo and sank in 20 minutes. The Cressy tried to zigzag to safety but two more torpedoes sent her to the bottom "with a loud sound, as if from a creature in pain," according to an eyewitness. In the three ships 1,459 British fighting men died within a single hour, victims of one of the most spectacular feats of destruction achieved by any submarine during World War I—or since.

Britain was stunned. And she was stunned again three weeks later when the cruiser Hawke and 500 more men went down to a torpedo. Then, on October 27, the full-fledged, 13.5-inch-gun dreadnought Audacious, the first ship of her class to receive so much as an enemy scratch, blundered into a German minefield (page 92) off the tip of Ireland, struck one of the floating bombs and sank. She stayed afloat long enough for all hands to be rescued, but her loss was so horrendous a disaster that the Admiralty kept it secret until after the War. Finally, a periscope fright in Scapa Flow sent Jellicoe steaming off with the entire Grand Fleet to safer anchorages, first on Scotland's west coast at Loch Ewe and then all the way to Lough Swilly in Ireland, where they remained for nearly a month before returning to Scapa Flow.

At this point the east coast of Britain lay wide open to Germany's High Seas Fleet, and if the Kaiser had borrowed an ounce of courage or advice from old Tirpitz and some dash from Hipper, England might have been made to suffer grievously. The High Seas Fleet now had 15 dreadnoughts and five battle cruisers in full fighting trim, to Jellicoe's 17 dreadnoughts (the rest were on distant patrol or in for repair) and five battle cruisers—and Jellicoe was on the run.

Britain had to do something, and quickly. But what? Beatty wrote to his wife of "bungling in high places," and to Churchill that "we are working up for a catastrophe." Apparently the First Lord of the Admiral-

The audacious cruise of the raider "Emden"

As the mighty dreadnoughts awaited their call to battle, a small German vessel on the far side of the world was performing some of the most daring feats of the War. Prowling the Indian Ocean in the fall of 1914, the 3,650-ton light cruiser *Emden* struck at Allied shipping with such audacity that one of her exasperated British pursuers was forced to admit: "We admire her exploits as much as we wish the ship may be taken."

Commanded by Captain Karl von Müller, one of the German Navy's most brilliant officers, the *Emden* employed a simple but clever disguise to get near her victims without alarming them. Since like most German light cruisers she was distinguished by three funnels, while British cruisers ordinarily had four, Müller added a fake smokestack of wood and canvas to the *Emden.* For armament she mounted 10 rapid-fire 4.1-inch guns, and with a 25-knot top speed she could overtake merchantmen and outrace pursuit.

The *Emden's* career as a lone marauder began on September 10 in the crowded shipping lanes between India and Ceylon, when Müller boarded and scuttled his first ship, a 3,400-ton freighter. Within a week the *Emden* had sunk six Britishers, and after a month the toll had reached 11 vessels totaling some 50,000 tons.

Amazingly, not a single life was lost during these early raids. The chivalrous Müller always made certain that the merchant crews were safely away in lifeboats or had been transferred to the *Emden* before sending their ships to the bottom. And for this, he was nicknamed the "gentleman captain" by the first victims of his celebrated and increasingly daring forays.

Long, lean and graceful, the German light cruiser Emden glides through the Kiel Canal shortly after her commissioning in 1909. As part of the Imperial Navy's prestigious China Squadron, she was known to her crew as the "Swan of the East" before she became a sharp-taloned commerce raider under Captain Karl von Müller (inset) at the outbreak of war in 1914.

A price to pay for pilfered luxuries

The nerve of the raiders was phenomenal. Late on September 22, as 14 Allied ships scoured the Indian Ocean for the *Emden*, Müller brought her into Madras. Before the British could man their shore defenses he shelled an oil depot, destroying two huge tanks.

On October 28 the raider stole into an Allied harbor at Penang, Malaya. Easing up to point-blank range, the *Emden* bombarded and sank the Russian cruiser *Yemtschuk*, then dashed for the open sea, sinking a French destroyer encountered along the way.

Between actions the crew of the *Emden* enjoyed a cornucopia of luxuries, including coffee, candies, cigars and cigarettes removed from Allied ships. "Sometimes I felt as if I were at a great fair," an officer recalled. "Hams dangled from the engine skylight. There were stacks of chocolate and bottles labeled 'Cognac' with three stars." But despite the high living, every man knew that any day the *Emden* might meet a vengeful Allied warship.

On November 9 Müller anchored off Keeling Island, west of Australia, and sent 50 men ashore to demolish a British radio and cable-relay station. It was a fatal mistake. The moment the raider appeared, the operator recognized her and signaled an SOS: "Emden here."

The landing party reduced the station to rubble. But as the men prepared to return to the cruiser, they were greeted by a horrifying sight: the *Emden* was speeding out to sea as an enemy warship crested the horizon.

Smoke billows up into the evening sky as a British-owned oil tank, shelled by the Emden, blazes on the shore at the Indian port of Madras. Commented a jubilant German Naval officer: "A change is good for everyone. We sent millions of the enemy's property up into the sky instead of down into the sea."

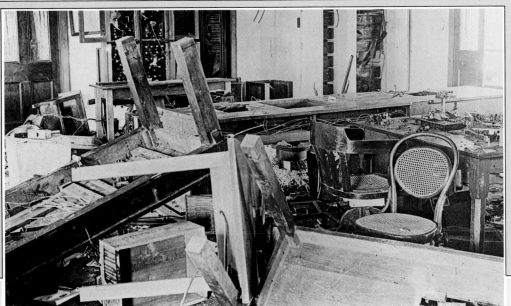

The British radio and cable station on Keeling Island is a tangled mess of severed wires and shattered panels after the attack by the Emden's raiding party. The Germans spent two hours destroying this important communications link between Great Britain and Australia.

Their mission completed but their own fate in doubt, the Emden's landing party waits at the dock on Keeling Island for their cruiser, which has put to sea to engage an Australian warship. Moored in the background is the Ayesha, an old schooner, which the men later seized for a bold trek back to the fatherland.

The incredible escape of a valiant few

Alerted by the radio operator's SOS, the Australian heavy cruiser *Sydney* had at once steamed for Keeling Island. With the superior firepower of her 6-inch guns, she attacked from just outside the firing range of the *Emden*, pouring shells into the German cruiser. After 90 minutes of uneven fight, the *Emden*, which had sent 23 Allied vessels to their graves, was a charred wreck wedged against a reef. Of the 325 men on board, 141 were dead; the rest, including Müller, were imprisoned for the duration of the War.

The only men to escape were the raiding party on shore. They commandeered an old schooner and slipped away. During the next eight months they sailed 4,300 miles to Arabia and then traveled on foot and by train to their allies in Constantinople. There, in June 1915, the valiant band saluted a German admiral as their leader announced: "I report the landing squad from the *Emden*, five officers, seven petty officers and 30 men strong."

Pummeled by shells from the Sydney (left), the listing Emden burns as desperate crewmen dive from the ship and swim for overloaded lifeboats. This dramatic rendering appeared in an Italian newspaper three weeks after the battle.

As newsreel cameramen record the stirring event, a pair of German sailors carry away the salvaged bow plaque of the Emden after it had been returned by Australia to Germany as a gesture of good will in 1933. Reichspresident Paul von Hindenburg personally accepted the name plate of the ship that the old Kaiser had at one time described as "filling all German hearts with pride."

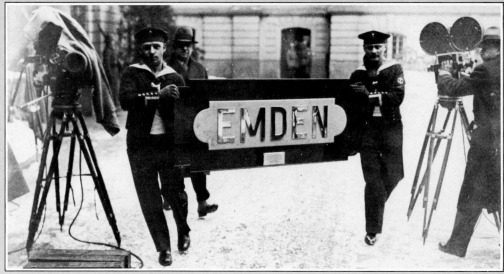

ty agreed, for on October 28 he sacked First Sea Lord Prince Louis of Battenberg—an easy scapegoat because of his German parentage. The new First Sea Lord was to be none other than Jacky Fisher, who, in Churchill's view, "was right in nine tenths of what he fought for."

Fisher and Churchill were an extraordinary pair to run the Royal Navy: the irascible, opinionated old admiral and the gifted amateur not much more than half his age. Many people predicted that it would not be long before they quarreled. But in the beginning, at least, they got on famously, and Fisher impressed everyone with his drive. The old man appeared to possess all the verve of his bygone youth, talking nonstop, using his favorite clichés and telling his favorite stories over and over again. One observer at the Admiralty, Baron George Riddell, called him "a wonderful old boy—full of life and energy. At lunch he got up and showed us how he taught a Polish countess dancing. He waltzed round the room in great style."

Scarcely had Fisher moved into his Admiralty office when he ordered a massive warship construction program. His plan included five battleships, five light battle cruisers, two light cruisers, five flotilla leaders, 56 destroyers, 65 submarines and numerous smaller vessels—for a total of some 600, all to be completed as quickly as possible. Instructions went out to block U-boats from the northern bases with minefields and jetties of sunken, concrete-laden merchant ships and with heavy submarine nets across the harbor entrances. Dirigibles would patrol the coastal waters; shore batteries were to be augmented. This was the sort of impetus the Royal Navy badly needed.

But Fisher was only four days in office when he received news of yet another devastating defeat for the world's largest and greatest navy. This time the calamity had occurred in the Southeast Pacific off the coast of Chile, some 7,000 miles away.

German Admiral Maximilian von Spee, commander of Germany's China Squadron, had spent the months since the beginning of hostilities moving his best ships eastward, to raid along the west coast of South America and possibly to round Cape Horn to harass British bases and shipping in the South Atlantic. By the end of October Spee had assembled a force of five vessels at the Juan Fernández Islands, some 400 miles west of the Chilean coast at about the latitude of Santiago. The two most formidable were the cruisers Scharnhorst and Gneisenau, both displacing 11,420 tons and built in 1907 with main batteries of eight 8.2-inch guns. Accompanying them were the light cruisers Nürnberg, Leipzig and Dresden, built between 1906 and 1909 with ten 4.1-inch guns apiece. All the ships could move at better than 20 knots, and their crews, after a couple of years together at sea, were superbly efficient.

Spee, a popular and admirable officer, was acting virtually on his own, unsupported by any clear order of record from his superiors, and he knew that his was an ultimately hopeless mission. "I am quite homeless," he noted at one point. "I cannot reach Germany. We possess no other secure harbor. I must plow the seas of the world doing as much mischief as I can, until my ammunition is finished, or a foe far superior in power succeeds in catching me."

The British Admiralty knew roughly where he was, from occasional sightings reported by agents in the Pacific islands. The British guessed that Spee would round Cape Horn into the Atlantic. But the ships the British had on hand to oppose him were not fit for the job. The Falkland Islands, east of Cape Horn, were part of the Royal Navy's worldwide network of coaling stations, and there Rear Admiral Sir Christopher Cradock was stationed with four vessels: his flagship the *Good Hope*, a 14,100-ton cruiser built in 1902 with a pair of 9.2-inch guns and sixteen 6-inchers; the *Monmouth* and the *Glasgow*, a pair of light cruisers with 6-inch guns; and an armed merchant ship named the *Otranto*, with eight 4.7-inch guns. Coming down the east coast of South America to join him was the battleship *Canopus*, even older than the others: she was laid down in 1897 and completed in 1900. She had four 12-inch guns and was designed for 18½ knots; however, her engines were worn out and at that moment she was limping along at scarcely 12 knots.

Although he was instructed to destroy German cruisers, Cradock had received orders from the Admiralty that were vague and confused. First he was warned that Spee's vessels were just around the Horn, and that "you must meet them in company"; in other words, he must fight. Next he was advised that his ships were "to search and protect trade"— which by British Naval tradition could also mean that he must fight if he spotted enemy warships of whatever strength. He was told that the *Canopus* was a "citadel around which all our cruisers could find absolute security"—which presumably meant that he was expected to wait around for the old bucket. When Cradock protested that the *Canopus* was useless and that he needed additional help from newer fleet units, he was turned down on the grounds that two Allied Japanese warships and one British light cruiser were on the way from the northern Pacific.

Cradock, an impulsive and brave man, angrily decided to go it alone. Handing the governor of the Falklands a sealed envelope to be mailed home "as soon as my death is confirmed," he set out around the Horn with his creaky little squadron, the *Canopus* wallowing 250 miles in his wake. Spee, meanwhile, had upped anchor and was steaming south from the Juan Fernández Islands. The squadrons met on the evening of November 1 off the port of Coronel, 1,400 miles north of Cape Horn, in rising winds and heavy seas.

As soon as Cradock spotted the smoke of the German ships, he made the worst conceivable move, turning southward to run a parallel course with the enemy. The German light cruisers were outgunned and they stayed clear of the action. But the two German heavy cruisers mounted 16 rapid-firing 8.2s, enormously superior to Cradock's one pair of old 9.2s on the *Good Hope*. What is more, the German gunners were superb (the *Gneisenau* had several times won the Kaiser's award for gunnery), while Cradock's men were green reservists. And the British ships were to the west, silhouetted against the sunset's afterglow, while Spee's ships were almost invisible against the darkening coastline.

There followed what one British survivor called "the most rotten show imaginable." At 7:00 p.m. Spee opened fire and with his third salvo destroyed the *Good Hope*'s forward gun. Meanwhile the *Gneisenau* began to chew up the *Monmouth*. Cradock desperately attempted to move the two beleaguered cruisers closer to the enemy to bring their 6-

Before the Battle of Coronel off Chile in November 1914, Admiral Christopher Cradock warned that he would be crushed by German Admiral Maximilian von Spee's cruisers. His pleas were ignored—and Cradock was proved right.

At a reception in Valparaiso after his victory at Coronel, Admiral von Spee had a premonition of death. Presented with a bouquet of roses by one of his sympathizers, Spee gloomily commented: "Better save them for my funeral."

inchers into play, but this meant going into the weather. The winds were now near hurricane force, and foam and green water swept over the bows so that the deck-mounted 6-inch guns were all but inoperable. Methodically the *Scharnhorst* pumped 35 hits into the *Good Hope*; at last one shot struck the British vessel's magazine. "At 1950," an officer aboard the *Glasgow* wrote of the *Good Hope*, "there was a terrible explosion between her mainmast and her funnel, the flames reaching a height of over 200 feet, after which she lay between the lines, a black hull lighted only by a glow." A moment later the *Good Hope* was gone, carrying with her Admiral Cradock and some 900 officers and men.

Meanwhile the *Gneisenau*'s expert gunners were inflicting much the same torture on the *Monmouth*, which the watch aboard the *Glasgow* reported to be "burning furiously, and heeling slightly." The severely damaged vessel turned away from the battle. So did the *Glasgow* and the *Otranto*, both of which fled southward in the darkness toward the battleship *Canopus*. The limping *Monmouth*, however, was overtaken by the Germans in the darkness at about 9 o'clock. She was sinking and could not fire her guns, but her flag was still flying and her engines were running. She turned toward the enemy as if to ram, and the Germans opened up at a range that began at 1,000 yards and mercifully ended at 600, when the *Monmouth* capsized and sank. Not a man among the 1,654 on board the two British cruisers had survived. The Germans suffered two men wounded from six inconsequential hits.

When the news reached Germany, the Kaiser announced the award of 300 Iron Crosses to the victorious crews. His ships and men had inflicted the first loss upon Britain in a high-seas battle between surface vessels in close to a century.

On November 4 Churchill proposed to Fisher that a battle cruiser with 12-inch guns should be sent to the Falkland Islands to avenge Cradock. "But I found Lord Fisher in bolder mood," wrote Churchill. "He would take two." The signal went to Admiral Sir John Jellicoe, Commander in Chief of the Grand Fleet: the *Invincible* and the *Inflexible* were to depart their North Sea base and "proceed to Plymouth with all dispatch." The two battle cruisers reached Plymouth on the 8th, and were put under the command of Vice Admiral Sir Doveton Sturdee.

A competent but overbearing and opinionated man, Sturdee was appointed for an unusual reason. Years before, he had been a supporter and protégé of Lord Charles Beresford, with whom Fisher had fought a vicious feud over the redeployment of the fleet. Fisher hated Sturdee, and he refused to keep that "damn fool" and "pedantic ass" at the Admiralty. With his usual finesse, Churchill eased Sturdee out of Fisher's way by proposing that he be appointed Commander in Chief, South Atlantic and South Pacific, with the important task of catching Spee.

Fisher agreed and ordered Sturdee and the battle cruisers to be ready to sail on the 11th—in three days' time. The *Invincible* needed new firebricks in her furnaces, and Plymouth dockyard reported that she could not be ready until the 13th. Fisher blew up: they *must* sail on the 11th. Besides, the 13th was a Friday: "What a day to choose!" Churchill supported him, signaling the Admiral Superintendent of the Dockyard, "Ships are to sail on Wednesday 11th. Dockyard arrangements must be

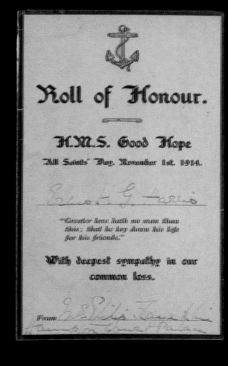

Blazing from stem to stern, the British cruiser Good Hope sinks with all hands after a battle off Chile with the mighty Scharnhorst and Gneisenau. The loss of 900 men occasioned an outpouring of sympathy: the family of each crewman, including that of engine-room technician Ernest Harris (bottom center), received a condolence card (bottom left) from the widow of the Good Hope's captain, as well as a plaque and medals (bottom right) as testimony that, in the words of an Admiralty official, "theirs is an immortal place."

made to conform. You are responsible." The admiral superintendent took a train to London to protest in person that it was impossible. Fisher ordered him back to his post, saying the ships would have sailed before he reached Plymouth. And so they had—taking with them, on Fisher's command, a number of extremely unhappy civilian bricklayers to fix the furnaces en route. The two battle cruisers picked up six lighter cruisers plus an armed merchantman, the *Macedonia*, on the way and reached the Falklands, where the *Canopus* was already moored, on December 7. Spee arrived off the islands at dawn next morning.

The German admiral had intended to destroy the coaling station and whatever ships he found nearby, and then start on the long and probably hopeless voyage up the Atlantic to Germany. He sent the *Gneisenau* and the *Nürnberg* ahead to reconnoiter. Their lookouts first saw black smoke that made them think the coal stocks were being burned in anticipation of surrender. Then they saw the masts and funnels of warships. The Germans held their approach course until, at 13,500 yards, two salvos of very heavy shells hurtled out of the harbor. One shell struck the *Gneisenau's* afterfunnel, blowing a large hole in it but not disabling her. At this, the *Gneisenau* and the *Nürnberg* turned sharply away, as did Spee astern in the *Scharnhorst*, trailed by the *Leipzig* and the *Dresden*.

The salvos had come from the 12-inchers of the old *Canopus*, which Fisher, in one of his inspirations, had grounded in the harbor mud to serve as a fort. And there were more surprises for the Germans. Just after the turnaway from the *Canopus'* salvos, German crewmen spotted tripod masts—a scarcely credible sight, because the only British ships with tripod masts were dreadnoughts and battle cruisers, and Spee had had no warning from usually reliable German intelligence that any such British vessels were about. Refusing to believe the evidence, Spee did not flee. Since he thought he was faster than any major British ship in the area, he could wait for a final assessment of enemy strength, then run if necessary. When the *Invincible* and the *Inflexible* appeared at the harbor mouth, with their engines winding up to a flank speed of some 28 knots and their main batteries of eight 12-inch guns apiece swinging to the ready, Spee knew he was doomed. Now the Germans fled.

The chase, in bright, clear weather, was almost leisurely. Sturdee, certain of his superior speed and armament, signaled his fleet to have the midday meal before battle was joined. By 12:45 p.m. he was in range of the rearmost German cruiser, and he signaled, "Engage the enemy." Thereupon, Spee ordered his three light cruisers to try to escape, while the *Scharnhorst* and the *Gneisenau* engaged the battle cruisers.

Within three hours, Spee's flagship, the *Scharnhorst*, outranged and overwhelmed by the British 12-inchers, had absorbed so many hits that she was listing badly and on fire. Sturdee signaled Spee to surrender but there was no reply. At about 4:15 the *Scharnhorst* rolled over and sank, taking the entire crew of 765 men, including the gallant Spee, with her.

For nearly three hours more, while the German light cruisers tried desperately to run to the safety of the South American coast, the *Gneisenau* fought on alone. It was an extraordinarily brave and hopeless struggle. The *Gneisenau* was hit by at least 50 British 12-inch shells. Still her captain refused to surrender. At last, at 5:40, she had fired all her ammunition, lost pressure in all her boilers, and some 600 of her crew of 850 were dead or wounded. Her captain now gave orders to hasten her end by scuttling, and hauled down her flags. "He called for three cheers for His Majesty," a surviving officer wrote, "and the *Gneisenau* was then abandoned. I fell into the water as she capsized."

The British picked up 190 survivors, floating in the chilly, oil-covered water "like a great patch of brown seaweed," as one rescuer recalled. Sturdee expressed admiration to the surviving Germans, especially for their gunnery. "We sympathise with you in the loss of your Admiral and so many officers and men," he said in a formal announcement. "Unfortunately the two countries are at war; the officers of both navies, who can count friends in the other, have to carry out their country's duties which your Admiral, Captains and officers worthily maintained to the end."

Yet the German sacrifice was useless. The British cruisers caught the *Nürnberg* and sank her at 7:27, saving only five among some 320 men (of whom a few were attacked by giant albatrosses as they died in the frigid water). An hour later the *Leipzig* went under, with all but 18 of 290 men. The *Dresden* got away but was hounded for months and was finally sunk in March by a British cruiser at the Juan Fernández Islands, where Spee had weighed anchor to start the fateful southern ocean action.

The tactical moral of the two battles was obvious. At Coronel the aging and obsolescent British ships had been no match for the newer Germans, and at the Falklands the Germans had been no match for the battle cruisers. On the high seas the fast, big-gun ship was supreme—as Jacky Fisher had always known it would be.

In terms of naval strategy, the Falklands action marked the end of fighting on distant seas. The last of the scattered German ships had been defeated, including a daring raider in the Indian Ocean named the *Emden*, which had been sunk a month earlier (*pages 75-78*); most British ships were called home, and the big-ship war was now concentrated entirely in the North Sea.

In that forbidding stretch of water, full of prowling U-boats and hidden mines, backed by the beetling armament of Germany's High Seas Fleet, even Fisher had been growing cautious. There would be no quick Armageddon to follow up the Falklands triumph: "No big ship of the Fighting Fleet should go into the North Sea," he had decided, and had written in his usual hyperbolic style, "WHEN the German Big Fleet comes out, THEN our Big Fleet will come out! WHEN the German battle cruisers come out, THEN our battle cruisers will also come out!"

Thus the initiative rested with Germany, if she chose to seize it. And so she did, through the efforts of Admiral Franz von Hipper, commander of the High Seas Fleet's battle-cruiser squadron and an officer who disliked the Kaiser's timorous doctrines.

Hipper had been born the son of a tradesman in Bavaria, far from the ocean, but when he was a child he had decided to go to sea. He had entered the Naval Academy at 17, and he became a cheerful but strong-willed officer. He detested paper work and avoided shore appointments—but this seems not to have damaged his career. When he made admiral at 49, he had little experience in administrative work. His flag

Vice Admiral Sir Doveton Sturdee stands on deck before the 12-inch guns of his flagship Invincible, which at the Battle of the Falkland Islands avenged an earlier humiliating British defeat by German cruisers Scharnhorst and Gneisenau. But Sturdee's longtime foe, First Sea Lord Jacky Fisher, disparaged the Falklands victory as a case of "criminal ineptitude" because one of five German ships managed to escape.

Fighting to stay afloat in the frigid South Atlantic, the survivors of the sunken German armored cruiser Gneisenau await rescue by lifeboats from the British Inflexible. But for many of the men, deliverance came too late: scores of them succumbed to their wounds or to shock after being pulled from the water.

captain called him a "lover of action, swift in decision, the most pleasant of superiors and always kindhearted." Hipper's first command had been a destroyer, and he probably always remained a small-boat man. But command of the German battle cruisers fulfilled the same need for him—to be independent, always out in front of the fleet, dashing ahead to find the enemy. At sea he was cool, clearheaded and a master of tactics; yet on the bridge of his flagship, with his short, thin hair and little goatee, he radiated an amiable air of humanity and enjoyment. Sailors loved him.

He had already mounted one battle-cruiser sortie against the British; on November 4 he had dashed across the Channel with four ships and shelled the town of Yarmouth with his 11-inch guns. The raid had scant military value, aside from knocking out a few shore batteries and sowing some mines in coastal shipping lanes. But as an "insult bombardment," as Jacky Fisher called it, the action infuriated the British and delighted the Germans. For the daring foray the Kaiser awarded the Iron Cross to Hipper; the free-spirited admiral refused to wear it "until I've done something." By that he meant taking some action against British warships, and he immediately started planning another raid to bring the enemy out once and for all. This one would be on December 16, against the English east-coast towns of Scarborough, Hartlepool and Whitby.

This time the Germans hoped to draw out units of the British Grand Fleet and catch them in a trap. Hipper secured permission to sortie with his five battle cruisers and the refurbished armored cruiser *Blücher*, plus a screen of light cruisers and destroyers. What is more, Ingenohl himself would follow in massive support with 14 dreadnoughts, eight predreadnoughts, nine lighter cruisers and 54 destroyers. He would advance to the eastern fringes of the Dogger Bank in the middle of the North Sea, farther from home than the High Seas Fleet had ventured before. The stage would be set for a classic ambush: Hipper would lure out a portion of the Grand Fleet, and it would be crushed between the jaws of a great vise that he and Ingenohl would clamp shut.

What followed instead was a comedy of errors that left both Germans and British grinding their teeth in embarrassment and frustration.

Unknown to the Germans, British intelligence had been decoding their radio signals; the British knew when Hipper was to leave the Jade, roughly where he was going, and when he would head home.

The radio intercepts were made and interpreted in Room 40 of the British Admiralty building in Whitehall. There the German code book and grid charts found on the dead signalman from the cruiser *Magdeburg* less than four months before had become the cornerstones of a brilliant intelligence complex under a blue-eyed, shaggy-browed Scot named Sir Alfred Ewing. In Room 40 the intercepts, called "Japanese telegrams" for security's sake, were deciphered, stuffed into red envelopes and given directly to Ewing or top subordinates, all sufficiently skilled in code work to keep up with the rotating changes in the German ciphers. The information was then passed on to the Naval commanders, though only the very top men—Jellicoe and a few others—knew where it came from. As an action developed, these critical data were supported by regular position reports on enemy ships flashed in from a chain of radio direction-finder stations along England's east coast. Thus, from early December of 1914 until the War's end, the Germans were unknowingly sharing most of their plans and ships' positions with the British.

Most, but not all. For some reason, Room 40 either did not pick up or failed to decipher any messages about Ingenohl's massive sortie with the bulk of the High Seas Fleet in support of Hipper. The British knew only half the plan, and that, had fate not intervened on their behalf, might have proved disastrous to a sizable portion of the Grand Fleet.

Believing Hipper's battle cruisers to be the main game on December 16, the British Admiralty sent four battle cruisers commanded by Vice Admiral Sir David Beatty, who had wreaked such havoc on the Germans at the battle at Heligoland Bight four months before. In addition, Vice Admiral Sir George Warrender was dispatched as backup with six heavy dreadnoughts, and a swarm of cruisers, destroyers and submarines.

Though Warrender was technically in charge of the force, he was actually playing second fiddle to Beatty, who, since his decisive action at Heligoland, had become the closest thing to a hero that the Navy had. And Beatty fitted the role perfectly. He was a dashing, square-jawed man with his admiral's cap set at a jaunty angle and with a reputation for fearless competence. At 13 he had left his rich, fox-hunting family to join the Navy, and as a young lieutenant in 1898 during the Sudanese rebellion he had taken his gunboat up the Nile to support the beleaguered 21st Lancers at the Battle of Omdurman. One of the Lancers had been Winston Churchill, who had been eternally grateful. At 29 Beatty had become the fleet's youngest captain, and at 39 its youngest rear admiral. He was the object of envy and gossip, especially after he married Ethel Tree, the divorced American heiress of the Marshall Field department store fortune. Once, when Beatty drove a ship so fast her engines were damaged and a court-martial was threatened, his bride supposedly said, "What—court-martial my David? I'll buy them a new ship!"

Now, as the German raiders under Hipper approached the English coast, Beatty and Warrender moved to cut them off. In so doing, Warrender without knowing it placed himself within 10 miles of the onrushing German High Seas Fleet. The opposing outrider destroyers exchanged light fire; Warrender supposed that he had encountered a minor force, and prepared to fight. In fact, the Germans outnumbered him by almost 3 to 1 in heavy ships. A catastrophic defeat was in the making for the British—if Ingenohl had only seized the moment.

But Ingenohl did not know his enemy's strength any more than the British knew the strength of the Germans. And now his natural timidity overcame him. Suddenly afraid that he might be facing the entire Grand Fleet and that he would be overwhelmed and lose the war at sea for Germany, he turned tail and with his vast armada ran for home.

Left on his own, Hipper sped along in the coastal fog, firing on the three towns long enough to kill 140 civilians. Then he headed back into a squall of wind and rain. En route he was nearly cut off by the now-superior British force. In fact, a pair of British light cruisers, the *Southampton* and the *Birmingham,* had sighted some of Hipper's ships and rushed to engage them. But Hipper got a reprieve when Lieutenant Commander Ralph Seymour, Beatty's signal officer, who would cause no end of trouble before long, sent a confusing message by signal light. It read, "Light cruisers—resume your position for lookout. Take station five miles ahead." The message was not meant for the *Southampton* and the *Birmingham*, but for two other cruisers that were not engaged, the *Nottingham* and the *Falmouth*. Beatty expected to come on Hipper's main force shortly, and he wanted additional scouts. But since the message was addressed simply "light cruisers," it was assumed to mean all light cruisers. The *Southampton* and the *Birmingham* reluctantly broke contact. And Hipper was thus allowed to escape. Armageddon had failed to occur. A feeling of shattering anticlimax afflicted both fleets; everyone was left with a sense of failure and missed opportunities.

In the aftermath, the same caution that from the start had ruled both the British Admiralty and the German Supreme Headquarters prevailed once more. Beatty quietly diverted any wrath from his signalman. Jellicoe grumbled privately about his fleet's confused signals but publicly wrote it off to a bad turn of weather, and Churchill made some statesmanlike comments about not attaching blame. On the other side, the Kaiser turned his usual deaf ear to an explosion by Tirpitz against the extreme caution of Ingenohl. Then all hands settled back to await the next stroke.

They did not wait long. On January 23, 1915, Room 40 signaled directly to Churchill: "Those fellows are coming out again." The report was relayed to Jellicoe and Beatty, with critical details: "Four German battle cruisers, six light cruisers and 22 destroyers will sail this evening to scout the Dogger Bank." The force contained four battle cruisers as reported, but the support was four light cruisers and 19 destroyers. Other intercepts from the too talkative German radio operators turned out to be dead accurate. The Germans, with Hipper in command, would be at a spot 30 miles north of the Dogger Bank at 7 o'clock next morning.

Sure enough, Hipper left his anchorage at 5:45 that evening, heading north of the Bank. Minutes later, Beatty, with five battle cruisers and four light cruisers, steamed out of the Firth of Forth; to support him, a second force of three light cruisers and 35 destroyers departed from Harwich. "Only one thought could reign," Churchill wrote later. "Battle at dawn. Battle for the first time in history between such mighty super ships."

The rendezvous was precise. At dawn the two forces met. Hipper was horrified. He surmised—correctly—that the interception was no accident. Who had betrayed his plans? He suspected the neutral fishing boats that were still all about the war zone. But neither he nor anyone else in the German high command dreamed that the British were using the *Magdeburg* windfall to monitor virtually every move of the Imperial Navy. The British knew that the *Von der Tann* was in dry dock, that Hipper was using the *Seydlitz* as his flagship, that his other battle cruisers were the *Moltke* and *Derfflinger*, plus the older *Blücher*, whose 8.2-inch guns really did not qualify her as a battle cruiser.

Visibility was poor because of funnel smoke, so Hipper could not tell exactly what type of enemy vessels he had encountered, or how many of them—possibly dreadnoughts, possibly many. At this point, caution overcame even this combat-minded officer, and he turned for home. But he was not to escape without a scalding.

Beatty in the *Lion*, leading the *Tiger* and the *Princess Royal*, all with eight 13.5-inch guns, plus the *New Zealand* and the *Indomitable* with eight 12-inchers apiece, ordered 29 knots. This was more than his ships could really do, but the three lead ships managed 27, with the two other battle cruisers, the seven light cruisers and 35 destroyers in the screening force keeping pace as best they could. Backing up Beatty to cut off the Germans if they swung north were seven predreadnoughts and a light-cruiser squadron of four ships. And still farther away the bulk of the Grand Fleet—some 60 strong, including 21 dreadnoughts—steamed grandly out of Scapa Flow, in case the action blew up into Armageddon.

As the British battle cruisers raced along, a young lieutenant on the bridge with Beatty wrote: "The enemy appeared on the eastern horizon in the form of four separate wedges or triangles of smoke. Suddenly from the rearmost of these wedges came a stab of white flame."

The Germans had opened fire. Following the muzzle flash, the young officer continued, "We waited for what seemed a long time, probably about 25 seconds, until a great column of water and spray arose in the sea at a distance of more than a mile on our port bow. The first shot had been fired, and another epoch in the history of war begun."

Hipper was limited to 23 knots, the best that the *Blücher* could do. "The pace at which the enemy was closing in was entirely unexpected," he wrote subsequently, and enviously. Toward 9 a.m. on this bright winter day, at the unprecedented range of 22,000 yards—more than 12 miles—Beatty snapped, "Open fire and engage the enemy."

The *Blücher*, the trailing ship in Hipper's retreating line, was engaged by three of Beatty's ships in turn, the *Lion*, the *Tiger* and the *Princess Royal*, pouring salvos of 13.5-inch shells at her. A survivor recalled: "The British guns were ranging. Those deadly waterspouts crept nearer and nearer. Men on deck watched them with a strange fascination."

Just before 9:30 the *New Zealand* also came in range of the unfortunate *Blücher*. "Now the shells came thick and fast with a horrible droning hum," the same German survivor recollected. "At once they did terrible execution. The electric plant was soon destroyed, and the ship plunged into a darkness that could be felt. Belowdecks there was horror and confusion, gasping shouts and moans as the shells plunged through the decks, even bored their way to the stokehold. Coal in the bunkers caught fire. Since the bunkers were half-empty the fire burned furiously."

At 10:30 a.m. the *Blücher* took a terrible salvo that knocked out her forward 8.2s, hit the boilers and crippled the steering gear. "In the engine room a shell licked up the oil and sprayed it around in flames of blue and green," the account continued, "scarring its victims and blazing where it fell. In the terrific air pressure of explosions in confined spaces, the bodies of men were whirled about like dead leaves in a winter blast, to be battered to death against the steel walls. As one poor wretch was passing through a trap door a shell burst near him. He was exactly halfway through. The trap door closed with an awful crash. In one of the engine rooms men were picked up by that terrible whirlwind and tossed to a horrible death in the machinery."

That was an aspect of battle that navies seldom dwelled on, since they saw themselves fighting against ships, not men. Hipper's flagship, the *Seydlitz*, "suffered a heavy direct hit aft," the German commander

Vice Admiral Sir David Beatty, the commander of British battle cruisers in what the press mislabeled a smashing victory at the Dogger Bank, always felt that circumstance had cheated him out of a far greater triumph. "The disappointment of that day," he wrote, "is more than I can bear to think of."

wrote, "and a serious fire broke out in turrets C and D. The after engine room had to be abandoned for some time owing to gas danger. The magazines were flooded."

His professional language masked the fact that the entire crews of his two afterturrets—159 men in all—were trapped belowdecks and burned to death or drowned. It also neglected the heroism of a chief petty officer who grabbed the red-hot wheels of the valves that flooded the magazines and, while the flesh burned from his hands, let in the sea water that saved the ship and its crew from a cataclysmic explosion.

But meanwhile the British had blundered anew into the communications mix-ups that had plagued them throughout the naval war. Beatty radioed his ships to "Engage corresponding ships in enemy line." As the match-up was five ships against four, the captain of the *Tiger*, second in line, decided that two ships should concentrate on Hipper's *Seydlitz*. Consequently the *Moltke*, second in the German line, was free to take target practice on the *Lion*—which she did forthwith. Moreover, in the recently commissioned *Tiger*, the gunnery officer mistook the *Lion's* fall of shot for his own, and his salvos fell 3,000 yards beyond the target.

Despite her own wounds, that target—the *Seydlitz*—joined the *Moltke* and the *Derfflinger* to pound away at Beatty's *Lion*. One salvo slowed the *Lion's* port engine, which soon stopped altogether. The *Lion* began to lag behind her sisters. Another series of shots knocked out two of her three dynamos, which dangerously overloaded the ship's electrical power system. At 10:47 Beatty told all ships to "Close the enemy as rapidly as possible," and an instant later ordered the newly arrived *Indomitable* to finish off the *Blücher*. Beatty's report of the battle stated: "At 10:48 the *Blücher*, which had dropped considerably astern of the enemy's line, hauled out to port, steering north, with a heavy list, on fire, and apparently in a defeated condition. Yet she still continued firing."

Now, suddenly, Beatty's last dynamo went out, leaving the *Lion* with no internal electric power and the admiral with no means of signaling his fleet save with flags.

Shortly after 11 a.m. Beatty again signaled his ships to close the enemy. To transmit the order, Lieutenant Commander Seymour selected signal flags that indicated "Course N.E." and "Attack the rear of the enemy." But the *Lion* now had only two flag halyards that had not been shot away, and Seymour hoisted these two signals in such a way that the other ships read them as: "Attack the rear of the enemy, bearing N.E." That, by coincidence, was the bearing of the *Blücher*, and Beatty, too far astern by then to do anything more, was stunned to see his squadron break off the chase and converge on the wreckage of the *Blücher*.

Despairing, he called a destroyer alongside the *Lion*, jumped on board it, steamed at flank speed to the *Princess Royal* and by radio ordered the squadron to resume the chase. But it was too late. The time was now noon. The *Blücher*, under the point-blank fire of four battle cruisers and several destroyers, was going down, and Hipper's three surviving ships had a head start of 12 miles. At 12:13 the gallant old *Blücher* sank, one or two guns blazing to the end. The battle was over. The Germans had lost 951 dead, all on the *Blücher* and the *Seydlitz*. The British, despite the *Lion's* heavy damage, had lost fewer than 50 killed and wounded.

Admiral Franz von Hipper, the commander of a reconnoitering force from the German High Seas Fleet, inflicted 22 hits on Beatty's cruisers at the Dogger Bank, and escaped with all but one of his own ships. Upon Hipper's death in 1932, Beatty referred to him as "a gallant officer and a great sailor."

The British press made a noble victory of the Dogger Bank action. And one admiral, Sir William Pakenham, commander of a cruiser squadron, privately said the inevitable of Beatty to the First Lord, "Nelson has come again." But Beatty, an honest man in assessing his own achievements, knew that he was no Nelson, that no Trafalgar had taken place, but only the sinking of one old battle cruiser. "We ought to have had all four," he noted gloomily. Subsequently he wrote to a friend, "Everybody thinks it was a great success, when in reality it was a terrible failure."

The Germans, despite the loss of the *Blücher* and nearly 1,000 men, drew some profit from the Dogger Bank. The near-disaster to the *Seydlitz* revealed a fault in her design. If a shell penetrated a gun turret, the flash of the explosion could go down to the handling room below and up into the neighboring turret. Only immediate flooding of the magazine could stop an explosion that would instantly sink the ship. The Germans modified all their battle cruisers with extra bulkheads and decking. But the British battle cruisers, which had the same defect (perhaps worse), took no major hits. The weakness remained undetected—and uncorrected.

The need for that technical modification was apparently the only lesson of the Dogger Bank learned by the Germans. The Kaiser was furious at the loss of the *Blücher*. Perversely, after a solid year of insisting upon caution, he now turned on Ingenohl for not properly supporting the sortie, and removed him from command. On several occasions Tirpitz had recommended his own appointment as Commander in Chief, that office to be combined with Chief of Naval Staff and Naval Secretary, thus ensuring absolute authority for himself over the Navy. The Kaiser ignored the idea of a unified and aggressive command, and pointedly turned his back on Tirpitz for good. Worse yet, instead of installing a man like Hipper as the new Commander in Chief, the Kaiser chose a sickly, inconsequential admiral named Hugo von Pohl, a gloomy yet arrogant man, unpopular in the fleet—but a person who could be relied on not to risk his ships. Under Pohl, a whole year went by in which the High Seas Fleet never ventured out beyond its coastal defenses.

Neither did the Grand Fleet, although the residue of excitement from the Dogger Bank stirred the offensive spirit in Beatty and Fisher. "At times our inactivity frets me to such an extent that I can hardly bear it," Beatty wrote to his wife. With Fisher, this frustration ignited the quarrel, foreseen by so many people, between himself and Churchill. Both now chafed to use the dreadnoughts for some positive aggressive aim. "When the Germans kick our bottoms, then we move, but d----d slow at that!" Fisher wrote to Churchill, bowdlerizing his mild profanity with Edwardian restraint. "DO SOMETHING!!!!!! *We are waiting to be kicked!!!*"

But they could not agree on what to do. Fisher's favorite scheme was to force a way into the Baltic, use the British fleet to land Russian troops in Germany, and meanwhile immobilize the High Seas Fleet by an immense minefield. No other Naval expert thought this idea was practical. But it became Fisher's obsession, and a futile one. In May 1915, after a stormy meeting with Churchill, he resigned. "Fisher is always resigning," Prime Minister Herbert Asquith said. "This is nothing new."

But the old man, now 74, dramatically left his office at the Admiralty, refused to do any work and announced that he was going to Scotland at

Crewmen desperately scramble over the hull of the capsized armored cruiser Blücher after she was shattered by 70 British shells and seven torpedoes at the Battle of the Dogger Bank. The Blücher, with 8.2-inch guns, was no match for the British heavyweights with their 13.5-inch guns, leading German Admiral von Hipper to the rueful conclusion that "only completely efficient ships should be included in battle squadrons."

once and would never return. The Prime Minister had to write to him: "Lord Fisher, in the King's name I order you to remain at your post." Jellicoe, Beatty and others begged Fisher to stay: the press unanimously said he must not go. The furore threatened to topple the government, which was already in trouble because of divisions within the Cabinet.

Convinced that he was indispensable, Fisher wrote a foolish letter to Asquith. "If the following six conditions are agreed to," it began, "I can guarantee the successful termination of the war." Among the conditions were that Churchill be removed from the Cabinet, and that he, Fisher, have "absolute sole disposition of the fleet, the appointment of all officers of all ranks whatsoever, absolutely untrammeled sole command of all the sea forces, sole absolute authority for all new construction," and the same for "all dockyard work of whatever sort whatsoever."

Fisher was demanding from a Parliamentary government infinitely more than it could—or should—give. It was madness to think that such powers, and the work of a dozen men, could possibly be given to one man, 74 years old. In his megalomania Fisher had lost all touch with reality; the Prime Minister remarked to the King that the document "indicated signs of mental aberration."

Asquith's reply was terse: "Dear Lord Fisher, I am commanded by the King to accept your resignation of the office of First Sea Lord of the Admiralty." That was all. In his annoyance, Asquith had failed to thank Fisher for his lifetime of service, or extend good wishes for his retirement. But Asquith's omission was understandable. The Allies had a war to win, and there was no more time to indulge a senile old man, no matter how much he had done for the Navy or the safety of the country. Fisher was replaced by Admiral Sir Henry Jackson, who was reputed to be competent in administrative matters and was experienced in the fleet.

In Germany, Admiral von Tirpitz lasted a little longer. But in March 1916 he also resigned, chagrined at the Kaiser's contemptuous disregard, exasperated that the High Seas Fleet was not being used, and infuriated that he, Tirpitz, was powerless to do anything about it. So both of the men who had created the dreadnought fleets had gone from the scene, and the dreadnoughts still lay idle in their harbors.

The deadlock was broken by, of all things, a medical report. Admiral von Pohl was found to have an internal disease—probably cancer—in a critically advanced stage. On January 8, 1916, he reported in sick to undergo an operation, and a man of a very different stamp was appointed Commander in Chief of the High Seas Fleet. He was the tough-minded and aggressive Admiral Reinhard Scheer, the officer who had so heartily cheered the prospect of combat at the outset of the War but who had been obliged ever since then to command an inactive battle squadron.

With these changes among the principal actors on each side, together with the mounting pressures in both countries to break free of the infuriating stalemate of blockade and counterblockade, the climate was set for a genuine confrontation. After all the months of waiting, on May 30, 1916, Room 40 at Whitehall reported that the High Seas Fleet would put to sea next morning. This time the full Grand Fleet embraced the challenge. The dreadnoughts at last were to be turned onto a real collision course for Armageddon.

Mine warfare: seeds of death planted in the sea

Of all the naval weapons of World War I, the most diabolical by far was the mine. Floating silent and invisible 10 to 15 feet beneath the surface of the water, these marine bombs, each carrying 350 pounds or more of high explosive, could rip open the underside of any vessel afloat. Laid in fields of 25 to 100 mines, they were employed to turn wide stretches of strategic sea-lane into hideous deathtraps.

To the British, with their superior fleet, the mine was at first a despicable and barbaric "weapon of the weak"—though as the War went on, the Royal Navy laid its full share of mines, particularly in defensive arrays around its fleet anchorages. But from the very start the Germans saw the mine as an offensive weapon of great effectiveness, an inexpensive equalizer with which, as a German Naval officer put it, "to bring the War to the enemy's coasts."

Stealthily slipping through the night, specially outfitted German submarines, destroyers and cruisers sallied forth to lay their murderous cargoes all along the Channel and North Sea coasts of England. Scores of British vessels, both warships and merchantmen, were sunk in the first few months of the War. On October 27, 1914, the spanking-new 23,000-ton dreadnought *Audacious* struck a mine and sank, touching off a panic wave of "mine-itis" among the Grand Fleet's staff. Wrote Admiral John Jellicoe: "It will be pure suicide taking the fleet out without sweeping, and I have nothing with which to sweep."

Desperate for minesweepers, the British fitted hundreds of fishing trawlers with devices to snare and cut mine-mooring lines. It was dangerous work: there were times, before sweeping techniques were perfected, when one trawler was sunk for every two mines swept up.

All told, the Germans laid more than 43,000 mines in four years of war, and by 1918, more than 210 British minesweepers had been lost trying to cope with them. In one case, the salvaged bow and stern halves of two destroyers that had struck mines, the *Zulu* and the *Nubian*, were hastily joined to produce a new sweeper: the *Zubian*.

At the peak of the British campaign against the mines, 725 minesweepers turned out each day to clear a 540-mile "war channel" between the Firth of Forth and Dover. Yet the sweepers could never get all the mines. By War's end, one million tons of Allied shipping, including 588 British ships, had fallen to the seeds of death planted in the sea.

On a moonless night, faintly illuminated by starshine, a converted German light cruiser, accompanied by an escorting destroyer, sows a field of high-explosive contact mines in the North Sea shipping lanes off the English coast. The mines are dropped overboard through a pair of transom portals in the minelayer's hull at intervals precisely calculated to form the largest and most impenetrable barrier with the fewest mines.

Working in the dim, eerie glow of
blue blackout bulbs, the crewmen of the
German minelayer gingerly roll the
crated mines, attached to their mooring
blocks, along steel rails to the
minelaying apertures. Each minelayer
carried up to 400 mines, stored in a
miniature railroad yard of tracks running
the length of the ship. A British sailor
held prisoner aboard a German minelayer
remarked that the deadly mines,
"standing lashed down in long rows,"
resembled nothing more than "black,
barrel sized eggs in eggcups."

As the minelayer disappears into
the distance, its mines drop to the seabed
and—as seen in this time-compressed
view—deploy themselves. Within five to
25 minutes, sea water dissolves salt
plugs that hold the retaining bars of the
mine cradles in place. As the bars fall
away, the mines rise to predetermined
depths on their mooring cables. The
"horns" on each mine are electrically
activated triggering devices sensitive to
the slightest contact with a ship's hull.

As mines severed from their moorings
bob to the surface, crewmen on board a
sweeper dispose of them by rifle fire,
exploding one mine in a geyser of smoke
and spray. A British officer described
an explosion of this kind as "an enormous
mushroom 300-500 feet high." More
often, a mine would simply sink harmlessly
to the bottom of the sea after a number
of bullets had punctured its air chamber.

Steaming in a formation of overlapping
pairs, a squadron of six minesweepers
(five of which can be seen here) clears a
passage about half a mile wide through an
enemy minefield. The ships of each
pair dragged between them a "sweep wire"
300 to 500 yards long and fitted at
intervals with steel cutting jaws to sever
mine-mooring cables. A wedge-shaped
device called a "kite" (inset), which
planed downward underwater, held the
wire taut at the depth of the mine cables.

Ripped by a thunderous blast from an exploding German mine, the bow of a trawler-minesweeper is blown out of the water and the doomed ship is rocked back until her stern is almost awash. In the foreground, crewmen watch helplessly from one of a new class of paddle-wheel minesweepers, designed with extremely shallow drafts to ride safely over the mines. This and other advances made it possible for the British to destroy more than 30,000 German mines by the War's end.

Chapter 4

A fierce skirmish of scouts at Jutland

ice Admiral Reinhard Scheer, the new commander of the High Seas Fleet, was a creature of conflict. His every instinct was that of the fighting man, and he had been thoroughly frustrated during a long and discouraging peacetime career. The son of a Bavarian schoolmaster (and therefore considered hopelessly middle class by aristocratic colleagues), Scheer had entered the Imperial German Navy at the age of 16 and was a ripe 39, veteran of 23 years' service, before becoming so much as a ship's second-in-command.

But as it became increasingly clear that the time was approaching for more serious business than regattas and reviews at Kiel or Spithead, family wealth and social status gradually gave way to professional ability as a prerequisite for Naval advancement, and preferment for Scheer came faster. By 1907, at 44 years of age, he was commander of a destroyer flotilla and the author of a competent if little-noticed treatise on torpedo tactics. In 1914 he took over the predreadnought Battle Squadron 2 — forming an attachment for the old warships that would later cost him dearly. And after a brief stint in command of the new dreadnoughts of Battle Squadron 3, he was named chief of staff to the commander of the High Seas Fleet. It was from that job that he was promoted to command of the fleet in January 1916.

Scheer was confident of his own capabilities — and overconfident of those of his fleet. "When I consider my entire Navy," he said, "I am forced to the belief that it is equal to Britain's." In that frame of mind he attended a February 23, 1916, naval conference in Wilhelmshaven and urgently sought the Kaiser's consent to use the High Seas Fleet more aggressively. It was in tribute to his forceful persuasion — and perhaps because the erratic monarch was distracted by preparations for a massive land offensive against the French at Verdun, only three weeks away — that the Kaiser agreed.

For a start, Scheer wanted to mount an operation much like the one tried by Ingenohl with such embarrassing results in December 1914. Only this time there would be no panicky retreat by the dreadnoughts at the first sign of the enemy. Like Ingenohl, Scheer would use Franz von Hipper's battle cruisers as bait. While Hipper bombarded East Anglian towns his own dreadnought force would trail 60 miles astern. Then, when Beatty and the British battle cruisers came hallooing down from their anchorage in the Firth of Forth to defend their coast, Scheer's main force would fall upon them before Jellicoe could arrive with the Grand Fleet from distant Scapa Flow. Eighteen submarines were assigned to skulk outside Scapa, Cromarty and the Forth, where they could harass

Dwarfed by massive 12-inch guns, crewmen on the afterdeck of the German dreadnought Ostfriesland scan a line of battleships stretching to the horizon as the High Seas Fleet steams toward Jutland on the morning of May 31, 1916. All told, 99 German ships sallied forth — to meet a British fleet more than half again as big.

and delay Jellicoe's southerly movement, and Zeppelins would be used for aerial reconnaissance. The operation was scheduled for May 17. To goad the British into a proper fury and ensure that they would jump into the trap, Scheer sent Hipper on two preliminary hit-and-run raids against the coastal towns, the first on March 6, the second on April 24.

That, as it turned out, was a mistake. During the second raid, the *Seydlitz* struck a British mine and returned home crippled. Since Scheer could spare not a single one of the five new battle cruisers, he postponed his main operation for several more weeks while the damage was repaired. By the time the *Seydlitz* was ready, the German submarines, which had sortied out so as to be on station under the original schedule, were running short of fuel for their diesel engines, and only four remained for the Scapa ambush.

Another delay was perfectly feasible, but patience was not one of Scheer's primary virtues—and at 9:48 on the morning of May 30, from the wireless room of the *Friedrich der Grosse* came the fateful signal for the warships of the High Seas Fleet to assemble in the outer roads of the Jade by 7 p.m., prepared to set forth before sunrise, seeking battle.

During the day of May 30, Scheer changed his mind as to the fleet's destination. Navy meteorologists predicted adverse winds for the Zeppelins, which meant that these fragile, lighter-than-air craft could not be used for reconnaissance as the fleet approached the British coast. Scheer decided instead to use a previously arranged alternative plan that would keep him closer to his own side of the North Sea, with less need for aerial reconnaissance. And at 3:40 p.m. the radio operator on the *Friedrich der Grosse* tapped out the signal—31 Gg 2490—that put the new plan into effect.

Under this scheme, Hipper's Scouting Group 1 (battle cruisers), Scouting Group 2 (light cruisers) and three destroyer flotillas would thrust northward, remaining just out of sight of the neutral Danish coast, then advertise their presence by attacking merchant shipping off Norway before dusk on May 31. In a later change, Scheer decided to follow only about 25 miles behind Hipper instead of the originally planned 60 miles; since he would have no air search, he thought it best to remain closer to Hipper and his battle cruisers in case something went wrong. And, finally, he succumbed to pleas from Battle Squadron 2 that he take along the six outdated battleships that had made up his first major command. These vessels mounted only four 11-inch guns apiece and were known in the German Navy as the "five-minute ships," because that was about how long they might be expected to last in a major fleet action. By agreeing to include them in his fleet, Scheer displayed an unsuspected streak of sentimentality—and diminished the speed of his main force by at least three knots.

Scheer's signals were, of course, intercepted and decoded by the British boffins in Room 40 at the Admiralty. By noon on May 30, Admiral Sir John Jellicoe knew that the High Seas Fleet was gathering for a sortie. At 5:40 p.m. the Admiralty ordered Jellicoe and the Grand Fleet to raise steam, following a few minutes later with instructions to "concentrate to eastward of the Long Forties ready for eventualities." In the chartrooms of Jellicoe's dreadnought *Iron Duke* and Vice Admiral Sir David Beatty's

Prelude to battle

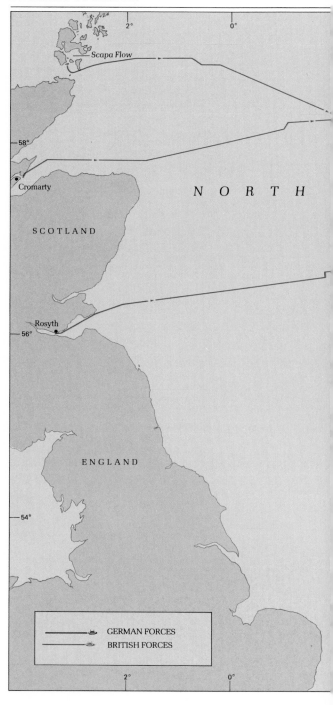

9:30 P.M., MAY 30, TO 2:15 P.M., MAY 31. At 9:30 p.m. Admiral John Jellicoe orders his 16 dreadnoughts out of Scapa Flow, and Admiral David Beatty's six battle cruisers and four new superdreadnoughts leave Rosyth, while eight dreadnoughts clear Cromarty. Admiral Franz von Hipper's five battle cruisers leave the Jade at 1:00 a.m. on May 31, and Admiral Reinhard Scheer leads his 16 dreadnoughts and six predreadnoughts out at 2:30. Almost 12 hours later, at 2:10 p.m., the British cruiser Galatea sights a German force, led by the cruiser Elbing, that has halted a merchant ship.

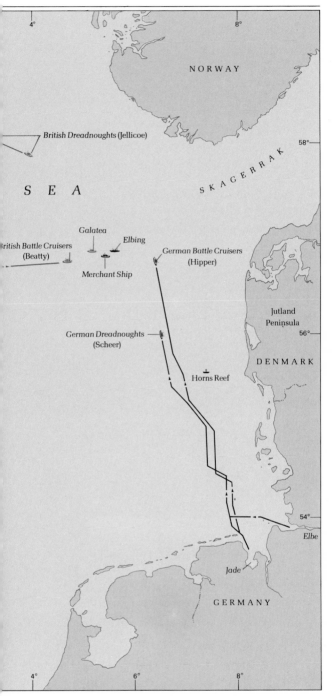

battle cruiser *Lion*, navigators laid their courses across the North Sea toward Norway and Denmark.

At 9:30 o'clock in the long summer dusk of the far north of Scotland, Jellicoe put to sea, his flag—a red St. George's cross on a white ground—snapping from the gaff of the *Iron Duke (chart, left)*. Joining in the silent procession of blue-gray warships were 15 other dreadnoughts, three battle cruisers, eight smaller armored cruisers, 11 light cruisers, 51 destroyers and a minelayer. Few on Scapa's desolate shores watched the warships go and, as darkness fell, even the admirals and captains on the bridges, the navigating officers, signalmen and upper-deck crews saw no more than the shadowed loom of the nearest ships, the dim blue sternlights of the next ahead, and the disembodied flashes of the flagship's signal lamps. Most of the crews witnessed little or nothing of the somber journey through the night; they were belowdecks, in a separate world of brilliant light and throbbing machinery, or off watch in the mess decks, asleep in the rows of swaying hammocks. By 10:30 the Grand Fleet had passed the Pentland Skerries at 17 knots, course 61°.

Beatty, in the *Lion* and commanding a 52-ship force, left Rosyth at about 9:30, steaming beneath the massive tubular girders of the Forth Bridge and past slumbering Leith and Edinburgh. Accompanying his six battle cruisers, 12 light cruisers, 29 destroyers and a single seaplane carrier were the four most modern and powerful superdreadnoughts then existing—the *Barham*, the *Valiant*, the *Warspite* and the *Malaya*, each mounting eight 15-inch guns and capable of 25 knots. But their presence with Beatty's battle cruisers was a fluke that would weigh heavily, and adversely, on British fortunes in the forthcoming battle. Because there was insufficient protected water at Rosyth for gunnery practice, Beatty's 3rd Battle Cruiser Squadron, under Rear Admiral Sir Horace Hood, had been sent to Scapa for training. Given to Beatty in temporary exchange were the four dreadnoughts of the 5th Battle Squadron, commanded by Rear Admiral Hugh Evan-Thomas. That officer was unaccustomed to working with Beatty and, as it turned out, was of the unfortunate sort who, when in doubt, went by the book—which called for strict adherence to orders, even when common sense dictated individual initiative.

Despite—or perhaps because of—the strangers in his midst, Beatty was inordinately proud of his array. "Here," he wrote to his wife, "I have the finest striking force in the world." In that attitude lay a mistaken understanding of his primary mission, which was less one of striking than of scouting. "Battle cruisers," Jellicoe wrote later, "were designed and built in order that they might keep in touch with the enemy and report his movements. They were intended to find the enemy for the Battle Fleet and to ascertain the enemy's strength for the Battle Fleet."

At 10:15 p.m., 45 minutes after Beatty had weighed anchor, the third and last major element of the British force—the 2nd Battle Squadron, with eight dreadnoughts under Vice Admiral Sir Martyn Jerram—commenced its departure from Cromarty, located at one end of the swift-running and extremely deep Moray Firth. The British had previously managed to avoid operating at night in these tricky waters, and the lighthouse on Kinnairds Head had been turned off. At 1 a.m. it flashed

The flagships at Jutland

As surprising as it may seem, H.M.S. *Dreadnought* was not among the ships in the British battle line at Jutland. In the 10 brief years since her commissioning, the great warship had become obsolete and unsuitable for combat in the Grand Fleet. Consequently, the *Dreadnought* was relegated to duty in her home waters.

In the main battle fleets at Jutland were dreadnoughts half again heavier than their older sister, with protective armor almost a third again as thick and cannon that hurled shells almost two and a half times heavier than those of the *Dreadnought*. These modern warships had power plants that delivered more than twice the horsepower of the *Dreadnought*'s engines, enabling them to move at 25 knots, some four knots faster than the older ship.

Faster still were ships of a new type known at first as dreadnought cruisers, and by the time of Jutland as battle cruisers. These vessels were larger and up to six knots faster than the dread-

Prized for her top speed of 35 knots, the British Lydiard led a combined destroyer flotilla of 22 ships at Jutland. One of the new, slender L-class vessels, she was 260 feet long and only 27 feet on the beam, and displaced 807 tons. She carried three 4-inch guns and four torpedoes.

With ten 13.5-inch guns capable of launching a broadside of 14,000 pounds, the 25,000-ton dreadnought Iron Duke served as Grand Fleet flagship for Admiral John Jellicoe. She carried 12-inch armor, was 620 feet long and 89½ feet abeam, and could reach a speed of 21 knots.

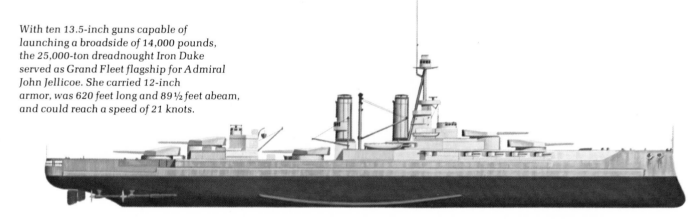

Flagship of Admiral Beatty's battle-cruiser fleet, the 26,350-ton Lion carried eight 13.5-inch guns and a crew of 1,000. Shielded by armor nowhere more than nine inches thick, she was 675 feet long and 86½ feet abeam, and her turbines could deliver a flank speed of 29 knots.

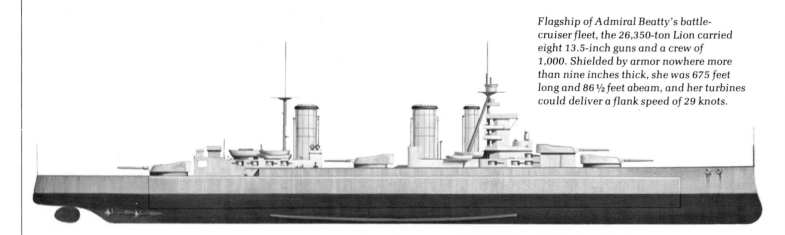

noughts, and while they were almost as heavily armed, they forfeited much of their armor for speed. Their mission was to act as scouts and decoys for the dreadnoughts, and their commanders sought to engage one another and to avoid the dreadnoughts themselves.

Ship for ship in such vitals as size, speed, cruising range and crew, the fleets were about equal. The British boasted more ships, carrying heavier guns. But the German ships were better armored, with thicker turret and deck armor and flashproof magazines. Belowdecks, they were honeycombs of bulkheads and watertight doors.

Dwarfed by the capital ships were the swarms of light, fast escorting destroyers. The Germans, who opted for offensive capability, called their destroyers torpedo boats and fitted them with as many torpedoes as practical. British destroyers, on the other hand, carried fewer torpedoes but were better armed with guns to form a defensive screen for the fleet.

Designed for 32.5 knots, the V-29 and her five sister ships in the Schichau class could get up to 36.5 knots at top speed. With approximately the same dimensions as her British destroyer counterparts, she carried only two 3.5-inch guns, but made up for it with eight torpedoes.

Admiral Reinhard Scheer's High Seas Fleet flagship, the 24,700-ton Friedrich der Grosse, carried ten 12-inch guns that could fire an 8,500-pound broadside. Shorter (594 feet) and wider (95 feet) than the Iron Duke, she traded a knot of speed for two inches more armor.

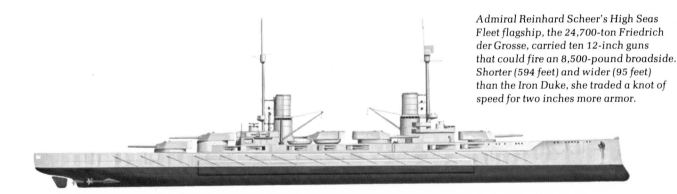

The newest of the German battle cruisers, Admiral Franz von Hipper's 28,000-ton Lützow carried eight 12-inch guns. She was 692 feet long and, even though weighted by armor that amidships was a comfortable 13 inches thick, she could make 27 knots.

for the first time since 1914, showing for 40 minutes, until the last of the warships slipped safely past the headland into the darkness beyond, heading for rendezvous with Jellicoe. The King's Navy was now at sea.

So, within a few hours, was the Kaiser's. At 7:50 a.m. on May 31, Hipper's battle cruisers, with pale-gray hulls and funnel bands of blue, red, white or yellow, according to each ship's position in its squadron, cleared the swept channel through the Heligoland Bight minefields and turned north. At that moment, despite the dour forecasts, the morning mist lifted. Recalled Commander Georg von Hase, the gunnery officer of the battle cruiser *Derfflinger:* "The sun rose magnificently, covered the sea with its golden rays and soon showed us the picture of the High Seas Fleet proceeding to meet the enemy, always a wonderful sight. Far ahead of us steamed the small cruisers in line ahead, surrounded by a cordon of destroyers. Then came the battle cruisers. Five powerful ships with imposing names, the pride of the fleet. Far astern the clear weather enabled us to see the main fleet, our ships of the line. These numbered 22, a proud armada."

The armada was badly outmatched. In all, the Germans had 99 ships, with a total tonnage of 660,000, and about 45,000 men, as against the Grand Fleet's 149 warships, a combined tonnage of nearly a million and a quarter, and some 60,000 men. The best of the German dreadnoughts had only 12-inch guns against the standard British 13-inchers and the 15-inchers of the superdreadnoughts. All the British ships were modern; only the armored cruisers were more than seven years old. Even the original *Dreadnought,* then 10 years old, was considered too outdated to sail with the fleet. Scheer's main force, on the other hand, was hampered by the six elderly battleships of his old squadron.

The British, morever, enjoyed the immense intelligence advantage of Room 40's operations—an advantage that, in a scandalous performance, they managed to throw away. Before Scheer's flagship *Friedrich der Grosse* left to follow Hipper's force, Scheer had transferred his harbor call sign, which was DK, to a shore station and had taken another operational sign. He did this to obscure the fact that the fleet was at sea. He had done the same thing on several previous occasions, and Room 40 was aware of his trick.

This time, the switch was quickly picked up by Room 40, which now was not only deciphering German signals but was using directional receivers to track the whereabouts of enemy ships. However, a gulf of Naval snobbery existed between the Operations Division of the Admiralty and the code breakers. The line officers regarded the Room 40 denizens as a donnish lot who could do wonders with ciphers but could hardly be expected to analyze or interpret their findings in a proper Naval fashion. Through repeated rebukes, the men of Room 40 had become chary of volunteering any information or advice for which they were not specifically asked. And when, at 11:10 on the morning of May 31, Rear Admiral Thomas Jackson, the Director of Operations, went into Room 40 and requested the location of call sign DK, he got exactly what he asked for—and no more. "In the Jade," he was told, and he duly signaled to Jellicoe and Beatty that while Hipper and the battle cruisers were at sea, Scheer and the dreadnoughts were still in base.

Thus, with each commander in chief contentedly confident that the other's dreadnoughts were beyond supporting range, the dark-gray British fleet and the pale-gray German fleet, carrying a total of no fewer than 25 admirals between them, groped toward what Winston Churchill would shortly call "the culminating manifestation of naval forces in the history of the world." The Battle of Jutland—or, as the Germans called it, the Battle of the Skagerrak—was the only full fleet action of World War I, the last that either the Royal Navy or the Imperial Navy would ever fight, and indeed the final fleet engagement of great magnitude for any nation in which air power played little or no part.

It was also, despite Churchill's magniloquence, a most confused and confusing affair, with two major phases—the first, a running fight between battle cruisers; the second, a clash pitting dreadnoughts against dreadnoughts—subdivided into dozens of smaller, swirling melees. Admiral von Hipper, the only ranking commander on either side whose performance was nearly flawless, had it just about right when, during a lull in the battle, he turned to his staff and said: "I bet the armchair experts at the Naval Academy will be scratching their heads one day as to what we have all been thinking about. I say we haven't done any thinking. We've all been too busy trying to carry out sound tactics."

The fleets very nearly missed each other. Beatty's orders were to steam to a point 100 miles northwest of the minefields at Horns Reef. If, by 2 p.m., he had not caught sight of the enemy, he was to turn north to meet Jellicoe, who would be 65 miles away. Beatty was at his decision point on the dot, his screen of light cruisers spread on a line eight miles ahead of him. He had found nothing on the cruise thus far, and still he saw nothing. Reluctantly, he signaled the northward turn that would break off the hunt. At that point Hipper's battle cruisers were 40 miles to the east, with Scheer about 50 miles astern of Hipper to the south. And through the open sea between Hipper and Beatty plowed a dingy Danish tramp steamer, the *N.J. Fjord*—whose innocent presence was to be the immediate cause of the Battle of Jutland.

At 2 o'clock, even as Beatty was arriving at the easternmost reach of his assigned sweep, the German light cruiser *Elbing*, part of Hipper's west flank screen, spotted the *N.J. Fjord* and sent two destroyers to stop and investigate the tramp steamer. Meanwhile, on the eastern wing of Beatty's screen, the British cruiser *Galatea* had missed the signal to steer north and was continuing on her original eastward course.

Thus at 2:10 the *Galatea*, proceeding on her solitary way, sighted the *N.J. Fjord*, stopped and blowing off steam. This was unusual, and worth looking into. As the *Galatea* approached, the two destroyers scuttled away from behind the tramp steamer; the destroyers were clearly identifiable as German by their stubby foremasts and tall mainmasts. The *Galatea* instantly sounded action stations (which were still, as they had been for centuries, signaled by bugle), turned up her speed to 28 knots, and opened fire from a 6-inch fo'c's'le gun.

The blast nearly blew the *Galatea*'s unsuspecting wireless officer off the deck. Possibly because of tight security, he was unaware that the Grand Fleet was embarked on anything but another boring and uneventful sweep of the North Sea, and he had been enjoying the sunshine on the quarter-deck. Even when the bugle sounded, he assumed it was for a practice exercise he had heard would be called that afternoon. But his leisurely stroll to the wireless office was dramatically broken by the roar of the nearby gun. "I nipped into my little W/T rabbit hutch quicker than it takes to tell," he recalled, "and as I entered there rattled down the communication tube from the upper bridge, in a small brass case, the first enemy report of the Battle of Jutland—'Enemy in sight.' "

The *Galatea*'s destroyer chase was brought up short by the sight of two German cruisers, which immediately opened fire. The *Galatea* reported them by wireless, but soon took a hit near her bridge from the *Elbing* at a range of about 14,000 yards. The *Galatea* hastily retired to the northwest, in the direction of Jellicoe's main force.

It took 12 minutes for the *Galatea*'s cruiser-sighting signal to be encoded, transmitted, decoded, written out and delivered to Beatty on the bridge of the *Lion*. At 2:31 the battle-cruiser fleet's teatime was rudely interrupted by the call to action stations and Beatty, hoping to cut the German warships off from their base, hoisted, "Alter course to S.S.E."

Although the *Galatea*'s signal to the *Lion* had been made by wireless because the ships were out of visual range, the British avoided the use of the radio in combat whenever possible. It was unreliable. The fragile wires and tubes of transmitters and receivers were easily damaged; even the concussion of a ship's own gun could put them out of commission. At Jutland, therefore, Beatty's orders were transmitted by flags, even though the *Lion*'s design made her halyards notoriously difficult to read and even though she was obscured by her own funnel smoke, as Beatty pressed on steam for full speed.

The results were swift, and grievous. The four superdreadnoughts under Evan-Thomas missed Beatty's signal to turn south-southeast and, since Evan-Thomas was no man to play follow-the-leader without orders, stubbornly continued on course. Six minutes passed before the superdreadnoughts, realizing their mistake, made their turn—by which time they were 10 miles astern and completely out of the first action.

The Germans reacted much more smoothly to the initial encounter. At 2:27, only a moment after receiving the *Elbing*'s wireless report of the brush with the *Galatea*, Hipper swung his battle cruisers into a west-southwest heading and a collision course with the British. On seeing the flagship turn, German light cruisers and destroyers followed without waiting for further orders. The German and British battle-cruiser fleets, though still beyond sight of each other, would soon be on converging courses—speeding south directly toward Scheer's dreadnoughts.

The British advantage had already begun to diminish, if only because Hipper knew what he was heading toward and Beatty did not.

Beatty made only a feeble effort at long-range reconnaissance. He ordered the seaplane carrier *Engadine* to send one of its two-seater floatplanes on a scouting expedition (*chart, page 110*). The little plane, lowered overboard, took off successfully from the calm sea and flew to the north, where it saw only enemy light cruisers and several destroyers. It had to fly so low beneath the gathering cloud cover that the Germans were able to shoot at it with their anti-torpedo-boat armament. But it

Soaring above a German cruiser during maneuvers in World War I, the Zeppelin at left and others like it were supposed to be the eagle eyes of the High Seas Fleet. But at Jutland the fragile, hydrogen-filled craft were hampered by fog and high winds, and played no useful role. The British also had little success with aerial reconnaissance. The seaplane carrier Engadine (below) dispatched one aircraft, which was forced down by mechanical failure after scarcely 40 minutes aloft.

survived, and reported what it had seen by wireless to the *Engadine*, whose erratic transmitter failed to relay the signal to Beatty. After a short time a fuel line broke in the seaplane's engine. The pilot, Lieutenant Frederick J. Rutland (later known as "Rutland of Jutland"), managed to bring his craft down within sight of the *Engadine*. He had mended the pipe with a rubber tube and was ready to take off again when he was told to come alongside the *Engadine* and be hoisted in. He was no longer needed. Guided by their outlying cruiser screens, the battle-cruiser fleets were in sight of each other—and so ended the only part that aircraft played in the battle.

Visibility was better to the west than to the east, where mist was forming. At 3:20 Hipper's fleet, 11 miles to the east-northeast of Beatty, was the first to sight its enemy, now steaming in a northeasterly direction. Commander Georg von Hase on the battle cruiser *Derfflinger* saw the British battle cruisers through the periscope of his gun sight. "Black monsters," he wrote, "six tall, broad-beamed giants steaming in two columns. They showed up clearly on the horizon, and even at this great distance they looked powerful, massive. Our flagship *Lützow* immediately ahead of us swung round on a southerly course. The enemy also altered to a converging course. Admiral von Hipper's intention was clear: he meant to engage the enemy battle cruisers and draw them on to our main fleet."

Only a few weeks before, Beatty had boasted, "If I meet Hipper and his battle cruisers, I can deal with them." Upon sighting the German battle cruisers, he had increased speed to a maximum of 25 knots and ordered Rear Admiral Sir William Pakenham's 2nd Battle Cruiser Squadron to fall in behind the first, forming a line led by the *Lion*, which was followed in order by the *Princess Royal*, the *Queen Mary*, the *Tiger*, the *New Zealand* and the *Indefatigable*. As Pakenham completed his move, Beatty signaled his battle cruisers to change course in succession to 100°, a converging course. The four superdreadnoughts were still hurrying desperately to catch up.

Hipper's response was simpler and more direct: knowing that he was outranged by the British guns, he closed by steering diagonally toward Beatty. Behind him, the *Derfflinger*, *Seydlitz*, *Moltke* and *Von der Tann* conformed to the flagship *Lützow*'s movement, each presenting an oblique angle to the British guns. At 3:48 o'clock, when Hipper's fleet was doing 18 knots—good for accurate gunnery—and had closed to a range of about 15,000 yards, flags were hoisted on the *Lützow*'s halyards, and the five German battle cruisers simultaneously opened fire.

Soon after, Beatty turned sharply to a course of about 180° to parallel Hipper's ships (*chart, far right*). The British were now caught in the middle of a complicated maneuver at high speed and they returned fire slowly, raggedly and inaccurately. Around them, the towering columns of water thrown up by shells crept ever closer as the German gunners corrected their range. To an officer on the *Tiger*, the projectiles resembled "big bluebottles flying straight towards you, each one seeming certain to hit you in the eye. Then they would fall, and the shell would either burst or else ricochet off the water and lollop away above and beyond you, turning over and over in the air."

The first battle-cruiser action

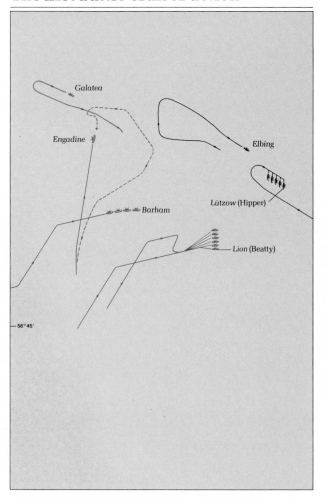

3:15 P.M. TO 3:48 P.M. Lacking precise knowledge of enemy strength, Beatty in the Lion orders the seaplane carrier Engadine to launch an aerial scout. Though the plane (dotted line) spots enemy cruisers at 3:30, signaling difficulties prevent word from reaching the British squadrons. To the north the Elbing chases the Galatea west and then turns southeast to lure her back toward Hipper's battle cruisers, led by the Lützow. Meanwhile Beatty, knowing only that the Germans are somewhere to the north and east of his position, turns to intercept them; his superdreadnoughts, led by the Barham, follow. At 3:20 Hipper sights Beatty and swings south. At 3:30 Beatty spots Hipper and at 3:48 the action begins.

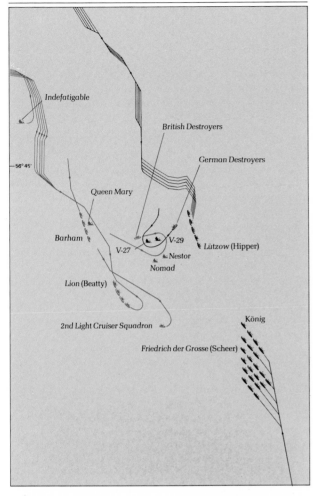

The Run to the South

3:48 P.M. TO 4:48 P.M. Hipper in the Lützow, outgunned by Beatty's battle cruisers and superdreadnoughts, runs south toward Scheer's approaching dreadnoughts, led by the König. But while the battle-cruiser squadrons steam south on roughly parallel courses, German gunnery has a devastating effect as three shells slam into the Indefatigable, sinking her at 4:05. Scarcely 20 minutes later the Queen Mary also explodes. Smaller ships between the battle lines engage, and each side loses two destroyers. At last at 4:40, having received the report from the light-cruiser squadron steaming before him that he is about to run smack into the High Seas Fleet, Beatty orders a 180° turn to the north, back toward his own dreadnoughts.

At 3:52, just four minutes after the shooting started, a shell from the *Moltke* struck the *Tiger* in the forecastle, wrecking her range finder. Worse, much worse, followed fast. Two of the *Moltke*'s 11-inch shells pierced the *Tiger*'s main forward turrets, cutting her rate of fire by half; at 3:56 another salvo smashed deep into the *Tiger*'s hull, breaking several steam lines; only heroic efforts by the boiler-room crew kept the vessel under way. During the next seven minutes, the *Tiger* suffered five more hits from the *Moltke*.

Meanwhile, the *Derfflinger* took the *Princess Royal* under fire, putting one 12-inch shell into the British ship's forward A turret and scoring with another that disabled the vessel's main control station in her engine room for 20 minutes, during which she could be steered only with difficulty. As if that were not enough, other *Derfflinger* shells hit the *Princess Royal*'s forward B turret and went through the foremast and funnel.

In a running duel between flagships, Beatty's *Lion* took distinctly the worst of it from Hipper's *Lützow*. Hardly had the battle begun than the *Lion* suffered two hits; one splintered a ship's boat and the other inflicted equally trifling damage. The *Lion*'s luck held through a third shell that, because it was not armor-piercing, exploded harmlessly. But the fourth hit from the *Lützow* was disastrous, and an officer on the *Lion*'s bridge recalled the awful occasion. He was observing the firing when a sergeant of the Royal Marines, burned, dazed and bloodstained, staggered onto the bridge. "I asked him what was the matter. In a tired voice he replied, 'Q turret has gone, sir. All the crew are killed and we have flooded the magazines.' I looked over the bridge amidships. The armoured roof of Q turret had been folded back like an open sardine tin, thick yellow smoke was rolling up in clouds from the gaping hole. Strange that all this should have happened within a few yards of where Beatty was standing, and that none of us on the bridge should have heard the detonation."

The *Lion* had suffered exactly the same misfortune that had befallen the German *Seydlitz* at the Dogger Bank: a shell had penetrated the turret, killed the gun crew and set fire to some cordite charges. The Germans had learned from the Dogger Bank experience and had corrected the design defect in their battle-cruiser turrets with antiflash precautions, such as double interlocking magazine doors that were closed before battle. But the British had not suffered the same disaster, and they had no way of knowing the flaw in their turret design. The cordite flash had passed down the turret's central trunk; it would have ignited the magazine and sunk the ship had it not been for the quick reaction of Major Francis J. W. Harvey of the Royal Marine Light Infantry, who was serving as turret commander. Although mortally injured, Harvey gave the order to shut the magazine doors and flood the magazine. Some of the men who carried out Harvey's command—and saved the *Lion*—were later found dead with their hands still clutching the door clips.

So far, the British had dealt out relatively little punishment. Their first shells had landed far off target near the light cruiser *Regensburg*—some 2,000 yards astern of Hipper's battle-cruiser line. Then the *Seydlitz* was hit, suffering a damaged electrical switchboard. Finally, after eight minutes of furious firing, the *Queen Mary* scored on the *Seydlitz* with another 13-inch shell. This one ripped through eight inches of steel on the German's C turret amidships; it exploded ready powder charges that killed the gunners, but because of the new antiflash doors and partial flooding the explosion did not reach down the turret's central core to the magazine.

The opening phase of the Battle of Jutland had been hopelessly one-sided. Although David Beatty's judgment may sometimes have been faulty, his courage was beyond question. It was a tribute to the accuracy and intensity of the German gunnery that throughout the action Beatty had steadily been giving way—first by five points (each point representing 11° 15′ on the compass), then by another, then by three more, until his course was to the southwest, and the distance between the battle lines had widened to more than 20,000 yards.

That put the British out of range of all the German battle cruisers save one, the *Von der Tann*. Though she was the oldest and smallest of the German battle cruisers, she possessed one feature that her newer sisters lacked. Her four 11-inch guns could be elevated to 20°, compared with 16° for the other ships. Tactical exercises had convinced the Germans that visibility in the North Sea and the Baltic would seldom permit battle ranges beyond 14,000 yards. It seemed pointless, therefore, to continue to face the engineering complications involved in high elevations for extreme range, and they had lowered the elevation of the guns on newer ships. But the *Von der Tann*'s guns could still reach out to a maximum range of 22,400 yards. At that distance, she opened fire on the *Indefatigable*—with devastating results. After an arcing flight of 30 seconds, three of the four shells from her 11-inch guns slammed down into the British battle cruiser's quarter-deck. A minute or so later, the *Von der Tann* loosed another salvo, and drove home three more 11-inchers, piercing the *Indefatigable*'s forward turret.

For perhaps half a minute nothing more seemed to happen. Then, at 4:05, a cordite flash reached the *Indefatigable*'s magazine and, with a stupendous roar, the great battle cruiser disappeared in sheets of flame and vast billows of thick, black smoke. Tossed above the smoke cloud and at least 200 feet in the air could be seen a 50-foot steam picketboat, apparently intact, but upside down.

It all happened so suddenly that many men in both fleets missed it entirely. When the superdreadnought *Malaya* came up astern—Admiral Evan-Thomas was at last getting close to the action—and passed over the spot where the *Indefatigable* had been, crewmen topside assumed that the floating debris was German and cheered at the sight. "We never dreamed it was one of our own battle cruisers," a midshipman wrote, "but it was the *Indefatigable,* and over 1,000 men lay in her wreck." On the *Lützow,* Hipper at first refused to believe that a modern battle cruiser could have been instantly demolished. Only after peering through a telescope, counting and finding that there were now only five instead of six ships in the enemy line was he satisfied. He then lit a fresh cigar.

But even as Hipper congratulated himself, the Germans saw and identified the four British superdreadnoughts arriving. They had all heard of these ships and often talked about them—ships with the speed of a battle cruiser and the colossal armament of eight 15-inch guns apiece.

Smoke towers over the British battle cruiser Lion as the "Q," or midship, turret goes up in a fiery blast after a direct hit by a 12-inch shell from the German battle cruiser Lützow. The shellburst, which sent flames down the turret's ammunition hoist to the magazine, would have triggered an even greater explosion on the Lion, Admiral Beatty's flagship, had it not been for the turret officer, Royal Marine Major Francis J. W. Harvey (inset). With his dying breath Harvey ordered the flooding of the magazine.

Their arrival, the captain of the *Seydlitz* wrote, "was a mighty but terrible spectacle." And Commander von Hase wrote in awe: "Their speed was scarcely inferior to ours, but they fired a shell more than twice as heavy. They engaged at portentous ranges."

The recently victorious *Von der Tann*, last in Hipper's line, was the first target of the superdreadnoughts, and a direct hit by one of the *Barham*'s 15-inch shells holed her on the water line aft, flooding her stern compartment. "The terrific blow at one end," the *Von der Tann*'s captain wrote, "caused her to oscillate backward and forward violently. The bow and stern dipped in and out five or six times." Before long the *Von der Tann* was under simultaneous fire from the *Barham*, the *Warspite*, the *Malaya* and the battle cruiser *New Zealand*—whose captain, John Green, was exotically clad in a black-and-white Maori kilt, or piupiu, made of woven rushes and worn over his uniform. It had been presented to the *New Zealand*, during a round-the-world voyage in 1913-1914, by a Maori chief who promised that the peculiar garment would bring good luck. Perhaps it did. When a shell from the *Von der Tann*, still firing although two of her four big guns were out of action, struck the *New Zealand* it caused only superficial damage.

Now that the superdreadnoughts were in action, Beatty ordered his battle cruisers to close again with Hipper, turning toward them first by two points and then by three. The British fire had steadied—in addition to the damage to the *Von der Tann* and *Seydlitz*, the *Lützow* had suffered a disabled turret and some casualties—and Beatty had ample reason to believe the fight was finally turning his way. Then, at 4:26, only a bit more than two hours since the *Galatea* had begun the battle, came catastrophe for the British.

An officer in the conning tower of the *Tiger*, just astern of the *Queen Mary*, saw it happen. As he watched in fascinated horror, three shells from the *Derfflinger* and the *Seydlitz* struck the *Queen Mary*, and then two more. "As they hit," the officer recalled, "I saw a dull red glow amidships and then the ship seemed to open out like a puff ball, or one of those toadstool things when one squeezes it."

Like the *Indefatigable* before her, the *Queen Mary* was lost behind a curtain of flames and smoke. A few minutes later the *New Zealand* passed by the scene. One of her officers later wrote: "The stern of a ship projecting about 70 feet out of the water, with the propellers revolving slowly, drifted into the field of my glasses; clouds of white paper were blowing out of the after-hatch, and on her stern I read, 'Queen Mary.'"

On the bridge of the *Lion*, Beatty reacted to the *Queen Mary*'s death with superb aplomb. "Chatfield," he said to his flag captain, "there seems to be something wrong with our bloody ships today. Turn two points to port"—toward Hipper. He also ordered his destroyers to launch a torpedo attack.

At the signal, 12 British destroyers in three divisions peeled off from the van of the British line and headed for the German battle cruisers. Hipper saw them coming and ordered a counterattack by 15 German destroyers. The destroyers clashed in a fierce independent battle, by far the fastest that had ever been fought at sea, the opponents closing on each other at a combined speed of 60 knots, all firing "rapid indepen-

How to hit a thimble on the horizon

It was a matter of little concern to Horatio Nelson in 1805 that the cannon on board his warships at Trafalgar had no gun sights. The limited range and accuracy of his guns made battle simply a business of facing off point-blank against the enemy and pounding away until one of the combatants was reduced to kindling.

But during the 19th Century, the state of the arms maker's art changed dramatically: muzzle-loading cannon gave way to the more sophisticated breechloaders made with rifled barrels that could hurl a conical shell many miles—and with great accuracy on land. But aiming these guns at sea was another matter entirely.

The task of firing a gun at sea has been likened to that of a man with a pistol rocking in a rocking chair and trying to shoot a thimble off a mantelpiece at the opposite end of the room. Even this is an oversimplification; it might be added that at sea both marksman and target usually have a horizontal movement, described in terms of their course and speed—as if man and thimble were in separate, moving cars. In fact, so great are the complications that it was usual at the turn of the century for a naval gunner to miss his target about seven out of every 10 times he fired.

It was such dreary statistics that prompted a Royal Navy captain named Percy Scott to start a crusade in 1898 to sharpen the marksmanship on board his own ship, the *Scylla*. During firing practice one day Scott noticed that one of his gunners at a 4.7-incher consistently scored two or three times higher than all the rest. The seas were choppy and the ship was rolling broadly. "I watched this man," Scott recalled afterward, "and saw that he could work his elevating wheel with such dexterity as to keep his sight on target notwithstanding the rolling of the ship."

With this clue Scott devised an ingenious training apparatus that he called a "dotter." Constructed of pipes, wires and a bicycle chain, the contraption was mounted just in front of a practice gun, where it moved a small paper target rhythmically up and down in a perfect simulation of the view through a gun sight on a rolling ship. The gunner's task was to keep the target in his sights by cranking the barrel up and down with the motion of the target. When Scott called "fire," the gunner squeezed his trigger. Instead of a shell,

Captain Percy Scott directs practice with his "dotter" firing simulator. The gunner in the foreground must hold his sights on the target, which is kept in motion by another sailor.

Dots made between the bars on the dotter card count as hits. The two cards above show the remarkable progress made by one William Bates, a gunner, in six months of practice.

Through binocular lenses—one at either end of the nine-foot range finder— the operator sees a split image of a ship (inset). The target's distance is found by aligning the halves of the image.

a pencil popped forward and made a mark on the dotter card, thus recording the "shot."

Scott drilled his men incessantly on the dotter and, when it came time for the annual prize firing of 1899, the gunners on the *Scylla* scored an incredible 80 per cent.

Although Scott's training technique performed miracles with the smaller guns, it was manifestly impossible to keep the heavy barrels of the mammoth 12- and 13.5-inchers constantly moving up and down with the motion of the ship. Some method had to be contrived to enable the great guns to fire at precisely the right setting to hit the target.

In 1906 the optical firm of Barr & Stroud perfected a "coincidence range finder." This was a device through which the distance of a ship spotted far off at sea could be estimated accurately to within a few yards.

Then, in 1913, the Admiralty was shown a device known as the Dreyer Fire Control Table, a bewilderingly complicated machine that performed much like a modern-day computer, except that its operation was purely mechanical. Dials on the table were set

with the estimated speed, bearing and range of the target ship, and the known speed of the attacking ship. Weighted in with these were figures for wind force and direction, drift (the corkscrew curve imparted to a shell's trajectory by the rifling in the gun barrel), and air temperature, which affected the propelling powers of the cordite.

After juggling all these factors in its spindles for a moment or two, the table produced a set of instructions that gave the gunlayer the degree of barrel

elevation required, told the gun trainer the degree of deflection the barrel was to be turned from the ship's center line, and finally gave a rate of change of range to keep the shells falling on target as the two ships diverged.

Duly impressed, the Admiralty ordered a Dreyer Table installed in each of its new dreadnoughts. But one problem remained: how best to orchestrate firing the big guns. For the solution the Navy again turned to Percy Scott of dotter fame—now Admiral Sir Percy.

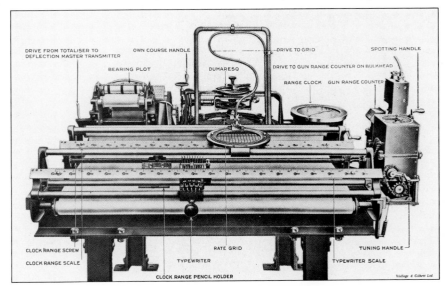

The Dreyer Fire Control Table, a miracle of mechanical ingenuity, plotted ship movements with great accuracy.

Director firing: 10 guns roaring as one

On a winter's day in 1912, Admiral Sir Percy Scott strode through the doors of the Admiralty office in London carrying under his arm a miniature wooden model of a dreadnought. He had an appointment with First Lord Winston Churchill, and he intended to demonstrate with the model a new system of gun control called director firing.

To Scott's mind the standard practice at the time—letting each turret officer on a battleship aim and fire his gun independently—simply frittered away the warship's great power. How much more effective the guns would be if they could all be aimed and fired together at the command of a single directing officer located in an observa-tion booth high up on the mainmast.

From Scott's sketches the Vickers Company had devised a control chair fitted out with telescopes, controls for both deflection and elevation, and a pistol-grip firing mechanism. Aiming instructions were relayed to this control center from the Dreyer Table in the transmitting room below the water line of the ship.

As the director set his control dials, a small red arrow traveled around the outer edge of identical dials in each turret, indicating the director's dial settings. The turret officer aligned his own pointers with the red arrow and signaled back to the director. When the ready light from all the turrets glowed red in the control tower, the director would squeeze his firing trigger, letting go a salvo of shells that would rain down miles away with unspeakable devastation.

Churchill was so impressed that he arranged for a competitive trial. On November 13, 1912, the dreadnought *Thunderer*, fitted out with a director firing system, was pitted against the *Orion* in a big-gun contest in which both ships, steaming at top speed in rough seas, were to fire at a moving target more than four miles away. The *Thunderer* swept the day, pouring one broadside after another into the target, while the *Orion* fired only ragged individual shots, most of which fell wide.

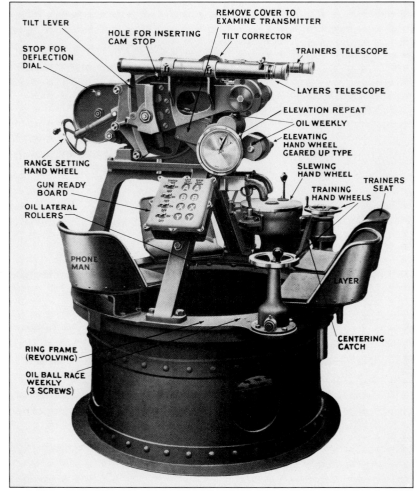

An annotated page from a 1917 gunnery manual (left) shows the control station of the Scott / Vickers gun-director system that could aim and fire all a battleship's large guns from a position aloft on the mainmast. A receiver dial (above) in each turret registered the degree of gun elevation selected by the director.

The score card from the match between the Orion and the Thunderer shows the advantages of director firing. In the three-and-a-half-minute test, the director-guided Thunderer fired 39 times, hitting the target ship 8,500 yards away 23 times, while the Orion, without a director system, managed to get off 27 shots, only four of which hit the target.

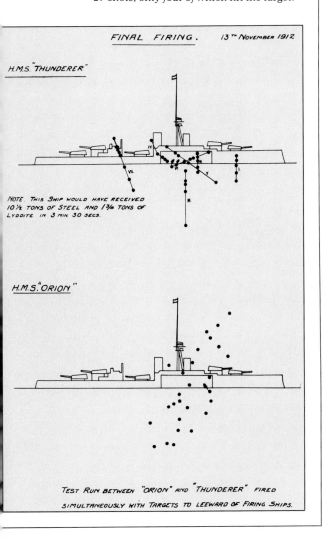

FINAL FIRING. 13ᵀᴴ NOVEMBER 1912

H.M.S. "THUNDERER"

NOTE. THIS SHIP WOULD HAVE RECEIVED 10½ TONS OF STEEL AND 1¾ TONS OF LYDDITE IN 3 MIN 30 SECS.

H.M.S. "ORION"

TEST RUN BETWEEN "ORION" AND "THUNDERER" FIRED SIMULTANEOUSLY WITH TARGETS TO LEEWARD OF FIRING SHIPS.

dent"—their maximum rate—and passing at point-blank range before swerving around to do it all over again.

From the big ships, officers watched transfixed by the destroyer struggle taking place between the battle-cruiser lines. "It was a wild scene," one of them wrote. "Groups of long low forms vomiting heavy trails of smoke and dashing hither and thither at thirty knots or more through the smother and splashes, and all in a rain of shell from the secondary armament of the German battle cruisers, with the heavy shell of the contending squadrons screaming overhead." Recalled another: "At times their high white bow-wave was the only part of them visible, and a tornado of shells was falling all round them. It seemed impossible that they could escape as time after time they were obliterated from sight by salvoes, but presently their bow-waves would appear again and they would emerge, only to be blotted out once more a moment later."

The British destroyer *Nicator* came through it all untouched, and a junior lieutenant put it down to the way his captain handled the ship: "His idea was to chase each salvo—that is to say, when a salvo fell short he would alter course to starboard towards it, so that after the Germans had applied an 'up' spotting correction and fired another salvo, instead of hitting us it would go over. Then we would alter to port towards where that salvo fell, and so on." Throughout the entire action, he added admiringly, the captain leaned coolly against the front of the bridge, smoking his pipe.

During the melee, two German destroyers, the *V-27* and the *V-29*, were sunk, and two British destroyers, the *Nomad* and the *Nestor*, were disabled by hits in their engine rooms and lay stopped and helpless between the big-ship lines. Both sides fired about 20 torpedoes, but all of them missed except one, which hit the *Seydlitz*. She went through the rest of the battle with—by German accounts—a hole "the size of a barn door" in her bows, and slowly sinking by the head. But the toughness bestowed by German shipbuilders kept her afloat till the fighting ended.

In the British order of battle, the proper place for Beatty's four light cruisers was ahead of the fleet as a scouting screen. His abrupt change of course when the enemy was sighted had put them out of position, and all through the fighting they had been steaming flat out, and cutting the corners, to get back where they ought to be. By 4:30 the cruiser *Southampton* was at last on station, two or three miles ahead of the *Lion*. And eight minutes later the *Southampton* sent a wireless signal that transformed the Battle of Jutland: "Urgent. Priority. Have sighted Enemy battle fleet bearing approximately S.E., course of Enemy N."

It was, of course, Scheer, and he was coming as fast as the laggardly 16-knot predreadnoughts of the second squadron would travel. Beatty instantly realized that Hipper had been luring him into the guns of the High Seas Fleet. He set about at once to reverse the situation by enticing the Germans—all of them—north into a meeting with Jellicoe, whose approach, he correctly believed, was still unknown to the enemy. Since his own wireless transmitter in the *Lion* had been hit and was out of action, he signaled the *Princess Royal*, next in line, to transmit the news to Jellicoe. Then, by flag, he ordered his fleet to wheel northward. Hipper did the same. Jutland's famed Run to the South was over. The Run to the North was beginning.

But not for everyone. Beatty's light cruisers went south for a closer look at the new enemy force. Later, a young lieutenant on the *Southampton* told of the harrowing experience: "It was a strain steaming at 25 knots straight for this formidable line of battleships, with our own friends going fast away from us in the opposite direction. Seconds became minutes, and still they did not open fire." In the confusion and with a rising mist that was to plague both fleets for the rest of the day, the Germans mistook the British squadron for one of their own. The *Southampton* was already flying the flag that meant reverse course, and crews waited breathlessly for Commodore William Goodenough to haul it down—the signal to execute the command. Not until the *Southampton* was at 13,000 yards did the flag finally flutter down. "Over went the helms, and the four ships slewed round, bringing our sterns to the enemy. As we turned, the fun began, and half a dozen German battleships opened a deliberate fire on the squadron."

That young man's action station was in the after control position with an even younger sublieutenant and half a dozen men. Since the Germans were out of range of the cruiser's guns, the two youngsters had nothing to do. So, trying hard to appear casual, they crouched down behind $1/10$ of an inch of plating and ate their bully-beef sandwiches, which "didn't seem to go down very easily. It seemed rather a waste of time to eat, for surely in the next ten minutes one of those 11-inch shells would get us."

The lieutenant and the sub agreed not to look at the enemy line. But the temptation was overwhelming, and they always seemed to peek just as two or three of the battleships flickered flames from their guns. From the sub's wrist watch, they soon learned that the time of flight was 23 seconds: "At the twenty-third second the Sub would make a grimace, and as if in reply a series of splitting reports and lugubrious moans announced that the salvo had arrived."

The four light cruisers escaped, but the two disabled destroyers, the *Nomad* and *Nestor,* were doomed. Unable to get their ships under way, the destroyer crews had seen the British and German battle cruisers reverse course and disappear beyond the northern horizon, still blazing away at each other. The crippled destroyers were left with the ocean to themselves—but not for long. The yeoman-of-signals reported to the captain of the *Nestor,* "German battleships on the horizon, shaping course in our direction."

The German dreadnoughts' course took them first past the *Nomad.* "The slaughter began," wrote the captain of the *Nestor.* "They literally smothered her with salvoes." Mercifully, the *Nomad* went down within minutes. "Of what was in store for us," the captain continued, "there was now not a vestige of a doubt. From a distance of about five miles the Germans commenced with their secondary armament. We fired our last torpedo at the High Seas Fleet. The *Nestor,* enwrapped in a cloud of smoke and spray, the centre of a whirlwind of shrieking shells, began slowly to settle by the stern. I gave my last order as her commander—'Abandon ship.' "

John Cornwell: a first-class Boy First Class

Among the many British heroes at Jutland the youngest was a 16-year-old named John Travers Cornwell. Newly enlisted, Cornwell held the rank of boy first class, just below ordinary seaman, and his job on board the light cruiser *Chester* was to assist in sighting the forward 5.5-inch gun.

At 5:35 p.m. the *Chester* suddenly found herself under fire from four German light cruisers. Within five minutes the entire crew of the forward gun was cut down—except for Cornwell who, though terribly wounded by a shell fragment in his chest, somehow managed to stay on his feet.

For the next 15 minutes, Cornwell stuck to his gun. "He felt he might be needed, as indeed he might have been," the *Chester*'s captain wrote to the lad's mother. "So he stayed there, standing and waiting, under heavy fire, with just his own brave heart and God's help to support him."

At last the *Chester* limped home and Cornwell was rushed to a hospital, where he died on June 2. He was buried with full honors and was posthumously awarded England's highest medal for valor, the Victoria Cross.

A heroic poster signed not only by the artist but also by two admirals and the First Lord of the Admiralty shows young John Cornwell mortally wounded but still cleaving to his gun. His courage earned him the Victoria Cross (below), one of 634 awarded in the War.

Miraculously, most of the 150 men on board the two ships survived; they were picked up by German boats and were prisoners—"the Kaiser's guests," they called it—for the next two and a half years.

As Beatty's battle cruisers turned north they left behind them not only the scouting light cruisers and wounded destroyers—but also Admiral Evan-Thomas with the *Barham*, the *Malaya*, the *Warspite* and the *Valiant*. Incredibly, the lordly superdreadnoughts had once again failed to read Beatty's flag-given signal for a change of course. Not even the startling sight of Beatty's battle cruisers passing him in the opposite direction deterred the single-minded Evan-Thomas as he headed full steam into the War's—and the world's—first direct confrontation of dreadnoughts, four British against 12 Germans.

In the ensuing 45 minutes the outnumbered Evan-Thomas engaged the enemy briefly at close quarters, then wisely came about and followed Beatty, fighting off Scheer's pursuit in a blazing rear-guard action. That three quarters of an hour was heavy with portent for the dreadnoughts. The great ships demonstrated that they were able to withstand a tremendous battering without any material effect on their fighting ability. The men in one part of the ship sometimes did not even know that another part had been hit until they saw the damage afterward. "Felt one or two very heavy shakes," wrote the *Warspite*'s executive officer, "but didn't think very much of it at the time, and it never occurred to me that we were being hit. I saw two of our salvoes hit the leading German battleship. Sheets of yellow flame went right over her mastheads, and she looked red fore and aft like a burning haystack. Told everybody in the turret that we were doing all right and to keep her going; machinery working like a clockwork mouse."

Among the exec's duties was supervision of the fire brigades and damage-control parties, and he soon learned that the *Warspite* had been taking a pummeling as well as handing one out. He was going forward on his rounds when a 12-inch shell came through the side armor only a few feet above the water line. "Terrific sheet of golden flame," he later wrote, "stink, impenetrable dust, and everything seemed to fall everywhere with an appalling noise." Going aft, he found water pouring into the admiral's cabin and a foot of water on the deck. All told, he found at least a dozen hits, which had started leaks and fires and had killed and wounded a number of men. Nevertheless, everybody "was very cheery and anxious for news which I couldn't give as I hadn't the faintest idea what was happening."

Although the leading German dreadnoughts were in much the same condition—the Germans rarely reported specific damage details—none of the huge ships, German or British, was anywhere close to being put out of action or sunk. This first running engagement proved that in dreadnoughts, unlike battle cruisers, defense was stronger than attack. Shellfire could damage them locally and cause ghastly suffering, but it would have taken hours of concentrated fire to inflict mortal damage on them. The only thing that could stop a dreadnought quickly was a torpedo hit on a vulnerable point—rudders, propellers or possibly an engine room.

The tables are turned

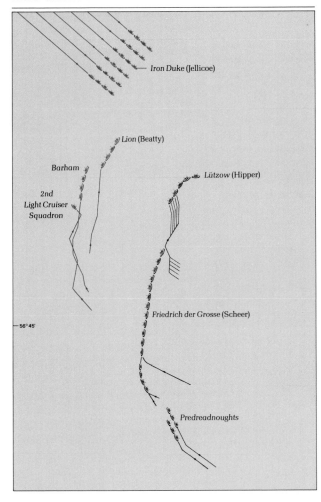

Iron Duke (Jellicoe)

Lion (Beatty)

Barham

2nd
Light Cruiser
Squadron

Lützow (Hipper)

56°45′

Friedrich der Grosse (Scheer)

Predreadnoughts

5:35 P.M. TO 6:00 P.M. Running north toward Jellicoe's dreadnoughts, Beatty tempts the German fleet into an ambush of his own. His gunners, gaining in accuracy, begin to punish Hipper's battle-cruiser squadron. By 6:00 p.m. Hipper has altered course eastward to escape Beatty's fire and thus cannot see Jellicoe's approach in time to warn Scheer, who is rushing from the south with the main German dreadnought fleet. The battle-cruiser action at Jutland now ends. And Scheer is headed unawares into the world's mightiest navy.

Meanwhile, to the north, Beatty continued to steam toward Jellicoe and the Grand Fleet *(chart, left).* Thus far in the battle, Beatty's performance, for all his courage, had been considerably less than distinguished. At first sight of the enemy he had gone tallyhoing over the horizon, away from Jellicoe and toward Scheer, and in the process he had taken an awful drubbing. Now, streaming north with Hipper on a parallel course to starboard, he brought off a maneuver that made up for at least some of his previous deficiencies. In spite of the damage to their turrets and upper works, Beatty's remaining ships could still do their top speed of 28 knots. He opened to the extreme range of his 13-inch guns—out of range of Hipper's 12-inchers—and drew well ahead of the German battle cruisers. Then he altered course to the eastward, and by heavy bombardment forced Hipper also to turn to the east. His object was to get the Germans' battle cruisers out of the way, to destroy their usefulness as scouts so that they could not warn Scheer of Jellicoe's approach. Hipper and his officers did not recognize the British purpose. But afterward, when he understood it, Hase wrote of Beatty's "excellent tactical movement" and "admirable feat of technique."

Scheer was also deceived. Although he did not expect his 10 obsolete predreadnoughts to be much help in battle, he could not leave them alone to look after themselves. So that they might keep up, he held the speed of his 12 dreadnoughts to 15 knots—while the fast-moving battle-cruiser brawl almost vanished to the north. "The wind had changed from northwest to southwest," Scheer recalled, "and the clear weather had become misty. Cordite and funnel smoke hung over the sea and cut off all view to the north and east. Only now and then could we see our reconnaissance forces." In this predicament, the wireless was no help: like the *Lion's,* the *Lützow's* had been put out of action, and now neither Beatty nor Hipper could report to their commanders in chief.

At the close of the Run to the South, Hipper's men had been jubilant. The British battle cruisers had been severely punished; two had been sunk, and now the dreadnoughts of the High Seas Fleet were coming into the fray. In the *Derfflinger,* Commander von Hase wrote, the crew had been "filled with the proud joy of victory and hoped to accomplish the destruction of the whole force opposed to us. We were burning to win fresh laurels." Now the vision of laurels was gone and, outranged by the British guns, Hipper's force was struggling for its existence.

At 5:45, the German official account reported, the *Lützow* was struck twice more; the *Seydlitz* took several hits and was on fire; and the *Derfflinger* was hit in the bow and "began to sink by the head." All the big guns of the *Von der Tann* were out of action but "the captain decided to stay with the squadron so that the enemy, having to take this ship into account, would not be able to strengthen his fire against the others." The report went on: "hard pressed and unable to return the fire, the German battle cruisers soon found their position unbearable." They were forced by Beatty's maneuver to retreat farther and farther eastward.

Ahead of Scheer to the north, the sea was left empty. Deprived of his scouts, he was advancing blindly, still totally unaware of what lay ahead in the smoke just beyond the horizon: the overwhelming force of Admiral Sir John Jellicoe and the British Grand Fleet.

Chapter 5

A duel of dreadnoughts: 50 minutes of fury

Spewing clouds of smoke, the Friedrich der Grosse, one of Germany's newest dreadnoughts, opens fire with 12-inch guns at the Battle of Jutland.

ven at sea, Admiral Sir John Jellicoe was ordinarily an inconspicuous sort. He kept mostly to his sea cabin, his gold-rimmed half-spectacles set solidly on his prominent nose as he dealt with the profusion of paper that represented the Grand Fleet's business. Thrice daily he emerged to preside amiably and abstemiously over his staff mess.

But today—May 31, 1916—was different. As he approached the supreme crisis of a career that had begun 44 years before, John Jellicoe was on the *Iron Duke*'s forebridge, garbed in a homely blue Burberry raincoat, an undersized, old-fashioned cap with tarnished braid, and a white muffler knotted around his neck. As always, he was outwardly in total self-possession, and only the quickening clicks of the metal taps on his heels as he paced betrayed his gathering anxiety.

Jellicoe had more than enough cause to worry. On his slight shoulders rested a burden few men are called upon to bear. The consequences of a German naval victory, disabling a major part of the Grand Fleet, were unthinkable. The sea-lanes to Scandinavia would be wide-open to the enemy. The Russian ally would be isolated. The British coast would lie naked to invasion; troops diverted to home defense might throw the stalemate in the trenches of the Western Front into fatal imbalance.

To avert such a calamity, Jellicoe needed every scrap of information he could get—the number and types of the enemy warships, their bearing, course and speed. Through an extraordinary blunder, he had already lost one set of eyes. The seaplane carrier *Campania*, with 10 aircraft, had been anchored at the north end of Scapa Flow and had missed the signal for the fleet to sail. When her watchkeepers looked about two hours later, the Flow was empty and the fleet had gone. The *Campania* weighed anchor and steamed full speed to catch up. But by wireless, Jellicoe ordered her back to her harbor. He had been told she could do only 19 knots, and he did not want her exposed alone to submarines. In fact, the *Campania* could make 20½, and with that extra speed she could, barring accidents, have caught up in plenty of time to help. But back she went.

Still, it was basically Admiral Sir David Beatty's mission to provide Jellicoe with the intelligence he so urgently required, and the battle-cruiser commander badly botched the job. As Jellicoe's agonizing day wore on, his reports from Beatty were scanty, ambiguous, misleading or, for stretches that seemed interminable, entirely absent.

At 2:18 p.m., with the Grand Fleet zigzagging at 14 knots on a placid sea amid forming patches of mist, Jellicoe was handed a wireless message from one of Beatty's scouts, the cruiser *Galatea*, whose chance encounter with the enemy had opened the Battle of Jutland: "Urgent. Two cruisers, probably hostile, in sight bearing E.S.E., course unknown. My position lat. 56°—48′, long. 5°—21′." Then, for more than an hour, all scouting activities were cloaked in a cathedral silence.

Jellicoe did what he could. He ordered a course change to southeast by south. He moved the fleet's speed up to 18 knots, then to 19, then 20. He called for action stations. His ships were steaming in six parallel columns of four dreadnoughts each (Vice Admiral Sir Martyn Jerram having joined with his eight dreadnoughts from Cromarty shortly before noon). Jellicoe increased the intervals between these columns from

Vice Admiral Reinhard Scheer, commander of the German High Seas Fleet at Jutland, believed that the primary issue of World War I was Britain's "claim to unrestricted primacy in sea power"; Jutland, he declared, proved "to the world that the English Navy no longer possesses her boasted irresistibility."

Admiral Sir John Rushworth Jellicoe, commander of the British Grand Fleet, was hounded for years by critics who thought that Jutland should have resulted in the absolute destruction of the enemy. "A victory is judged not merely by material losses and damage, but by its results," he replied, observing that after the battle the German fleet only once ventured outside its home waters.

1,500 to 2,000 yards so as to give them sea room for the maneuver that would take them into line of battle. Beyond that, he could only wait.

And wait. It was 3:21 p.m. before Jellicoe again heard from the battle-cruiser force, and then the news came by an intercepted radio message, in which Beatty informed his squadron commanders of his own position, course and speed. Since such a transmission would have been unnecessary under ordinary circumstances, Jellicoe deduced that Beatty was involved in some sort of action. What sort? Jellicoe had no idea.

By 3:27, other bits and pieces had come in: an intercepted report that the *Galatea* had seen, to the east-southeast, the smoke of ships steering west-northwest; another from the *Nottingham*, also in Beatty's cruiser screen, which had spotted five columns of smoke bearing east-northeast. Two minutes later, word came from the *Galatea* that she was running ahead of German ships—of unreported size and number—to the north-west. From these fragments, Jellicoe formed his own estimate of the situation, which he signaled to the commodore of his destroyer flotilla on the *Castor:* "Enemy cruisers and destroyers are being chased to the northward by our battle cruiser force and should be in touch with our cruisers at about 4 p.m." Jellicoe could hardly have been more mistaken: Beatty and Hipper were turning for their blazing Run to the South.

The accuracy of the information Jellicoe received did not improve. At 3:40 Beatty's first direct message to Jellicoe reported five German battle cruisers and many destroyers bearing northeast; it neglected to give speed or course. At 4:38 separate signals came from two of Beatty's commanders saying that the German dreadnought fleet had been sight-ed; they differed in their estimate of the enemy position by 25 miles. At 4:45, Beatty sent: "Have sighted enemy's battle fleet bearing S.E."

It was at best a feeble report, and it was horribly garbled in transmis-sion by flags to the *Princess Royal* (the *Lion*'s wireless being out of commission), which then passed it on to the *Iron Duke*. By the time the message had been enciphered, transmitted, retransmitted and then deci-phered, it was positively ludicrous: "26-30 battleships, probably hostile, bearing S.S.E. steering S.E." No explanation has ever been given how the "26-30 battleships" got in there, nor how the course information crept into the message. And there was no "probably" about the hostility of the vessels: the approaching dreadnoughts could only have been German. Far from steering southeast, they were heading northward toward Jelli-coe. And the "26-30" led Jellicoe to believe, through the battle, that he was confronted by a much more numerous force than in fact he was.

"I have never felt so 'out of it,' " he later wrote to Beatty in remon-strance. "I could not make out the situation a bit. Whether the enemy battle fleet was ahead, abeam or on the quarter."

Finally, at 5:55, word came not from Beatty but from the *Marlborough*, the leading dreadnought in Jellicoe's own starboard column: "Gun flashes and heavy firing on the starboard bow." In moments, Jellicoe could hear the roar of guns for himself, but in the mist he could not make out its direction. For an instant, his nerves showed. "I wish," he barked, "someone would tell me who is firing and what they're firing at."

Just then Beatty's ships came charging out of the gloom five miles off Jellicoe's starboard bow. Thick smoke billowed from the *Lion*'s forecas-

The main fleets meet

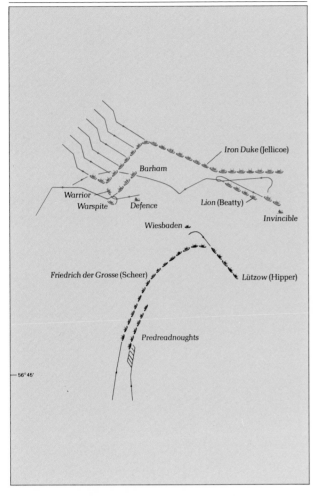

6:00 P.M. TO 6:30 P.M. Scheer races his dreadnoughts northward to aid the beleaguered battle cruisers, led by the Lützow. The British cripple the cruiser Wiesbaden. The Germans sink the Defence and riddle the Warrior, which is spared only when the dreadnought Warspite, circling crazily because of a jammed rudder, draws off the German fire. Meanwhile Jellicoe is masterfully deploying the Grand Fleet in a line ahead, crossing Scheer's "T"; at 6:30 Scheer's van comes under fire from 24 British dreadnoughts while only his most advanced ships are in range to reply. In the continuing battle-cruiser duel, the Germans sink the Invincible.

tle on the port side, her guns were blazing and huge plumes of water rose from the splashing of enemy shells around her. Jellicoe immediately signaled, "Where is the enemy's battle fleet?"

Beatty replied, as his four surviving battle cruisers rushed flat out across Jellicoe's front: "German battle cruisers bearing S.E." This was useless to Jellicoe, who was looking for dreadnoughts. But in fact, Beatty had not seen Scheer's force, which he was supposed to be scouting, for more than an hour. Not until 13 minutes after Jellicoe's plea for information did Beatty glimpse Scheer through a break in the mist, and signal: "Enemy's battle fleet bearing S.S.W." Still, no course, no speed, no indication of distance. But John Jellicoe had run out of time. He had to act now if he was to deploy his ships to meet the enemy.

As the signalman repeated each word of Beatty's message, Jellicoe, his heels tapping on the deck, walked briskly to the compass platform and for nearly half a minute gazed at the magnetic compass card. "I watched his face with tremendous interest, wondering what he would do," wrote Flag Captain Frederick Dreyer. "I realised as I watched him that he was as cool and unmoved as ever. He looked up and broke the silence with the order in his crisp, clear-cut voice to Commander A.R.W. Woods, the Fleet Signal Officer, who was standing a little abaft of me: 'Hoist equal-speed pendant S.E.'" In the Royal Navy's signal book this pendant ordered the ships of a fleet to fall out of their cruising columns into a single line ahead. In this case the course of the column was to be southeast to cut across the van of Scheer's force, coming from the southwest.

Since the fleet was already steaming in a southeasterly direction, there might have been some confusion as to which of the outside columns Jellicoe wished the dreadnoughts to form on. Woods offered a suggestion: "Would you make it a point to port, sir, so that they will know it is on the port-wing column?" Jellicoe pondered briefly and replied: "Very well. Hoist equal-speed pendant S.E. by E." By adding a point to port and ordering southeast by east, Jellicoe made it unmistakenly clear that he wished the fleet to form on the port column led by the King George V. As the ships of the Grand Fleet began to acknowledge, Jellicoe commanded: "Dreyer, commence the deployment."

To accomplish the deployment, the port column held its course. The leaders of the other five columns sounded two short blasts on their sirens and, followed by their squadrons, turned 90° to port, then to starboard, thus falling into a single line nearly seven miles long (chart, left). On Jellicoe's part, the decision was mostly instinct. His purpose was to cross Scheer's "T," thereby bringing the broadsides of all 24 of his dreadnoughts to bear on a German line able to answer with only its forward guns. But Jellicoe knew pitiably little about Scheer's location, course and speed. He had chosen to form a line on his port wing because it would remove the fleet by five miles from Scheer's presumed position to the southwest, and thus give the fleet both time and room to complete the maneuver. Had he deployed on his starboard column—the wing nearer to Scheer—he would have risked being caught and hammered by the oncoming enemy while in the midst of his maneuver.

Jellicoe's 24 dreadnoughts finished deploying soon after 6 p.m., forming a curved, single-line wall that extended in almost a quarter of a circle from north to east. Scheer, in the *Friedrich der Grosse*, with 15 dreadnoughts in his line, was still unsuspecting as he approached this awesome arc from the south. Between the two main forces, the battle cruisers, cruisers and destroyers from both fleets, badly scrambled in the earlier fighting, rushed to take station—the British on Jellicoe's flank, the Germans in Scheer's van—and began firing savagely. The place where they clashed, around lat. 56° 57' N. and long. 5° 43' E.—a desolate North Sea tract about 85 miles from Danish Jutland—would henceforth bear a name denoting, in British slang, a fearful place: Windy Corner.

"The whole surface of the sea was heaving up and down," wrote a *Southampton* officer, "in a confused swell caused by the wash created by the two hundred odd ships which were moving about at high speeds." Although the British dreadnoughts were still out of sight of Scheer's battleships, some of them had a grandstand view of the Windy Corner. "The light cruisers and destroyers," an officer of the *Malaya* wrote, "were twisting and turning, endeavouring to avoid each other and the big ships. It will never cease to be a source of wonder to me that so few ships were hit and that there were no collisions."

Enough were hit. The sea was soon littered with war's wreckage: flaming ships, vast patches of burning oil, men swimming for their lives. Rear Admiral Sir Horace Hood's 3rd Battle Cruiser Squadron blasted the German cruiser *Wiesbaden* and left her dead in the water. In the armored cruiser *Defence*, Rear Admiral Sir Robert Arbuthnot saw the helpless *Wiesbaden* and led the *Warrior*, the *Black Prince* and the *Duke of Edinburgh* in for the kill. From at least 50 ships, hundreds of men—some exhilarated, some horrified—watched what happened next.

Arbuthnot charged from north to south past the *Wiesbaden* and suddenly came within sight and range of German battle cruisers and the leading German dreadnoughts. All four of his armored cruisers immediately came under fire. The *Warrior* and the *Black Prince* were both severely hit; the *Duke of Edinburgh* escaped with minor damage. But Arbuthnot's *Defence* was doomed. Three quick salvos of 12-inch shells rumbled toward the *Defence*, the first over, the second short and the third a hit. The ship heeled to the blow, righted herself and steamed on. Then followed three more salvos. Again the first was over, the second short and the third a hit. The *Defence* "completely disappeared in a mass of spray, smoke and flame," wrote one observer. "But she came through it apparently intact, only to disappear a few seconds later in a tremendous belch of vivid flame and dense black smoke, from which some dark object, possibly a boat or a funnel, was hurled through space, twirling like a gigantic Catherine wheel." The smoke "rose to a height of some hundred feet and quickly clearing, left no sign of a ship at all." Admiral Arbuthnot and all 900 men aboard the *Defence* were dead.

While the doomed *Defence* had been moving to its last attack, Beatty and his battle cruisers had come careening into the Windy Corner from west to east, and they had to sheer violently away to avoid Arbuthnot's armored cruisers. "There was handling of ships in that ten minutes," wrote a witness, "such as never been dreamed of by seamen before."

The confusion was compounded by the *Warspite*, one of the four superdreadnoughts with 15-inch guns, which had been trailing Beatty all afternoon. Now ordered to leave Beatty and fall in astern of Jellicoe's line, the squadron was steaming north-northeast when the *Warspite* was hit heavily, jamming her rudder. For the next 15 minutes the dreadnought sailed at full speed—25 knots—in two giant circles that took her within 10,000 yards of the head of Scheer's battle line. If there had been any doubt about a dreadnought's toughness, it was now dispelled. During her concentric travels, the *Warspite* was taken under fire by the *Friedrich der Grosse, König, Helgoland, Ostfriesland, Thüringen* and *Kaiserin*. She was hit 13 times but was still in fighting trim, and only because her steering gear continued giving trouble did Admiral Hugh Evan-Thomas, the squadron commander, order her back to base. The Germans, finding the *Warspite* had vanished when the smoke cleared, presumed they had sunk her, but she eventually reached Rosyth, after narrowly avoiding torpedo attacks on the way.

The preliminaries were now over. At 6:30 p.m., the two dreadnought fleets sighted each other. Jellicoe in the *Iron Duke*, now in the middle of the British line, saw the leaders of the German line come looming through the mist from the southwest—exactly abeam of him, exactly where he wanted them to be. His deployment had been correct. At last, after two years of waiting, the British had brought the Germans to battle, and Jellicoe had achieved the classic maneuver of crossing their "T." The *Iron Duke* and at least a dozen other dreadnoughts instantly opened fire on the dim shapes of the German leaders.

To Scheer, the shock was devastating. For half an hour, confused reports had come from his cruisers, which here and there had briefly seen the shadowed forms of big ships through the mist and smoke. The first thing Scheer himself saw was "rounds of firing from guns of heavy caliber on the horizon directly ahead of us. The entire arc stretching from north to east was a sea of fire. The flash from the muzzles of the guns was distinctly seen, though the ships themselves were not visible. More than a hundred heavy guns joined in the fight on the enemy's side."

Reinhard Scheer had set a trap—and had fallen into another. His tactical position could hardly have been worse. Every one of the British dreadnoughts was able to bear its broadsides on the leading battle cruisers and dreadnoughts in Scheer's column. Moreover, visibility favored the British. As his dreadnoughts had begun to deploy, Jellicoe had asked his flag captain to decide on the direction in which visibility would be best to engage a fleet heading north. "I reported to him," Captain Dreyer said later, "that the most favourable direction was to the southward and would draw westward as the sun sank." Now, by his careful foresight, Jellicoe had gained that advantage. The official German history described Scheer's predicament: "The German van was faced by the belching guns of an interminable line of heavy ships extending from northwest to northeast. Salvo followed salvo almost without a pause. The impression gained in power from the almost complete inability of the German ships to reply, as not one of the British dreadnoughts could be distinguished through the smoke and fumes."

Within 10 minutes, the British fired 40 salvos, scoring 12 hits on the dreadnoughts *Markgraf* and *König*, and on the battle cruisers *Lützow* and

Derfflinger. The *Lützow,* now with 20 hits from the afternoon's fray, was struggling to stay in line, and the *König,* Scheer's leading dreadnought, was listing 4½°. Georg von Hase, the observant gunnery officer on the *Derfflinger,* said later: "It was clear the enemy could see us better than we could see them. Several heavy shells pierced our ship with terrific force and exploded with a great roar that shook every seam and rivet."

To the men on the beleaguered *Derfflinger,* what happened next could only have seemed an act of God. The baffling mist suddenly parted, leaving a sunlit corridor, at the other end of which appeared the *Invincible,* Admiral Hood's battle-cruiser flagship. "Her guns were trained on us," wrote Hase, "and immediately another salvo crashed out, straddling us completely. 'Range 9,000!' roared Leading Seaman Hämel. '9,000—salvos, fire!' I ordered, and with feverish anxiety I waited for our splashes. 'Over. Two hits!' called Lieutenant Commander von Stosch. I gave the order: '100 down. Good. Rapid!' and 30 seconds after the first salvo the second left the guns. I observed two short splashes and two hits. And then for the third time we witnessed the dreadful spectacle that we had already seen in the case of the *Queen Mary* and the *Defence.*

"As with the other ships there was a rapid succession of heavy explosions, masts collapsed, debris flew into the air, a gigantic column of black smoke rose skyward, and from the parting sections of the ship, coal dust spurted in all directions. Flames enveloped her, fresh explosions followed, and behind the murky shroud our enemy vanished. I shouted

into the telephone, 'Enemy has blown up!' Above the din of battle a great cheer thundered through the ship and was transmitted to the fore-control by the gunnery telephones and flashed from one gun post to another. I sent up a short fervent prayer of thanks to the Almighty.''

The third British battle cruiser to be destroyed by identical explosions, the *Invincible* split into halves, both of which sank and remained for at least half an hour standing vertically on the bottom of the shallow sea, the bow and stern projecting straight up above the surface like gravestones. A few minutes later Jellicoe passed by in the *Iron Duke*, saw the macabre monument and signaled a nearby destroyer: "Is this wreck one of ours?'' "Yes,'' came the answer, *"Invincible.''*

The destroyer *Badger* rescued two officers and four ratings; the other 1,026 men of the *Invincible*, including Admiral Hood, were dead.

But Hipper's battle cruisers had little time to savor their victory over the *Invincible*. All of them had been badly damaged, and the flagship *Lützow* was on fire forward, listing heavily, and so much down by the head that her foredeck was awash. When Hipper's staff begged him to transfer his flag, he at first refused: "I cannot leave my flagship.'' "She is sinking, Your Excellency!'' "But I cannot leave.'' "Your Excellency, you must. The fleet needs you.'' At that, Hipper consented to go to a nearby destroyer. While the *Lützow* left the line and set a slow course southward, in hope of reaching home, the German battle-cruiser commander embarked on a three-hour odyssey in search of a new flagship.

Standing on the bed of the shallow North Sea, the bow and stern sections are all that remain of the British battle cruiser Invincible. Struck repeatedly by heavy shells from five German ships, the Invincible exploded in a great flash, broke in half and sank within two minutes. Wrote a stunned observer: "One moment she was the flagship leading her squadron; the next moment she was merely two sections of twisted metal."

First, as his destroyer passed the *Derfflinger*, Hipper signaled, "Captain of *Derfflinger* will take command until I board." But the *Derfflinger* was, as Georg von Hase said, "a pretty sorry sight." Her masts, rigging and wireless aerials were in a tangle, she could not transmit signals, and she had a hole "six by five meters" just above the water line in her bow. As she pitched, water surged in, and shortly she had to stop because her torpedo net had been shot away and was about to foul the propellers.

Hipper then approached the *Seydlitz*. She was awash up to the middle deck forward, and she also had no wireless. The *Von der Tann*, all her turrets still out of action, was powerless, and had only stayed with the fleet in a valiant effort to draw British fire away from the other German warships. Of Hipper's five battle cruisers, the *Moltke* was the only one still fit to act as flagship. But in the swirl of the battle, it would be 9:50 p.m. before Hipper could board her and regain control of his command.

Scheer was encountering equally desperate difficulties. As Jellicoe's Grand Fleet crossed in front of him, his ships could not bear up under the weight of British metal. One by one the German dreadnoughts began to veer off to the east on a course parallel to the British. This could only lead to a running battle, with numbers, range, speed and visibility all against Scheer. And he was still encumbered by his six predreadnoughts, slow and vulnerable ships with armament of only four 11-inch guns apiece. Scheer could either abandon them, risk the fleet by pausing to help them—or break off the battle. To his credit, he wasted no time in deciding. At 6:36 p.m. the signal mast of the *Friedrich der Grosse* showed, "*Gefechtskehrtwendung nach steuerbord*"—"Battle turn to starboard."

It was an unusual maneuver, calling for a 180° turn—a complete reversal of course—in the swiftest possible time. In the standard fleet turn, the vessels changed course in succession starting with the van, each ship swinging around as it passed over a designated point. This turn kept the chance of collisions at a minimum, but had the disadvantage of exposing each ship, at its turning point, to concentrated enemy fire. Scheer's order, on the other hand, required all the dreadnoughts in his line to make 180° turns simultaneously. It demanded the highest order of seamanship. But the High Seas Fleet had been practicing assiduously, and executed it superbly *(chart, right)*. The first confrontation between dreadnought fleets was over. It had lasted less than 30 minutes.

Scheer's maneuver took the British by surprise. To Jellicoe, the enemy had been there one moment and vanished the next. "I could not see him turn away from where I was on top of the charthouse," he wrote. "I imagined that it was due merely to the thickening of the mist, but after a few minutes had elapsed it became clear that there must be some other reason." Jellicoe signaled the *Marlborough*, leading the rear division, "Can you see the enemy?" Replied the *Marlborough*: "No."

In Jutland's aftermath, Admiral Jellicoe was bitterly criticized for his failure to seek out and, with his overwhelming dreadnought advantage, pursue the German fleet. But Jellicoe had given fair warning as to what he would—and would not—do in such a situation. On October 30, 1914, he had written to the Admiralty: "If, for instance, the enemy Battle Fleet were to turn away from an advancing fleet, I should assume that the intention was to lead us over mines and submarines, and should decline

Scheer's initial retreat

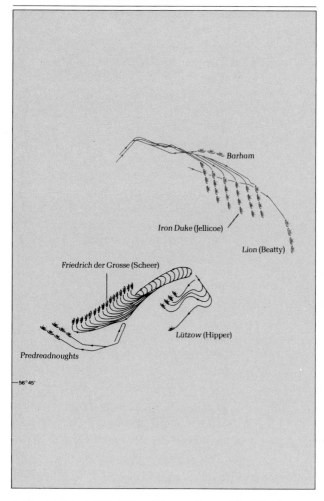

6:30 P.M. TO 7:00 P.M. Unable to withstand the British cannonade, Scheer at 6:33 orders a Gefechtskehrtwendung, a daring battle turn of 180°—a virtual about-face—that has been lauded by naval historians ever since. The flawlessly executed maneuver immediately plunges the German dreadnoughts back into the protective mist. Jellicoe, afraid that the retreating Germans are sowing mines in their wake, re-forms his ships into columns and swings east, then south, to flank the Germans and cut them off from their bases. After 20 minutes of steaming away from the British, Scheer decides to resume the engagement and orders another Gefechtskehrtwendung back toward the British fleet.

The second encounter

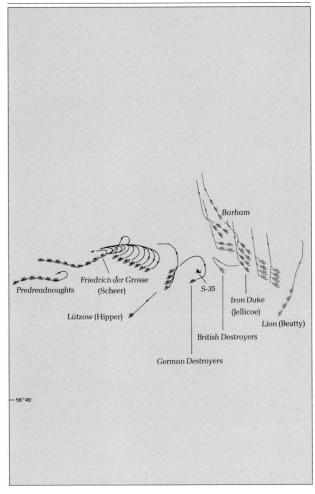

7:15 P.M. TO 7:25 P.M. Again the British gunners are devastatingly accurate, and Scheer suffers hit after hit on his König-class dreadnoughts. At 7:18 he orders a third 180° turn to escape from the enemy and calls for a smoke screen and torpedo-boat attack to cover his retreat. The British counter with a destroyer attack of their own. But the Germans, though they lose a torpedo boat, the S-35, succeed in their main objective. Sighting torpedo tracks, the British dreadnoughts turn their sterns toward the Germans and Scheer escapes.

Labels on chart: Barham; Friedrich der Grosse (Scheer); Predreadnoughts; Lützow (Hipper); S-35; Iron Duke (Jellicoe); Lion (Beatty); British Destroyers; German Destroyers; 56°45'

to be so drawn. I feel that such tactics, if not understood, may bring odium upon me, but so long as I have the confidence of their Lordships I intend to pursue what is, in my considered opinion, the proper best course." The letter was approved by the Admiralty, presumably including the then First Lord, the aggressive Winston Churchill.

In fact, the Germans had abandoned the notion of sowing mines in their wake during a chase as being just as likely to blow up their own ships as the enemy's. And Scheer had not a submarine nearby. But Jellicoe could hardly be expected to know this, and his fears did seem to be confirmed when, minutes after Scheer's withdrawal, the *Marlborough* took a torpedo hit. Fretful as he was about the threat of submarines, Jellicoe could only assume a sub was responsible, though the torpedo probably came from the German cruiser *Wiesbaden*, dying but still afloat, defiant and dangerous. The *Marlborough*, with a 70-foot hole yawning starboard, took a 7° list, which was reduced by flooding compartments to port. Her speed fell to 17 knots, but she limped home.

The *Marlborough*'s fate was more than enough for Jellicoe: instead of pursuing Scheer, he set a southerly course, hoping to cut the High Seas Fleet off from its base. For his decision he later received in full measure the odium he had predicted in his Admiralty letter. Beatty, too, was blamed for "failing to regain touch," a charge he churlishly laid off onto Jellicoe: "How could we know that as soon as we had brought the German battle fleet to the C.-in-C. the latter had lost it again. It was no longer the main duty of Battle Cruiser Force to alone keep in touch with the battle fleet of the enemy when C.-in-C. avoided doing so by retreating."

Such backbiting was, however, mostly academic—for at 6:55, only 20 minutes after he had so precipitately withdrawn from the action, Scheer again reversed his course and started steaming right back toward the British line. John Jellicoe was about to be granted the rarest of all gifts in warfare—a second chance.

No one would ever know for certain why Scheer did it. His official explanation was less than satisfying: "It was too early to assume night cruising order. The enemy could have compelled us to fight before dark, he could have prevented our exercising our initiative, and finally he could have cut off our retreat to the German Bight. There was only one way of avoiding this: to deal the enemy a second blow by again advancing regardless of consequences, and to bring all destroyers to attack." In private, he made even less sense. "I wanted to help the poor *Wiesbaden*," he told his staff after the battle. "The thing just happened."

Whatever the reason, the results were the same. The battle cruisers of Scouting Group 1, now under Captain Johannes Hartog on the *Derfflinger* (Hipper was still looking for a new flagship), led the way back into the fray. And it immediately became apparent that Scheer, for perhaps one of the few times in the history of conflict at sea, had managed to get his "T" crossed not once, but twice, in a single battle *(chart, left)*.

"The van of our fleet was shut in by the semicircle of the enemy," Hase of the *Derfflinger* wrote. "We were in a regular deathtrap." From the British Line, the *St. Vincent, Neptune, Revenge* and *Agincourt* opened fire, and the *Derfflinger* shuddered under their blows. At 7:12, Scheer and the dreadnoughts followed the battle cruisers out of the mist.

Within a minute of sighting the British, he sensed his perilous situation and signaled his dreadnoughts for another battle turn—"*Gefectskehrtwendung!*"—to take them back into the protective mist. At the same time, he issued a desperate order for rear-guard action to cover his escape. He signaled his battle cruisers, already under heavy British fire. "*Rein in dem Feind! Ran!*"—"Straight into the enemy! Charge!"

The battle cruisers responded with a gallantry that would forever after stir seafaring souls. One by one, the crippled battle cruisers moved toward the flaming British line. The *Derfflinger* led, followed by the *Seydlitz*, the *Moltke* and, finally, the *Von der Tann*, her guns out of action, unable to fire but unwilling to abandon the fight.

The *Derfflinger* lurched toward the *Colossus*, 17th dreadnought in the British battle line, and even managed to drive home two shells, inflicting minor damage and wounding six men. She paid a price for her impertinence, and an officer on the bridge of the *Colossus* tersely recorded the event: "Observed *Lützow* class battle cruiser 10,000 yards on starboard beam, accompanied by two other large ships. Opened fire at 9,000 yards, closing at 7:16 p.m. to 8,400. Fired five salvoes, observed at least four direct hits. Enemy burst into flames, listed, disappeared in the flame."

A shell from the *Colossus* had pierced the armor of one of the *Derfflinger*'s turrets and burst inside, and the flames from burning cordite flared high into the air; of the 78 men in the turret, only five survived. Moments later, another turret was hit. "The same horrors ensued," Hase wrote. "With the exception of one single man, the whole turret crew of 80, including all the magazine men, were killed instantly. Whole sheets of the deck were hurled through the air, tremendous concussion threw overboard everything that could be moved. The charthouse with all the charts and other gear vanished forever."

Scheer soon changed his mind and signaled the reeling battle cruisers to "engage the enemy van." Hartog on the *Derfflinger* ordered a change of course from east to south at 23 knots, and as the battle cruisers turned in compliance they were virtually helpless before the British broadsides. The *Seydlitz* and the *Von der Tann* were hit, and the *Derfflinger* took six shells before she and her stricken mates finally broke off and escaped into a smoke bank laid by German destroyers.

Although the battle cruisers' suicidal attack drew the brunt of the fire, Scheer's dreadnoughts were by no means unscathed. The *König* was down by the head and the *Grosser Kurfürst*, listing 4°, was taking water forward up to her main deck. At 7:18, Scheer ordered his brave battle cruisers to break off their hopeless attack and signaled his destroyers to cover the general retreat with a torpedo attack.

All along the British line, men saw the destroyers coming. In the *Conqueror*, seventh ship in the line, an officer wrote that the lithe and lethal little warships were never on the same course for more than a minute at a time. They were constantly "turning, twisting, wriggling and disappearing into their own smoke, only to reappear again almost immediately at a different place, the result for us being rather like trying to hit snipe with buckshot." British destroyers were ordered out to counterattack, and the whole battle was soon obscured by a German smoke

Virtually awash, the damaged German battle cruiser Seydlitz labors homeward after Jutland, her flooded hull ripped open by 22 heavy shells and one torpedo. Unable to maintain the fleet speed of 16 knots during the night of May 31, the battered Seydlitz, at times making only seven knots, managed to slip past no fewer than five enemy warships on her way back to the safety of German waters.

screen. Then out of the murk sped the tracks of German torpedoes.

Big ships obviously ran less risk of being hit by torpedoes if they could avoid presenting a broadside target. They could turn toward the torpedoes, hoping to dodge them bow-on. But standard British tactics called for turning stern-on to a torpedo attack, an evasive maneuver that was considered safer for two reasons: the ships might outrun the torpedoes' range or, failing in that, they might stay ahead until the torpedoes, near the end of their runs, were traveling more slowly and were therefore easier to avoid. Jellicoe signaled his dreadnoughts to turn away from the enemy torpedoes—and from the retreating High Seas Fleet.

The torpedo attack caused great excitement, but little real damage. About 50 German destroyers armed with nearly 250 torpedoes were available. But in the face of gunfire, the counterattack by British destroyers, and the evasive action of Jellicoe's dreadnoughts, only 13 of the German boats reached firing positions—and then at the extreme range of 7,500 yards. They fired a grand total of 31 torpedoes. Twenty-one of these reached the British line, but not one ship was sunk.

To the pleased surprise of the British, the enemy torpedoes left a plainly visible track of bubbles. The British had remedied this defect in their own torpedoes, and intelligence had reported that the Germans had done the same. Not so. Lookouts could see the torpedoes coming from as far as two miles away, giving even the heaviest ships time to evade. There were, to be sure, some near-misses. One torpedo passed close under the *Neptune*'s stern, and a gunnery lieutenant in the foretop saw another coming straight for the ship. He bellowed, "Hard a-starboard," down the voice pipe, and a midshipman with him recalled the response, with the mast and top "groaning and vibrating under the strain of the ship turning at full speed with full helm on." The turn brought the torpedo exactly astern—and catching up. "We could do nothing," the midshipman wrote, "but wait and wait, mouths open. Nothing happened. The time passed when it should have reached our stern and there should have been a big explosion, but still nothing happened." It seemed to him a miracle, but the *Neptune*'s report explained it more prosaically: "Torpedo was either deflected by the wash from *Neptune*'s propellers or ran its range out. The latter is more likely."

At 7:31, the torpedo attack ended, the destroyers faded into their own smoke, and the great guns fell silent on the *Iron Duke*. She would never fire another shot in anger. The fact that the Grand Fleet had turned away in the face of such a puny attack was a terrible blow to British Naval pride, and one for which Jellicoe would not be forgiven by many of his countrymen. At 7:40 he signaled the fleet to resume its southerly course, but the German fleet was gone. The second encounter between the dreadnought fleets had lasted little more than a quarter of an hour. No vital damage had been done to any dreadnought on either side.

Most of the personal accounts of Jutland were written by men who could more or less see what was happening. But the great majority of the 105,000 men who were there saw nothing at all. These were the men belowdecks: engineers, medical staffs, damage-control and fire parties, wireless operators and cipherers, magazine and turret crews. Their experiences were all the more harrowing because they were fighting blind.

"I heard a tremendous explosion at the after end, a heavy jar went through the whole fabric, and most of the lights went out," wrote the engineering officer of the armored cruiser *Warrior*, which was hit by German dreadnoughts early in the battle. "The engines still went on running, which seemed to show that the cylinders had not been hit. But in the dim uncertain light I perceived what appeared to be Niagara, though whether the sheet of water was rising up from below or pouring down from above I couldn't be sure at the time. A blast of steam on my face warned me that I hadn't long to think about it, and I soon made up my mind that no pumps could deal with the quantity of water that was coming in, and that the only thing to do was to get the men out."

The two engine rooms, port and starboard, had a watertight door between them, but it was jammed shut. The officer hustled his men up a ladder and followed them himself. The last lights went out. It was pitch dark. He felt his way by the handrails along the platform at the tops of the reciprocating engine cylinders toward another door at the fore end. But when he opened it, a rush of smoke and blinding fumes came through. The mess deck beyond it was ablaze. "With this in front and the roar of steam behind me," he wrote, "I felt like a trapped rat, for there seemed no possibility of lifting the heavy armour hatches overhead, and a spasm of sheer terror came over me; but just then I realised a man was calling my attention to a glimmer of light above, and the next minute I found myself climbing out through a torn rent in the deck."

All told, the *Warrior* was hit 13 times, and for the next two hours her belowdecks men fought to control the fires. Every access to the other engine room was barred by flames, and steam was roaring out of its ventilators. The officer was agonizingly convinced that the entire port engine-room crew had perished, but one of the armored hatches was finally lifted and, astonishingly, shouts came from below.

In the port engine room, ladders had been inaccessible; water rose breast-high over the floor plates and the open cranks of the engine were racing round in it. The crew climbed up the engine, over pipes and condensers, holding hands to prevent the swirling water from carrying them away. Some fell and were mangled and drowned. About eight men reached the underside of the gratings above but could not budge them. Trapped between the gratings and the rising water, escaping steam almost suffocating them, they splashed oily water over their faces to keep from being scalded. In total darkness and hopelessness, they clung to one another. But one by one they dropped off and drowned. When the hatches at last were opened by their mates, only three were still alive.

These were the men who survived to tell their story, but hundreds and hundreds in the *Warrior* and other ships could not get out of their compartments when disaster came. Their bodies were found after the battle—drowned, burned, boiled, suffocated in the dark or, more mercifully, killed instantly by explosions.

To the British, darkness came as anathema. Before the War, the Royal Navy had held night exercises off the coast of Spain at Vigo; they had proved to be a shambles, leading an officer to comment that "the control

Honored mascot William the Hun, an English bull terrier, displays his distinctively ornamented neck as he stretches for the hand of Lieutenant King Harman on the British destroyer Swift. The metal plates on William's collar attest to his loyal presence at the Battle of Jutland and at two smaller engagements with German raiders in 1916 and 1917.

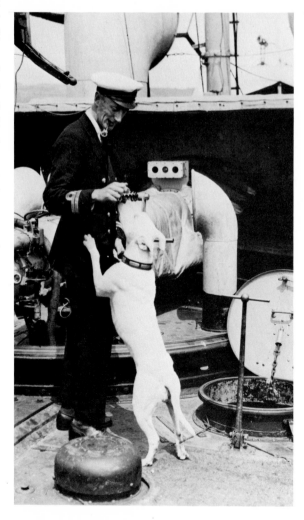

Scheer's run for home

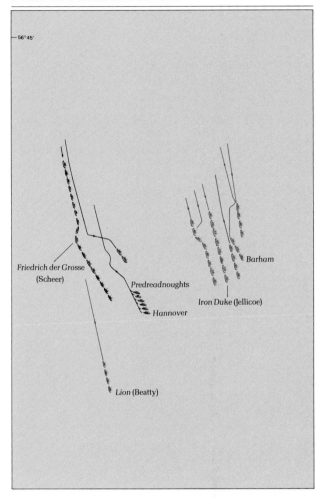

56°45'

Friedrich der Grosse
(Scheer)

Predreadnoughts

Hannover

Barham

Iron Duke (Jellicoe)

Lion (Beatty)

9:30 TO 10:00 P.M. Jellicoe now races south, intending to cut off the retreating Germans from the safety of their bases. Scheer knows that he cannot outrun the British, so he shapes a course to the southeast, hoping to let the enemy pass in front of him in the darkness; his six vulnerable predreadnoughts, led by the Hannover, wait for Scheer's main force to pass so they can fall in behind it. In the meantime the British battle cruisers, led by the Lion, have moved southwest in an effort to engage the enemy, but after a brief skirmish they have lost contact with the Germans again.

of British searchlights was so bad as to be laughable." Jellicoe emerged from this sorry experience convinced that night fighting was "a lottery" of which he wanted no part. A battle at night, with all its elements of chance, would favor the weaker fleet and nullify the British strength in long-range gunnery. The Admiralty had therefore decided to save strength for daytime and avoid battle at night. In his official report after Jutland, Jellicoe wrote: "I rejected at once the idea of a night action between the heavy ships, as leading to possible disaster, owing first to the presence of torpedo craft in such large numbers and, secondly, to the impossibility of distinguishing between our own and enemy vessels."

To the Germans, night offered opportunity for which they had fully prepared themselves. Unlike the British, they carried star shells, which could illuminate enemy ships without giving away their own position. The German searchlights were much more powerful and efficient: a pencil ray of light would first form on an enemy vessel; then a shutter would open to bathe the target in full beam and, in almost instant coordination, the German guns would open fire. Most important, the High Seas Fleet had developed a far superior system of night-recognition signals: patterns of colored lights in the riggings, which could be switched on and off so quickly that an enemy could not copy them. Against this, the British used letters flashed in Morse code, which took longer and could be picked up and used by hostile ships.

By the time night fell on Jutland, the day's fighting had carried the British fleet east of the Germans, between Scheer and his base. Jellicoe hoped and expected to keep that relative position, but to do so required an accurate estimate of the route Scheer would take while avoiding the minefields in the Heligoland Bight. There were two possibilities: the longer but less risky way was for the Germans to steer due south, then east past the Dutch coast and into the Jade estuary. The other was to take a direct line and cut southeast close to Horns Reef off Denmark.

For reasons that he never made clear, Jellicoe decided that the Dutch route was the more likely, and he accordingly set his own course to the south, sending only his minelayer, *Abdiel*, to sow more mines off Horns Reef. By 9 p.m., Jellicoe had his fleet in cruising formation on a southerly course, with his destroyers as a defensive screen five miles astern and Beatty with the battle cruisers, out on his own again, 13 miles to the west. In all, the fleet made a barrier about 25 miles long.

Jellicoe had guessed wrong. Ten minutes after he had started south, Scheer turned south-southeast at 16 knots, heading for Horns Reef (*chart, left*). Somewhere, the projected tracks of the two fleets would have to cross. Scheer made it grimly clear what his fleet was to do in such an event. "This course," he ordered, "is to be maintained."

Perhaps fittingly, the night action began with another ghastly mistake by Beatty's flag lieutenant, the feckless Ralph Seymour who, soon after dark, signaled by flashing light to the next ship astern: "Please give me challenge and reply now in force as they have been lost." This, as Jellicoe said when he first heard of it after the War, was simple idiocy. The other ship flashed back the secret recognition signals—while two groups of German cruisers, less than two miles away, read and copied the messages. Throughout the night, German ships were thus able to fire instantly on anyone who began to make the British challenge, and probably—although it was never proved—to reply correctly to British challenges and pass through the Royal Navy line.

As if Seymour's incompetence was not enough, the Admiralty now made its own contribution to the tragicomedy of British communications. Because of the misinformation given him that morning about Scheer's continuing presence in the Jade, Jellicoe had come to nourish a distrust of Admiralty intelligence. His suspicions seemed confirmed when, late in the evening, Operations passed on to Jellicoe a position for Scheer that Jellicoe knew could not be right. That information came from Room 40, using directional receivers that were sometimes unreliable. Yet at the same time, Room 40 was accurately deciphering Scheer's wireless message and relaying them to Operations. At about 10 o'clock, Operations transmitted to Jellicoe an intercepted signal ordering the course for the night—the route that pointed directly to Horns Reef. In his unbelieving frame of mind, Jellicoe concluded that this was more Admiralty twaddle. He continued to steer south.

In the next two hours, Room 40 deciphered six more of Scheer's signals—and two of them were vital. One, to the Zeppelin base in north Germany, read: "Early morning reconnaissance at Horns Reef is urgently requested." The other, to the German destroyers, ordered all flotillas to assemble by 2 a.m.—at Horns Reef. Together, they were conclusive, and almost certainly would have overcome even Jellicoe's considerable skepticism, causing him to alter course for Horns Reef.

But he never got the messages. They were dutifully sent by Room 40 to the Operations Room, which was controlled by the Chief of the War Staff. He had gone to bed. Left in charge was Captain A. F. Everett—the First Lord's naval secretary—who had no special knowledge of Operations work, and evidently very little sense to boot. He decided that the signals were not worth forwarding and filed them away. By the time they were found, there was no point in even censuring the man who had committed one of the most egregious mistakes in Admiralty history.

At about 10:00 p.m., elements of the German High Seas Fleet ran into destroyers screening the rear of Jellicoe's force, and the last and most desperate phase of the Battle of Jutland flamed in the darkness of a drizzling night. It was fought at point-blank range in separate unconnected actions that sometimes lasted no more than three or four minutes. Afterward, historians were able more or less to sort out what happened. But to those involved, it was complete and utter confusion. "We had absolutely no idea of where the enemy was," wrote a British destroyer captain, "and only a very vague idea of the position of our own ships."

The first real action began when the British *Castor*, leading a destroyer flotilla, came upon two ships that made the British recognition signal. The *Castor* approached to within 2,000 yards—and the ships suddenly switched on searchlights and opened fire. They were in fact the German light cruisers *Frankfurt* and *Pillau*. The *Castor* replied with gunfire and torpedoes, but she was badly damaged and had many casualties. Most of her flotilla failed to fire; they thought they were being fired on by friendly ships, and before they realized their error,

Making good the escape

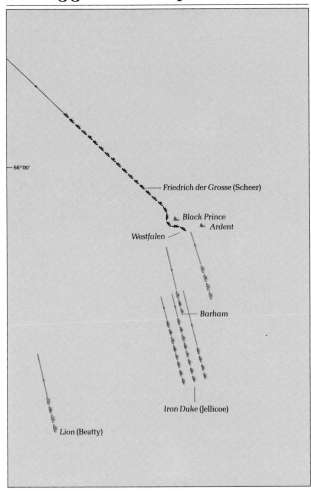

— 56°00'

— Friedrich der Grosse (Scheer)

Black Prince
Ardent
Westfalen

Barham

Iron Duke (Jellicoe)

Lion (Beatty)

12 MIDNIGHT TO 12:15 A.M. Scheer bears tenaciously southeast through the night, escaping by a narrow squeak. His lead dreadnought, the Westfalen, actually comes within three miles of the rearmost of Jellicoe's dreadnoughts. For two hours he has been fighting a series of furious night actions against a rear guard of British cruisers and destroyers. His fleet now sinks the destroyer Ardent and observes the armored cruiser Black Prince burning fiercely in her death throes. Three hours later, as the sun reddens the eastern sky, Scheer brings his High Seas Fleet safely into the protection of German waters.

the brief action was over and an uneasy silence fell upon the sea.

It was broken again at about 10:30, when the light cruisers *Southampton* and *Dublin* stumbled onto German cruisers. "A signalman and the navigator suddenly whispered, 'Five ships on the beam,'" wrote a *Southampton* officer. "We began to challenge; the Germans switched on coloured lights at their fore yard-arms. A second later a solitary gun crashed forth from the *Dublin*. Simultaneously I saw the shell hit a German ship just above the waterline and about 800 yards away. I caught a nightmare-like glimpse of her interior. At that moment the Germans switched on their searchlights, and we switched on ours. Before I was blinded by the lights in my eyes I caught sight of a line of light grey ships. Then the gun behind which I was standing answered my shout of 'Fire!' The action lasted 3½ minutes." In those three and a half minutes the *Southampton* fired a torpedo that hit the cruiser *Frauenlob* and blew her in half. But the *Southampton* herself suffered 89 casualties, with 75 per cent of the men on her upper deck killed or wounded.

An hour later, at about 11:30, the German dreadnoughts, steering slightly east of south for Horns Reef, began to cross the track of the British destroyers, still steaming south in the wake of their battle fleet, and five miles astern of it. Dimly sighting a shadowy line of ships very close at hand, the British flotilla leader *Tipperary* challenged—and the Germans instantly switched on their searchlights and opened fire.

The *Tipperary* caught fire almost at once and sank. The cannonading continued for more than 40 minutes, rising and falling in crescendo as more and more Germans came into contact with the light British ships and broke through their lines. The destroyer *Fortune* was shattered and sunk by the Germans. In the wild melee, the German cruiser *Rostock*, which was in company with the battle fleet, took a torpedo hit, and the German battleship *Posen* rammed the German cruiser *Elbing*. Both the *Rostock* and the *Elbing* were abandoned and sank later in the night. The British destroyer *Spitfire* collided bow to bow with the German dreadnought *Nassau*, which scraped down the *Spitfire*'s side. The huge *Nassau*'s guns roared over the heads of the destroyer's crew. "They could not depress them to hit us," a *Spitfire* survivor wrote, "but the blast brought down the mast, funnel and bridge." The *Spitfire* was left on fire, with a hole 60 feet long in her side. "In exchange the *Nassau* had left twenty feet of her upper deck inside our mess deck."

By now it was midnight, and the leading German dreadnoughts were almost across the track of Jellicoe's Grand Fleet *(chart, left)*. Yet another British destroyer, the *Ardent*, fell under the German guns and went to the bottom. On board the damaged *Spitfire*, a crewman heard a cry of "Look out!" from a dozen voices. "I saw what appeared to be a battle cruiser on fire steering straight for our stern," he later recalled. "We thought she was steering for us with the intention of cutting us in two. She missed our stern by a few feet, but so close that it seemed we were actually lying under her guns, which were trained out on her starboard beam. She tore past us with a roar, and the very crackling and heat of the flames could be heard and felt. She was a mass of fire."

The Germans also saw and reported this macabre apparition. "A burning ship drove past us," Hase of the *Derfflinger* wrote. "The whole ship was red hot. There could not have been a soul alive on board for some time." Neither the British nor the Germans knew what ship she was, but it was reckoned afterward she must have been the armored cruiser *Black Prince,* which, heavily shelled in the afternoon, had been caught alone and shelled again by the High Seas Fleet in the night. With dead men at her helm, she now drove through the center of the battle, disappeared into the darkness and was never seen again.

After the *Tipperary* sank, the destroyer *Broke* took over leadership of the flotilla. She was soon caught in the searchlights of the dreadnought *Westfalen,* leading the German line. The *Broke* fired her 4-inch guns at the searchlights and unleashed torpedoes, but a battleship salvo smashed her bridge, wheel and engine-room telegraph. She swung out of control and rammed the *Sparrowhawk,* next astern of her.

In the *Sparrowhawk,* a sublieutenant watched the *Broke's* bow coming straight for the bridge, where he was standing. It hit, and the young officer was flung off the bridge. When he came to his senses, he was lying on the foredeck—not of his own ship, but of the *Broke.* He struggled to his feet and was greeted by another sublieutenant, who said, "Who the hell are you?" The *Sparrowhawk* and the *Broke* were locked together, and each captain, thinking his ship was sinking, ordered his crew to cross to the other. Many men actually crossed in both directions before the orders were canceled. Each captain signaled, "Full astern," to his engine room, the ships drew apart and each, by great grace, floated. The *Broke* moved away, stern first into the darkness—whereupon a third destroyer, the *Contest,* rammed the *Sparrowhawk* in the stern. The *Sparrowhawk* was left dead in the water, crippled fore and aft.

The first faint streaks of daylight were appearing in the sky at 2 a.m., when the German fleet met still another destroyer flotilla, and this time a torpedo struck the predreadnought battleship *Pommern.* "It looked like a sheaf of flame from some gigantic firework," wrote Hase, coming up astern in the *Derfflinger.* "The ship must have been shattered to atoms, as only a few minutes later not the slightest trace of her could be seen." All hands—more than 800 men—perished on the *Pommern,* the only battleship sunk at Jutland.

Dead fish and dead men floated belly up in the oily sea, and dead ships haunted the surface. In the growing light a German battle cruiser approached the helpless *Sparrowhawk.* "Fellows went about sort of whispering that this must be the end," the sublieutenant wrote. The *Sparrowhawk's* men got up as much ammunition as they could and piled it around their only remaining gun. The enemy cruiser crept closer, still holding her fire. To some of the men on the *Sparrowhawk,* the strange ship seemed to be low in the water. Closer she came, and still closer. Then she stood on her head and sank.

The *Sparrowhawk's* men never knew what ship she was, and nobody can be certain now. By then, against all odds, Reinhard Scheer had broken through the tail of the British line and was heading for home. Throughout the deadly night, Britain's Jellicoe had sailed serenely south. Only one destroyer had so much as attempted to notify him by wireless that she was engaging dreadnoughts; that message failed to reach the *Iron Duke.* In a lapse for which there was no explanation,

A seaman on the German battle cruiser Derfflinger looks out through the jagged edges of a massive shell hole while his vessel awaits repair at the Wilhelmshaven dockyard after Jutland.

nobody else had thought to tell the Commander in Chief of the wild events taking place far to the rear—and he assumed that the thunder and lightning astern was the result of mere destroyer skirmishes.

Later a British officer sourly observed, "The flash of guns, display of searchlights, sudden glare of explosions and the blazing torches of burning destroyers marked the German escape route as unmistakably as the compass on the *Friedrich der Grosse*'s bridge."

The Battle of Jutland was over. Missing forever from the German battle array were the predreadnought *Pommern*; the battle cruiser *Lützow*; the light cruisers *Frauenlob*, *Wiesbaden*, *Elbing* and *Rostock*; and the destroyers *S-35*, *V-4*, *V-27*, *V-29* and *V-48*. The British litany was even more doleful: the battle cruisers *Indefatigable*, *Queen Mary* and *Invincible*; the armored cruisers *Defence*, *Warrior* and *Black Prince*; the destroyers *Nestor*, *Nomad*, *Tipperary*, *Ardent*, *Fortune*, *Shark*, *Turbulent*—and, after a weird and ghostly night, the *Sparrowhawk*, which was too badly mangled to save and was finally sunk by her own fleet. It was a fearful toll, but all the dreadnoughts—on both sides—were still afloat after the only battle they would ever fight against one another.

The drama of Jutland through a German's eyes

When the High Seas Fleet returned home from Jutland with its proud, if unjustifiable, claims of victory, the German Admiralty commissioned the foremost sea painter of the day, Claus Bergen, to recapture all the furious action and fierce beauty of that momentous battle.

Bergen had been born near the Black Forest, far from the sea, but he took no comfort in mountainscapes. In 1907 he visited Hamburg, Helgoland Island and the Norwegian port of Bergen—where he saw the English fleet—and was so enchanted that he made ships and the sea his specialty. His new work soon won acclaim, and commissions poured in from naval officers, shipping lines and governments.

Warships fascinated him. "I fell in love with those bulky gray shapes the first time I saw them," he said. His obsession with churning seas and belching guns made him a close friend of powerful admirals and captains. Bergen worked several years on his Jutland commission and produced hundreds of paintings. Each scene was a masterpiece of reconstruction. He began by making a painstaking study of battle maps and war diaries. In interviews with survivors of the battle, he obtained precise descriptions of shellbursts, the colors of different explosions and the terrifying appearance of gigantic shells hurtling toward the viewer.

At one point, Admiral von Hipper arranged a reenactment of German tactics during the Battle of Jutland for Bergen to witness from a light cruiser. "It was the only way to see it," said Bergen. Indeed, it would have done him no good to have been at the battle. "It is impossible to stand on deck when a salvo is fired," he explained. "The blast would blow you off the deck. And the gun flash is so blinding that you cannot see what is happening in that brief instant, so it is obviously only an impression that you finally put down."

Bergen produced watercolor sketches that he showed to each ship's commander for authenticity, incorporating any changes into his final oil paintings. The results were accurate down to the last brush stroke. During a showing of the completed art, an officer thought he had detected an error; he called attention to a huge puff of smoke in Bergen's gun flashes and advised that the flash should come first and then the smoke. Bergen politely replied that the smoke was not from the shot being fired but from the previous salvo.

Smothered by a lethal storm of German fire from the ships in the foreground, the British armored cruiser Defence, on the horizon at far left, blows up in a tiny flash of orange flame like a flaring match. Leading the column of German dreadnoughts steaming from left to right through seas pelted by enemy rounds is the König (far right), followed by the Grosser Kurfürst, the Kronprinz Wilhelm and the Markgraf. Between the Kurfürst and the Wilhelm a British shellburst raises a waterspout.

CLAUS BERGEN
MÜNCHEN

The predreadnought German battleship Pommern is depicted by
Bergen making a final flank-speed sprint toward hoped-
for safety — just moments before she was blasted to pieces by a
flotilla of pursuing British destroyers. Orange flashes piercing the

black smoke from left to right indicate the battle line of destroyers
as they zero in on the hapless old Imperial Navy vessel,
which was blown "literally to atoms," as one observer remarked,
ending the Battle of Jutland with one titanic detonation.

Chapter 6

Dishonor and suicide for the Kaiser's Navy

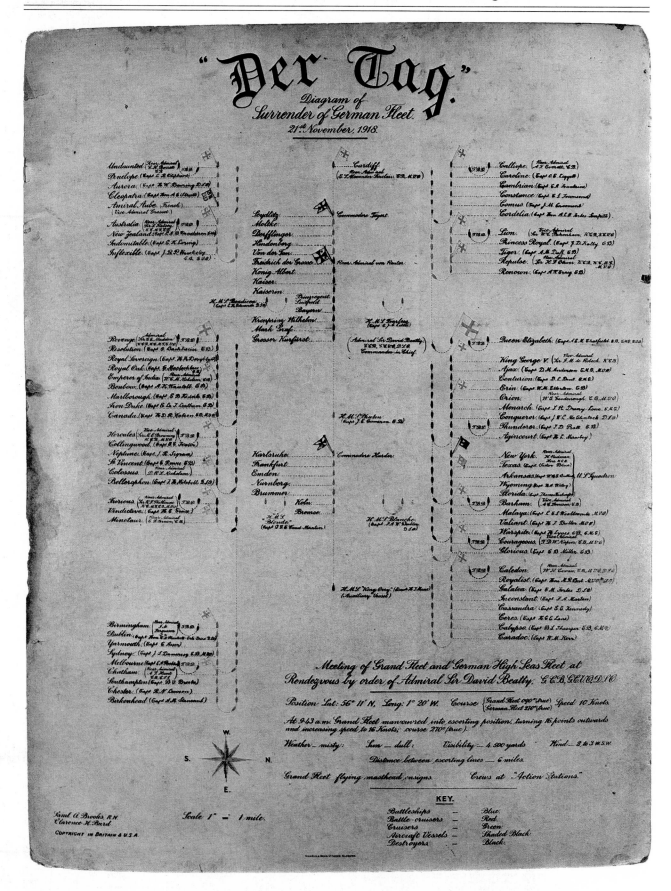

hroughout the melancholy morning of Thursday, June 1, 1916, the British Grand Fleet lingered on the North Sea battlefield in the forlorn hope of picking off at least a few German stragglers. Although rough weather was beginning to close in and the sky had turned leaden, the water's surface reflected vast oil slicks as the warships nudged through Jutland's pitiable flotsam: bits of wood and paper, cork life preservers and, here and there, floating corpses in the uniforms of both navies.

True to tradition, Jellicoe entrusted to the sea the bodies of those who had perished on board his ships—just as Sir Francis Drake had committed his dead to the sea after the defeat of the Spanish Armada more than 300 years before. All hands were piped on deck and the Royal Navy's dead, lashed in their hammocks and weighted at their heads and feet, slid overboard. Then at noon Jellicoe turned back toward Scapa Flow.

By that time the vessels of Scheer's High Seas Fleet, after posting five battleships at Schillig Road, outside Wilhelmshaven, to guard against an expected British foray, were beginning to arrive in their home harbors. Again and again throughout the day and into the night the huge Jade River locks opened and closed as the survivors of Jutland limped through. Last of all came the dreadnought *Ostfriesland*, crippled by a mine in the early morning. Remaining alone at hazard was the desperately wounded *Seydlitz*, which lay grounded on a sandbank in Heligoland Bight while repair ships worked furiously—and, after 36 hours, managed to tow her into the Jade, stern first.

Scheer's homecoming, while Jellicoe was still toiling at sea, gave Germany ample opportunity to stake prior victory claims—with results, compounded by British blunders, that created a myth about Jutland that has never been wholly dispelled.

Even before his flagship anchored, Scheer had sent a congratulatory message to his fleet that concluded: *"Deutschland und unser Kaiser über alles!"*—"Germany and our Kaiser over all!" He followed that with a terse preliminary battle report to the Emperor, who promptly responded with glee tempered by caution: "I am proud of our mighty fleet, which has proved by this feat of arms that it is a match for a superior enemy." The German Admiralty was less reticent about asserting a positive advantage. As early as noon on that first postbattle day—Jellicoe was just then starting his journey home—the German Naval command issued its first official communiqué, announcing that "a series of heavy engagements developed between the Skagerrak and Horns Reef, which were successful for us." The communiqué went on to give a fairly accurate list of British losses—but without mentioning German casualties.

"Successful for us." The news was the headiest the German people had received in a distressingly long while. Within minutes, extras were on the streets and crowds jostled around kiosks and outside newspaper offices; above the entrance to Berlin's daily *Tageszeitung* a giant placard proclaimed, "Trafalgar Is Wiped Out!" On the city's lovely Unter den Linden boulevard, excited throngs waved German flags, and a heavy-booted soldier, fresh from the trenches, was cheered as he emerged from a shop carrying a small anchor he had bought to celebrate the occasion.

By nightfall such newspapers as the *Berliner Tageblatt*, the *8-Uhr*

Issued to commemorate the German Navy's demise, this diagram illustrates the positions taken by the various ships during the surrender to the Royal Navy at the Firth of Forth on November 21, 1918. The heading "Der Tag"—The Day— was a barb directed at the Germans, who used that term throughout the War to describe the glorious day when Germany would gain final victory over her enemies.

Abendblatt and the *Vorwärts* were using the words triumph, annihilation and extinction in headlines, and one editor gloated about "the arrogant presumption of the British 'rats' who left their safe hiding places, only to be trapped by German efficiency, heroism and determination."

Friday, June 2, was declared a national holiday and Sunday, June 4, a day of mourning for the honored dead, who so far as possible had been carried home to be laid to rest amid appropriate ceremony in the Naval Cemetery at Wilhelmshaven. On Monday the Kaiser paid the fleet a formal visit, extolling the titanic struggle at sea and closing with the words: "The British fleet was beaten!" Vice Admiral Scheer was promoted to full admiral and Rear Admiral von Hipper to vice admiral. Both received the famed "Blue Max," Germany's Order of Merit, the highest military honor. Hipper, moreover, was elevated to a Bavarian barony.

Poor Jellicoe. He had no mind whatever for such matters. As the Grand Fleet, its wireless silenced for security reasons, labored through heavy seas toward Scapa Flow, he was utterly unaware of the commotion caused by the German claims. And he was not in the least inclined to issue any claims of his own. Thursday, June 1, passed without any sort of battle report from Jellicoe. That evening the Reuters News Agency in Holland picked up the text of the original German communiqué—complete with the boasts of British ship losses—and sent it to London, where it was rushed by messenger to the Admiralty. There it was immediately, completely and understandably suppressed; the newspapers would get wind of the German claims soon enough.

The Admiralty did, however, signal Jellicoe at 9:20 on the evening of June 1, asking him to report British losses. Inexplicably, there was no request for even an estimate of German casualties. But it hardly mattered: Jellicoe, ensconced in the war room beneath the *Iron Duke*'s bridge, was far too preoccupied with the myriad details of nursing his fleet to safety to bother about tally sheets. He put aside for the moment the Admiralty's demand for a report.

In the vacuum of information, dark and dismal rumors of disaster quickly swept throughout England and Scotland. And when, at 9 o'clock on Friday morning, Beatty's battle-cruiser force moved wearily but proudly to anchor at Rosyth, the tars were astonished to be greeted by jeers and hisses from civilian dock workers.

Still without word from Jellicoe, the Admiralty, shortly after 10 o'clock that Friday morning, decided to wait no longer: in a move probably without parallel in the history of warfare, it released, verbatim and without comment, the enemy's victorious communiqué. Hardly had it done so than Jellicoe's report arrived. It was less than a help: in strict adherence to the Admiralty's urgings of the night before, Jellicoe listed only British losses—thereby in essence confirming German claims. He said virtually nothing of the damage inflicted by the Grand Fleet. And though he certainly did not admit defeat, neither did he assert victory.

That afternoon the best brains of the Admiralty—including Arthur Balfour, who had succeeded Churchill as First Lord in 1915, Admiral Sir Henry Jackson, the First Sea Lord, and Admiral Sir Henry Oliver, the Royal Navy's Chief of Staff—struggled to produce an official explana-

Dressed in mourning as a token of respect for the dead of Jutland, villagers from the Danish coastal town of Skagen surround the flower-laden graves of a German officer and five sailors washed ashore after the battle. The neutral Danes had the unenviable task of burying scores of Germans and Britons whose bodies were carried by the currents onto the peninsula's northwest shore.

tion. In the end, they gave forth a squeak. "On the afternoon of Wednesday, May 31," their communiqué began, "a naval engagement took place off the coast of Jutland. The British ships on which the brunt of the fighting fell were the Battle-Cruiser Fleet, and some cruisers and light cruisers supported by four fast battleships." The report named most of the British ships that had been sunk; German losses, unspecified, were described merely as "serious." Lacking any expression of triumph or disaster, the British press and public were left to assume the worst.

Even while the Admiralty officials were in the throes of composition, Jellicoe's dreadnoughts, all the more majestic because of the scars they bore, steamed slowly into their haven at Scapa Flow. Between the slopes of the Orkney Islands, dotted by placid flocks of sheep to the north and the desolate Scottish coast to the south, the mighty procession passed through the antisubmarine gate at Hoxa Sound and dropped anchor. About three hours after the Admiralty's feeble communiqué was released, Jellicoe reported to the Admiralty that the Grand Fleet was ready to sail once again into battle on four hours' notice. Obviously this was not the sound of a defeated fleet. Yet even this gallant declaration, when it circulated, could not lift the pervasive gloom that had settled on England. And Jellicoe, six hours after his return, still had not rendered an account of enemy losses. That evening, however, he did send the Admiralty three further reports conservatively stating German casualties.

The next day, June 3, was George V's 51st birthday, and Jellicoe sent his monarch a message of congratulations. The reply, though gracious, was soured by disappointment. "I mourn the loss of brave men, many of them personal friends of my own, who have fallen in their country's cause," wrote the King. "Yet even more do I regret that the German High Seas Fleet, in spite of its heavy losses, was enabled by the misty weather to evade the full consequences."

As for the press, which remained singularly uninformed about the actual events of Jutland, it was already full cry in pursuit of a scapegoat—and Jellicoe nicely fitted the role. The quiet, gray little man had always held himself remote from the press; he permitted journalists to visit Scapa Flow with vast reluctance and under close rein, and he steadfastly refused to permit them to accompany the fleet to sea. Now, since none of his dreadnoughts had been sunk (much less had they sunk enemy dreadnoughts), it seemed fair to assume Jellicoe had idled about the Jutland periphery while Beatty's battle cruisers had fought to the death. "Where was Jellicoe?" became an overnight editorial cliché.

Beatty, on the other hand, with his mastiff look, his rakish ways and his devil-may-care thirst for combat, was a natural hero. Besides, since Beatty had suffered by far the heaviest losses, in both ships and men, of any of the British or German forces at Jutland, it seemed eminently evident that he had borne the brunt of the battle while Jellicoe had presumably dawdled on the sidelines. Soon editors were writing admiringly of Beatty's "gallant Balaklava charge"—recalling the bravery, if not the monumental stupidity, of the charge of the Light Brigade at Balaklava. Jellicoe himself praised Beatty for his "fine qualities of gallant leadership, firm determination and correct strategic insight."

Less than a week after the roar of Jutland's gunfire had faded in the North Sea mist came another blow to the prestige of the Royal Navy. Horatio Herbert Lord Kitchener, hero of Omdurman and now Great Britain's Secretary of State for War, was on board the cruiser *Hampshire* on a mission to Russia when the ship struck a German mine off the Orkneys and sank, taking with it Kitchener and all but 12 of the 655-man crew.

Such things happen in wartime. But the British mood in June of 1916 was hardly one of understanding. Kitchener's life had been entrusted to the Royal Navy; the Royal Navy had failed to protect that life; taken in conjunction with Jutland, Kitchener's death meant that the Royal Navy was no longer to be fully trusted. Q.E.D.

Thus, through an unhappy sequence of events and by the massive confusions that followed Jutland, the island nation's faith in the absolute invincibility of its fleets, for so long the anchor of British policy throughout the world, was eroded beyond complete repair.

If war were only a matter of numbers, Jutland certainly gave the British reason for dismay and the Germans cause for celebration: the Grand Fleet suffered losses of 6,097 killed, 510 wounded and 14 ships totaling 111,000 tons sunk. Against this, the High Seas Fleet toll was 2,551 killed, 507 wounded and 11 ships of 62,000 tons sent to the bottom. Yet in strategic terms Jutland was a British victory. Simple arithmetic said

A rain-soaked London newsboy carries the grim placard announcing that Britain's Secretary for War, Lord Kitchener, has been lost after the cruiser Hampshire, carrying him on a mission to Russia, struck a German mine off the coast of Scotland on June 5, 1916. The area was thought to be so secure that Admiral Jellicoe remarked before the Hampshire sailed that he would "not hesitate to take the Grand Fleet by the same route."

that the British, who still had more than twice as many modern capital ships as the Germans, could outlast the enemy in a struggle of naval attrition. And they were outbuilding the Germans at a rate of 3 to 1.

And not only was the Grand Fleet left in unchallenged possession of the battlefield, but the dreadnoughts and battle cruisers of the High Seas Fleet had been driven into ports from which throughout the rest of the war they emerged but thrice, on brief excursions that amounted to little.

Scheer himself tacitly admitted that the Imperial Navy could not rely on its capital ships to win the war at sea. In a report summarizing the development of the battle, Scheer ominously concluded, "The German national spirit can be impressed on the world only through a High Seas Fleet directed against England. If, however, as an outcome of our present condition, we are not finally to be bled to death, full use must be made of the U-boat as a means of war so as to grip England's vital nerve." It remained for a New York newspaper to offer the bluntest and most perceptive explanation of the meaning of Jutland: "The German fleet has assaulted its jailer, but it is still in jail."

Yet the British were profoundly shaken by the force of the assault and the losses shown possible in a dreadnought action like Jutland. It was widely believed that the fleet, indeed the War, could have been lost in an afternoon. Churchill later described the transcendent importance Great Britain attached to its warships: "All our long history built up century after century, all our great affairs in every part of the globe, all the means of livelihood and safety of our faithful, industrious, active population depended upon them. Guard them well, admirals and captains, hardy tars and tall marines; guard them well and guide them true."

Guard them well the admirals were more than willing to do; loath to risk the Grand Fleet in another Jutland, the Navy command not only cut down on the number of North Sea sweeps by the Grand Fleet but restricted their range to no farther south than lat. 55.30° N. (about that of Alnwick in Northumberland) and no farther east than long. 4° E. (safely west of the Jutland waters). Thus, though the German capital ships stayed home, light cruisers, destroyers and especially submarines could and did make their way into the Atlantic with relative impunity to prey on merchant shipping. In May, the month Jutland was fought, British losses to U-boats for the year to date had amounted to 64,000 tons; by October the cumulative toll was up to a staggering 176,000 tons.

Partly in response to this frightful exaction and partly in delayed reaction to British dissatisfaction with Jutland, a little-noticed event occurred on the blustery afternoon of November 26, 1916. As the Grand Fleet approached Scapa after one of its limited patrols in the North Sea, the slight, inconspicuous figure of Admiral John Jellicoe appeared on the afterbridge of the Iron Duke. Even as he gazed at the long line of ships he had loved so well and husbanded so carefully, the flagship's wireless signaled, "Good luck." Then the Iron Duke fell out of formation and steamed toward Rosyth, where on the following day Jellicoe met with Arthur Balfour and accepted appointment as First Sea Lord. David Beatty would succeed him as Commander in Chief of the Grand Fleet.

The strong implication was that Jellicoe was out of place on the flagship of a fighting fleet and would do better behind a desk, applying his tidy mind to what had become the Royal Navy's most urgent mission: organizing a defense against the submarine onslaught. Jellicoe did his devoted best. In April 1917, two months after Germany began unrestricted submarine warfare (and thereby drew America into the conflict), Jellicoe instituted a convoy system. Recruited for escort duty were warships of the Grand Fleet—including, occasionally, even the dreadnoughts, now called to play a role their designers had never dreamed of. It worked: by the end of September, Allied losses to German U-boats mounted to 4.7 million tons, but for the rest of the year losses declined steadily. Jellicoe's convoy system meant salvation for the Allies.

But Jellicoe had never been much of a hand at delegating responsibility, and the strain of directing the antisubmarine war told on him to the point where his heavy burden, in the words of a contemporary commentator, "could not be further prolonged with justice to himself or advantage to the Service." On Christmas Eve, 1917, Jellicoe was, as always, working late when he was interrupted by a messenger: "A note has just come in for you, sir." The note informed the man who had commanded the last Grand Fleet action the Royal Navy would ever fight that he was being retired. His successor was Admiral Sir Rosslyn Wemyss, known to the fleet as "Rosy," who had distinguished himself at Gallipoli.

Meanwhile the fire-breathing Beatty, now bearing the responsibility of command of the Grand Fleet, had become a model of prudence. Early in 1918 he committed his caution to paper in a memo to the Admiralty Board: "The correct strategy of the Grand Fleet is no longer to endeavour to bring the enemy to action at any cost, but rather to contain him in his bases until the general situation becomes more favourable to us."

Jutland therefore had the effect of deflecting the Grand Fleet from the purpose for which it had been created—fighting. Yet the British warships, including the mighty dreadnoughts, were free to patrol at least a restricted area of the North Sea. Not so the capital ships of the High Seas Fleet, which remained cooped up in port while Scheer was concentrating on Germany's U-boat offensive. In the German fleet's idleness lay the kernel of revolution. As Scheer later wrote with rueful retrospection, "The best distraction would have been active warfare."

One result of the virtual embalming of the capital ships was that the ablest and most dedicated of the officers and enlisted men soon volunteered for service on destroyers and submarines, leaving aboard the dreadnoughts and battle cruisers a disproportionate share of the inept and the sullen. Moreover, as befitted their inactive status, the enlisted men on the capital ships were now given reduced and inferior rations—turnips, bread, herb tea and very little meat—while their officers' shore-side messes remained stocked with liquor, tobacco and tasty food.

On August 2, 1917, some 350 men aboard the dreadnought *Prinzregent Luitpold* refused to stand watch, went ashore and marched in protest through the streets of Wilhelmshaven. Then, their grievances aired, they reported back for duty—only to see their leaders arrested and court-martialed. Several were sentenced to long prison terms while two, Reichpietsch and Kobis by name, achieved martyrdom when they were taken to Cologne and executed by an Army firing squad.

Holding weights, German crewmen go through calisthenics on a dock in the fall of 1917, during the long period of idleness following the Battle of Jutland. Officers tried to keep the men in some semblance of decent physical condition, but such exercises only lowered morale because they intensified the hunger pangs induced by short rations.

The Navy's high command insisted that the outbreak had been inspired by Communist agitators. It seems far more likely that the sailors' contacts with revolutionary elements were a result of the mutiny rather than a cause. Among the few concessions wrung from the Imperial Navy was one allowing sailors to elect food committees to oversee the distribution of rations on each ship. These groups did attract revolutionaries from Berlin and led to the formation of secret sailors' councils modeled after those already springing up in the Russian Navy.

And so, below the decks of the German dreadnoughts and battle cruisers, rebellion simmered for more than a year. In August 1918 Scheer succeeded the ailing Admiral Henning von Holtzendorff as the Imperial Navy's Chief of Staff, and Hipper assumed command of the High Seas Fleet. As a condition of taking his new job, Scheer demanded that the Navy be removed entirely from the Kaiser's control. It was a gratuitous slap: in fact, the Kaiser had been exerting less and less influence. Changing from one adviser to another, and accepting the advice of none, he was becoming politically paralyzed. With Germany in the tormented twilight of its war effort, he had entered a condition described by a top aide as "Cloud Cuckoo Land." Although he would later mutter that "my Navy has deserted me very nicely," he now agreed to Scheer's mandate.

On October 5, 1918, a new German chancellor, Prince Maximilian of Baden, requested that United States President Woodrow Wilson arrange an armistice. At that point the Germans still hoped for a negotiated peace instead of terms dictated by victor to vanquished—and the British Navy command feared that the Germans might attempt to improve their bargaining position by demonstrating that the High Seas Fleet was still a formidable fighting force. Explained a British admiral: "The enemy must realise that some, at any rate, of his fleet will be demanded of him in the armistice and peace terms. They may as well try to inflict some losses on us before they lose the power altogether of doing so."

That was just what Scheer planned. On October 21, without telling the government or the Army command (much less the Kaiser), he sent orders to Hipper at Wilhelmshaven: "The High Seas Fleet is to be made ready for attack and battle with the British fleet." His Operation Plan 19 called for destroyers to raid shipping off the coast of Flanders and the Thames estuary while the main battle fleet gathered at the Schillig Roadstead anchorage. The marauding destroyers would attract the Grand Fleet and draw it toward Terschelling, a Dutch island some 70 miles from the Ems River estuary. There, after mines and 25 lurking submarines had begun to destroy the British force, the dreadnoughts and battle cruisers of the High Seas Fleet would steam onto the scene and finish the job.

It was a desperate scheme for a desperate time and, fortunately for just about everyone, it was never given a chance. By the evening of October 29 the High Seas Fleet had assembled, scheduled to sortie at midnight. Yet despite Scheer's extraordinary efforts to maintain secrecy, signal lights blinked through the portholes of the anchored warships as crews passed the most fantastic rumors from vessel to vessel: the German command had accepted a formal British challenge to meet for a duel unto death; the 69-year-old Admiral von Tirpitz had come out of retirement and would lead the fleet to its *Götterdämmerung*; the Kaiser was aboard the dreadnought *Baden*, ready to inspire the fleet to victory.

It hardly mattered which, if any, of the tales was true. By clear consensus, the crews were unwilling to risk their lives in the last battle of a war already lost. At 10 o'clock, while Hipper was in conference aboard his flagship, an officer burst in with the fearful news that men aboard three dreadnoughts—the *Markgraf*, *König* and *Kronprinz Wilhelm*—were refusing to obey their officers. By midnight, the planned time of departure, the men on another three dreadnoughts—the *Grosser Kurfürst*, *Thüringen* and *Helgoland*—were in open mutiny, with stokers threatening to extinguish the boiler fires if the ships tried to sail.

Hipper temporized, postponing the fleet movement for a day. But next morning, when the hands of the *Thüringen* were piped to duty, several hundred sailors holed up in a huge belowdecks compartment and refused to raise anchor. Late that afternoon, when Hipper again tried to put the fleet to sea, this time under the flimsy guise of conducting a "fleet exercise," sailors on the *Thüringen* and the *Helgoland* smashed the anchor windlasses while stokers dumped coals from the boilers onto the floor plates and hosed them down. Hipper canceled his exercise.

On the morning of October 31, Hipper finally took repressive measures that led to a ludicrous yet potentially fatal confrontation. The submarine *U-135* was sent to lay off the *Thüringen*, menacing the mutinous ship with its torpedo tubes. Two loyal destroyers came alongside

In a show of solidarity, members of the People's Marine Division, the self-proclaimed elite of the sailors' and workers' councils that fomented mutiny on German battleships, parade through Berlin in December 1918. Shortly after, the division participated in an abortive attempt to topple Germany's government and establish a Communist regime.

and tied up to the *Thüringen*, while a steamer moved to the dreadnought's port side and put 200 marines aboard. The mutineers fled into the forecastle, leaving the marines and loyal officers and seamen in control abovedecks. At that point, rebellious crewmen on the nearby *Helgoland* trained guns on the submarine and the destroyers—only to find themselves threatened in turn by the after gun turrets of the *Thüringen*. And there they stood, muzzle to muzzle at point-blank range, with nobody knowing quite what to do. The mutineers buckled first: those belowdecks in the *Thüringen* surrendered when warned that in two minutes the marines would start firing into the forecastle; those on the *Helgoland* followed their comrades' example. Some 350 *Thüringen* seamen and another 150 from the *Helgoland* were taken off under arrest.

Confident that the mutiny had now been suppressed, Hipper made a grievous mistake: he dispersed the fleet. Among the units sent to Kiel was the mutinous Squadron 3—the *König, Grosser Kurfürst, Kronprinz Wilhelm* and *Markgraf*. And in Kiel mutiny flared anew. On November 3 some 500 sailors left their ships and assembled in a park outside town. There dockyard workers and other civilians joined the sailors until they became a chanting mob of perhaps 20,000 men. As they marched on Kiel's naval jail, intent on freeing some prisoners, a loyal shore patrol fired into the surging crowd, leaving a score of dead and wounded on the cobblestones. Returning to their ships and barracks, the sailors broke into armories and small-arms lockers. With the weapons they seized, they won control of Kiel with little opposition on November 4.

The rebellion spread, and within two or three days red flags flew over Wilhelmshaven, Hamburg, Lübeck, Rendsberg, Bremerhaven and Rostock. On November 9 the Kaiser abdicated and the government gave way to a Socialist regime. And at 5 a.m. on Monday, November 11, 1918, an armistice was signed.

In the British Grand Fleet the news was received with joy and an order to splice the main brace—double the rum ration. Yet even as sirens shrieked, whistles shrilled and foghorns blared, even as men and officers danced on the decks of their warships, there was, as First Sea Lord Wemyss put it, a bittersweet "feeling of incompleteness." The senior officers of the Royal Navy, he said, regarded the Armistice as unworthy. "They had looked for a Trafalgar—for a defeat of the German Fleet in which they would have played a prominent and proud part. What they got was a victory far more crushing than any Trafalgar and with none of its attendant losses on our part—but also without any of the personal glory which would have been attached to the survivors."

Under the Armistice terms the bulk of the German High Seas Fleet was to be turned over to the British for internment pending a final peace settlement. Thus, on November 21, led by the British light cruiser *Cardiff* as guide, 11 German dreadnoughts, five battle cruisers, seven light cruisers and 49 destroyers steamed slowly through the mist toward their last rendezvous. The capital ships bore not war's honored scars but the rusty patches of disuse and disrepair. For this appropriately named Operation ZZ, Vice Admiral Ludwig von Reuter, who had led a scouting division at the Battle of Jutland, had been placed in command, but his authority was

Following the November 11, 1918, Armistice, German crews unload ammunition from warships soon to be surrendered and interned at Scapa Flow. The vessels had to be disarmed at breakneck speed to satisfy the Armistice term that "all ships designated for internment must be ready to leave German ports seven days after the signing."

doubtful at best. Before the fleet sailed, crews had elected a "Supreme Sailors' Soviet," which recognized Reuter as no more than a "technical adviser." The sailors had agreed to go only after the award of a bonus, and even then had had to be dissuaded from flying the red flag. Yet no matter the low estate into which the once-proud fleet had fallen, it remained beloved by many, and upon its departure Hipper wrote simply in his journal: "My heart is breaking."

As the Germans moved out of the mist into autumn sunshine, the entire Grand Fleet loomed on the North Sea horizon in war's full regalia. Such a force had never before gathered. It had left the Firth of Forth before dawn, 90,000 men on 370 warships, with more than 30 battleships, battle cruisers and cruisers. Beatty, in command, was taking no chances on treachery: the men were at action stations, the guns loaded.

Slowly, silently, led by the *Seydlitz*, then the *Derfflinger*, then the *Von der Tann*, all valiant veterans of Jutland, the High Seas Fleet in single line ahead passed through the British gauntlet, which was formed in two lines, six miles apart, and reached beyond sight into the distance. At a signal from Beatty, the Grand Fleet turned 180° together—the same maneuver by which Scheer had so mystified the British at Jutland—and swung round to escort the Germans into captivity.

As they watched their defeated enemy, many of the British felt a certain compassion. Ernle Chatfield, Beatty's flag captain at the Dogger

Bank and Jutland, was present as captain of the dreadnought *Royal Oak*. The surrender, he wrote, "was to many of us a highly painful if dramatic event. To see the great battleships coming into sight, their guns trained fore and aft; the battle cruisers, which had met us twice under such very different circumstances, creeping toward us as it were with their tails between their legs, gave one a very real feeling of disgust. Surely the spirit of all past seamen must be writhing in dismay over this tragedy."

If Beatty felt any such sentiment, he managed to conceal it admirably. As the fleets came to anchor in the Firth of Forth, a signal went out from the *Iron Duke*: "The German flag will be hauled down at sunset, and will not be hoisted again without permission."

Worse, far worse, was yet in store for the High Seas Fleet. After undergoing rigorous inspection at the Firth of Forth to be certain that ships and men were entirely disarmed, the fleet was taken to Scapa Flow for internment—and quarantine. Fearful that the disease of German revolution might infect British seamen, Royal Navy authorities refused to permit the Germans so much as to set foot on Scapa's shore, confining them instead to the echoing caverns of their ships, which daily grew more rusty and filthy. The British understandably refused to recognize the Sailors' Soviet and, except for providing Admiral von Reuter with newspapers, had only infrequent contact with the German commander.

Reuter's problems were legion. Each German ship was ruled by a committee, and Reuter's orders were carried out—or defied—according to a majority vote. He was forced to transfer to the light cruiser *Emden*—namesake of the famous raider which had been sunk in 1914—after the crew of the *Friedrich der Grosse* spitefully took to tromping about on the deck above his cabin at night so that he could not sleep. Yet as the Versailles negotiations dragged on, with the fate of the German fleet in the balance, Reuter evolved a plan to salvage some of his Navy's lost honor: if the opportunity arose, he would scuttle his ships.

In June 1919 the British unwittingly gave him the chance. Early that month, repatriation ships took most of the German seamen home, leaving skeleton complements of scarcely a dozen or so officers and men on each destroyer and about 80 on each battleship. Whether by Reuter's design or simply because the most rebellious sailors were also the most anxious to return to civilian life, those remaining were mostly loyal.

On June 17 Reuter sent a secret letter to his commanders, ordering them to scuttle their vessels in response to a certain signal from the flagship. The loyalists immediately began their preparations. "It was very thorough," recalled one of Reuter's ship commanders. "We set the sea cocks on a hair turning and lubricated them heavily. We placed large hammers beside any valves that, when knocked off, would allow the water to rush in."

Four days later, on a sunny Saturday morning, the British fleet weighed anchor and, led by Admiral Sir Sydney Fremantle on the *Revenge*, steamed blithely out to sea. Confident that the Germans were beyond causing trouble, Fremantle, commanding the watchdog squadron at Scapa Flow, had ordered a day of torpedo practice, leaving behind only two destroyers, seven trawlers and some picketboats.

At 11:20 a.m. Reuter's flagship signaled, "Paragraph 11. Acknowledge." On 70 ships throughout the huge harbor, German seamen rushed below and awaited the action order, which came within moments: "Condition Z—Scuttle!"

In a burst of long-pent energy, the Germans opened sea cocks, pried out bulkhead rivets, and smashed valves, pipes and condensers with sledges. "Once the valves and sea cocks were wrenched open," said Captain Hermann Cordes, commander of the German destroyer flotilla, "their keys and handles were thrown overboard, as were entire intake valves of the condensers. Now they could not be closed again—ever."

Aboard one of the remaining British trawlers, a civilian artist was sketching the dreadnought *Friedrich der Grosse* and, as he drew, noticed to his bewilderment that the great ship seemed to be settling into the water. On a weekend sightseeing boat that had been meandering about in the midst of the High Seas Fleet, some 200 British school children, hitherto preoccupied mostly with floating candy wrappers on Scapa's waters, now turned their excited attention to the sight of German sailors leaping into lifeboats and fleeing their ships as the remnants of German bands played "Deutschland über Alles."

In a shoreside office Admiral Joseph Strauss, an American officer on a liaison mission, looked out a window and exclaimed, "Good heavens! They're sinking!" Beside him a British admiral glanced at the spectacle and, in an unparalleled display of phlegm, replied, "Aren't they, now?" Then he turned back to his paper work.

Other witnesses were far less indifferent. "The scene beggared description," said one. "What an hour before had been a stately fleet, riding calmly at anchor, now became an array of reeling and rocking battleships whose doom was written in their movements. Here a destroyer would disappear amid a cloud of steam; there a battleship would take her last plunge and disappear in a tumult of spray."

Alerted at last, the Grand Fleet came boiling back—too late. At 12:16 p.m. the *Friedrich der Grosse*, the proud dreadnought that had served as Scheer's flagship at Jutland, rolled over and sank. "The English Navy behaved as though insane," German Captain Cordes said later. "Sailors, engineers, officers and even civilian personnel with them shrieked and bellowed in a crazy discord." British warships and picketboats fired upon German picketboats under white flags, killing 10 and wounding 21. In one disgraceful episode a German sailor who had been aboard a British ship at the time of the scuttling was executed on the spot.

Even as they vented their rage, the British worked madly to tow ashore, beach and thereby save the sinking ships; they succeeded with one dreadnought, the *Baden*, four light cruisers, the *Emden*, *Franfurt*, *Bremse* and *Nürnberg*, and 18 destroyers. But Captain Cordes had the satisfaction of watching two British tugs struggle futilely to save the *Hindenburg*: with great effort they managed to right her and take her in tow—only to see her list again and go under. According to a German officer, "It was a marvelous sight. All over the vast bay, ships were in various stages of sinking. Everywhere cutters, whalers and rafts were being manned or were pulling or drifting away, and the British guard destroyers and drifters were hurrying about, giving the general alarm with their sirens. In the intervals, sounds of firings were to be heard."

Their faces reflecting the euphoria of victory, British gunners line the deck of a warship as they watch the German fleet surrendering in the North Sea on November 21, 1918. Grand Fleet Commander Beatty ordered the gas masks and combat garb in the event there was last-minute German treachery.

Before the dismal day was done, 51 ships, including 10 dreadnoughts and five battle cruisers, totaling nearly 500,000 tons—more than twice the toll borne by both sides at Jutland—lay on Scapa's bottom.

Admiral Sydney Fremantle was in a fine fury. Assembling all German officers on the deck of the *Revenge*, he insisted, with a logic that might have been laughable under different circumstances, that the German "vessels were resting here as a sort of good will from the German government until peace has been signed." Germany's Admiral von Reuter came in for a personal tongue-lashing: "I would like to express my indignation at the deed which you have perpetrated and which was that of a traitor."

Reuter and 1,860 men were taken ashore as prisoners of war, and the Admiralty twice attempted to bring the German commander to trial for the scuttling. Both times, the Judge Advocate of the Grand Fleet ruled that trying him was impossible: under the Armistice and until a peace treaty was signed, the High Seas Fleet had been interned, not surrendered—and in a legal sense, Reuter had merely destroyed property still belonging to his own government. To the British the fact that Reuter was beyond reach of legal reprisal made his act all the more frustrating: newspapers freely and fiercely used such adjectives as dishonorable, low, vile, treacherous and scandalous, and *Punch* carried a cartoon with the caption "Germany expects that every man this day will do the dirty."

Yet as days and weeks passed, a curious metamorphosis set in. One

The scuttling of the German fleet at Scapa Flow, recorded in these melancholy photographs, sent 15 capital ships and 36 other vessels to the bottom. The most valuable ships lost were the dreadnoughts, including the Bayern (inset, left) and an unidentified Kaiser-class vessel (bottom). The battle cruiser Derfflinger (top right) sank in three hours, while her sister ship the Hindenburg (inset, right) stayed afloat for five hours. The British beached some ships, like the light cruiser Frankfurt (top, far left), but had less success with the destroyers (top, near left), many so securely anchored that they could not be towed.

newspaper on reflection described the scuttling as "the only plucky and justifiable thing the Germans have done in the war." Once his initial choler had cooled, even Admiral Fremantle admitted privately that "I could not resist feeling some sympathy for von Reuter, who had preserved his dignity when placed against his will in a highly unpleasant and invidious position."

First Sea Lord Wemyss perceived the scuttling within the context of a problem posed for Britain by the peace treaty itself: the treaty required that most German warships be surrendered to the Allies and Associated Powers; it overlooked the subsequent division of the spoils, about which the Allies were already squabbling. "I look upon the sinking as a real blessing," Wemyss wrote in his diary. "It disposes of the thorny question of the distribution of the German ships. When the facts become known, everybody will probably think, like me, 'Thank the Lord.' "

As for German reaction, almost everyone could agree with Admiral von Hipper in his hope that the scuttling at Scapa showed a glowing ember "of the good old spirit." And when, in January 1920, the survivors of Scapa Flow were returned to Germany, they were hailed as heroes.

During 51 cruel months, dreadnoughts had fought dreadnoughts for less than an hour, and in that brief time at Jutland they had inflicted heavy punishment without mortal wound. The dreadnoughts had qualities no other weapon could match: a fierce, purposeful beauty, an air of majesty, pride and pageantry that inspired the hopes of men and of nations. Yet they were so precious, in terms of both cost and national prestige, that those who had them were unwilling to lose them. Created to control the seas through mobility and power, they became a force for static deterrence: just as the Grand Fleet had kept the High Seas Fleet penned in the Jade, so the German presence had fixed the British position.

After the War many of the magnificent ships were broken up under the terms of the Naval Disarmament Treaty of 1922. Even their formidable name fell into disuse; those that remained were, as in predreadnought days, called battleships. In the 1930s, as Europe fell under Hitler's gathering storm cloud and as the Japanese moved aggressively to fulfill a dream of empire, the disarmament treaty was scrapped and new, infinitely greater and more powerful battleships were built to join the remnants of the old fleet. (Britain's *Barham*, *Warspite*, *Royal Oak*, *Malaya* and *Revenge* were still in service.) Yet none of these vessels ever fought in the great cataclysmic action for which they were designed. There was no World War II Trafalgar. The battleships were mainly useful in shore bombardment, and as antiaircraft escorts in carrier task forces— and to an appalling degree they were destroyed by air power. To two uncommon men on opposite sides of the Atlantic—both dead before World War II began—that fate had long been writ.

Britain's Jacky Fisher, considered quite mad, had outlived World War I. In the darkening corridor of his sanity, the Lear of the rose garden had moments of frightful clarity. Just as he had once cried of Britain's aging predreadnought fleet, "Scrap the lot!" shortly before he died in 1920 he demanded, "Why keep any of the present lot? All you want is the present naval side of the air force—that's the future navy!"

In the United States, Army Brigadier General William "Billy" Mitchell, having commanded the fledgling American air arm in France during World War I, was obsessed with the idea that land-based air power could "almost make navies useless on the surface of the water." This, understandably, failed to endear him to the American or any other navy, and Mitchell's own infantry-minded Army superiors were hardly more enthusiastic about his theory. "The General Staff knows as much about air as a hog does about skating," he said—and for such statements he was court-martialed and cashiered in 1925. But first, he had his day of proof.

Mitchell's father had been a U.S. Senator, and the son had many friends and acquaintances in Congress. He lobbied them shamelessly to force the Navy to furnish an old battleship to serve as a target so he could prove the efficacy of airborne bombs. Finally, under heavy pressure, the Navy agreed. Selected as victim was the 27,000-ton German dreadnought *Ostfriesland*, built in 1911, the survivor of 18 British gunfire hits and a mine explosion at Jutland. She had been one of eight dreadnoughts left to the Germans when the bulk of the fleet was interned at Scapa Flow, and thus had escaped scuttling. After the War she had been surrendered to the Allies, and had been allotted to the United States.

On July 20, 1921, a stormy day with a northeast wind gusting to 30 knots, the *Ostfriesland* lay anchored amid hard-running whitecaps about 65 miles off Virginia's Cape Charles. Six twin-engined Martin MB-2 bombers, each armed with two 600-pound bombs, were followed by a number of Navy F5L seaplanes, each carrying two 550-pound bombs. As they attacked the *Ostfriesland*, Billy Mitchell circled the scene in an old two-seater DH-4B observation plane. To him the target ship appeared as "a grim old bulldog. She was sullen and dark and we knew we had a tough nut to crack." A tough nut indeed: out of 19 bombs dropped, the Army scored two hits and the Navy three; but Navy umpires who went aboard reported the ship "absolutely intact."

In fact, the *Ostfriesland* had settled a few feet at the stern by next day, when Mitchell's bombers tried again. This time they dropped five 1,100-pound bombs, scoring three hits. The umpires found heavy damage but ruled that the ship was "still in action." Aboard the observation ships carrying ranking military men, government officials and the press, a Navy captain exulted: "By Jove, they're not going to sink this ship."

But they were. Shortly after noon the Martins, given one last chance, attacked again—with 2,000-pound bombs. The first two missed, but at 12:21 a third struck the point of the bow, tearing a gaping hole; after another apparent hit forward, the fifth bomb landed in the water near the stern, lifting the wounded ship into the air. To one observer she looked like "some immense, round, helpless sea animal." At 12:38 the *Ostfriesland* turned on her beam-ends and slipped beneath the surface.

Admirals and captains wept openly. And a newspaper reporter felt that he had witnessed "the end of an era which began when Rome crossed the high seas and smote Carthage." That was nonsense, of course. Navies would continue to exist, and even grow in importance. But they would be navies in which the greatest striking forces were planes, transported on board giant aircraft carriers. The day of the superb dreadnought as the most feared of the world's naval weapons was done.

Her midships shrouded in the blast of an aerial bomb, the surrendered German dreadnought Ostfriesland endures her final humiliation, as a guinea pig for the U.S. Army Air Service off the coast of Virginia on July 20, 1921. The bombing, designed to test U.S. Brigadier General Billy Mitchell's gospel of the superiority of air power, ended the next day, after numerous hits, when the great warship turned bottom up and sank.

Bibliography

Bacon, R. H., *The Life of Lord Fisher of Kilverstone*, 2 vols. Hodder and Stoughton, 1929.

Barnett, Correlli, *The Swordbearers*. Indiana University Press, 1975.

Batchelor, John, and Antony Preston, *Battleships 1856-1919*. Phoebus, 1977.

Bennett, Geoffrey:
Coronel and the Falklands. Batsford, 1962.
Naval Battles of the First World War. Scribner's, 1968.

Campbell, N. J. M., *Battle Cruisers*. Conway Maritime Press, 1978.

Chalmers, W. S., *The Life and Letters of David, Earl Beatty*. Hodder and Stoughton, 1951.

Churchill, Winston S., *The World Crisis*, 3 vols. Scribner's, 1927.

Corbett, Julian S., *History of the Great War Based on Official Documents: Naval Operations*, 5 vols. Longmans, Green, 1920-1931.

Costello, John, and Terry Hughes, *Jutland 1916*. Holt, Rinehart and Winston, 1976.

Davis, Burke, *The Billy Mitchell Affair*. Random House, 1967.

Fawcett, H. W., and G. W. W. Hooper, *The Fighting at Jutland*. Macmillan, 1921.

Fisher, John Arbuthnot, *Memories and Records*, 2 vols. George H. Doran, 1920.

Gibson, Langhorne, and J. E. T. Harper, *The Riddle of Jutland: An Authentic History*. Coward-McCann, 1934.

Hansen, Hans Jürgen, *The Ships of the German Fleets 1848-1945*. Arco, 1973.

Hase, Georg von, *Kiel and Jutland*. E. P. Dutton, 1922.

Hoehling, A. A., *The Great War at Sea: A History of Naval Action 1914-18*. Arthur Barker, 1965.

Hough, Richard, *Dreadnought*. Macmillan, 1975.

Howarth, David:
"Fighting Admiral Fisher Scuppers the 'Fossil' Navy," *The British Empire*, No. 65, TIME-LIFE International, 1973.
Sovereign of the Seas: The Story of Britain and the Sea. Atheneum, 1974.

Hoyt, Edwin P., *The Last Cruise of the Emden*. Macmillan, 1966.

Jane, Fred T., ed., *Jane's Fighting Ships 1914*. Arco, 1969.

Jellicoe, John Rushworth, *The Grand Fleet: 1914-1916*. George H. Doran, 1919.

Legg, Stuart, *Jutland*. John Day, 1967.

Mackay, Ruddock F., *Fisher of Kilverstone*. Clarendon Press, 1973.

Marder, Arthur J:
The Anatomy of British Sea Power. Octagon Books, 1976.
Fear God and Dread Nought, 3 vols.

Jonathan Cape, 1952-1959.
From the Dreadnought to Scapa Flow, 5 vols. Oxford University Press, 1961-1970.

Morris, James, *Pax Britannica: The Climax of an Empire*. Harcourt, Brace & World, 1968.

Padfield, Peter, *The Great Naval Race*. Hart-Davis, MacGibbon, 1974.

Parkes, Oscar, *British Battleships*. Archon Books, 1970.

Reynolds, Clark G., *Command of the Sea*. Robert Hale, 1974.

Ruge, Friedrich, *Scapa Flow, 1919*. United States Naval Institute, 1973.

Scheer, Reinhard, *Germany's High Sea Fleet in the World War*. Peter Smith, 1934.

Steinberg, Jonathan, *Yesterday's Deterrent*. Macmillan, 1965.

Tirpitz, Alfred von, *My Memoirs*, 2 vols. Hurst & Blackett, n.d.

Trotter, Wilfrid Pym, *The Royal Navy in Old Photographs*. Naval Institute Press, 1975.

Waldeyer-Hartz, Hugo von, *Admiral von Hipper*. Rich & Cowan, 1933.

Woodward, E. L., *Great Britain and the German Navy*. Frank Cass, 1964.

Young, Filson, *With the Battle Cruisers*. Cassell, 1921.

Picture Credits

dence Loudon, Kent; Imperial War Museum, London. 127: Chart by Bill Hezlep. 130, 131: Imperial War Museum, London. 132, 133: Charts by Bill Hezlep. 134, 135: Foto Drüppel, Wilhelmshaven. 136: Library of Congress. 137, 139: Charts by Bill Hezlep. 141: Bundesarchiv, Koblenz. 142, 143: Foto-Lassen, courtesy Marine-Schule, Mürwik, Aula. 144, 145: Erich Lessing from Magnum, courtesy Dr. Bernartz Collection, Deutsches Schiffahrtsmuseum, Bremerhaven. 146, 147: Erich Lessing from Magnum. 148-151: Fischer-Daber, courtesy Dr. Bernartz Collection, Deutsches Schiffahrtsmuseum, Bremerhaven. 152: Derek Bayes, courtesy Rear Admiral Morgan-Giles, Norfolk. 155: Süddeutscher Verlag, Bilderdienst, Munich. 157: The Mansell Collection, London. 158-162: Süddeutscher Verlag, Bilderdienst, Munich. 165: National Archives. 166, 167: Top, Imperial War Museum (2); Bibliothek für Zeitgeschichte, Stuttgart, center, Ullstein Bilderdienst, Berlin; Süddeutscher Verlag, Bilderdienst, Munich, bottom, Imperial War Museum, London. 170, 171: U.S. Air Force.

Acknowledgments

The index for this book was prepared by Gale Partoyan. The editors wish to thank the following: John Batchelor, artist, and Antony Preston, consultant (pages 45-48, 104-105), Bill Hezlep, artist (pages 102-103, 110-111, 121, 127, 132-133, 137, 139), Peter McGinn, artist (end-paper maps), and Lloyd K. Townsend, artist, and Antony Preston, consultant (pages 92-99).

The editors also wish to thank: In Germany: Berlin—Dr. Roland Klemig, Heidi Klein, Bildarchiv Preussischer Kulturbesitz, and Axel Schulz, Ullstein Bilderdienst; Bremerhaven—Arnold Kludas; Cologne—Dr. Hanswilly Bernartz; Dresden—Konteradmiral Johannes Streubel, Armeemuseum der DDR; Flensburg—Franz Hahn, Marineschule Mürwik; Freiburg—Dr. Gert Sandhofer, Bundesarchiv, Militärarchiv; Karlsruhe—Rolf Liedke; Koblenz—Dr. Matthias Haupt, Bundesarchiv; München—Ulrich Frodien, Süddeutscher Verlag; Nürnberg—Dr. Lydia Bayer, Spielzeug Museum; Rastatt—Ulrich Schiers, Henning Volle, Wehrgeschichtliches Museum; Rellingen—Dr. Jürgen Meyer; Stuttgart—Professor Jürgen Rohwer, Bibliothek für Zeitgeschichte; Wasser-und Schiffahrtsamt Kiel-Holtenau—Karl-Dieter Jäger. In France: Paris—Denise Chaussegroux, Hervé Cras, Marjolaine Mathikine, Musée de la Marine. In the United Kingdom: London—Stephen Howarth; James Lucas and E. C. Hine, Department of Photographs, T. C. Charman and George Clout, Department of Printed Books, Miss D. M. Condell, Department of Exhibits and Firearms, J. O. Simmonds, Art Department, Imperial War Museum; Mrs. J. E. Tucker, Roger Quarm and David Taylor, Picture Department, David Lyon, Draught Room, Dr. R. J. B. Knight, Department of Manuscripts, Miss P. Blackett and T. H. Wilson, Department of Weapons and Antiquities, A. W. H. Pearsall, Historical Section, Joan Moore, Photographic Services, National Maritime Museum; Marjorie Willis, Radio Times Hulton Picture Library; Wilfred Pym Trotter; Dartmouth—R. J. Kennell, Royal Naval College; Portsmouth—Colin White, Assistant Curator, Nicola Fraser, Royal Naval Museum; Thetford, Norfolk—Lord Fisher.

The editors also wish to thank: In the United States: Washington, D.C.—Tobias Philbin, Defense Intelligence Agency; Jerry L. Kearns, Head, Reference Section, Sam Daniel, Reference Librarian, Prints and Photographs, Elena Millie, Curator of Posters, Library of Congress; William Leary, Still Pictures, James Trimble, Bureau of Ships, National Archives; John C. Reilly Jr., Ships History, Charles R. Haberlein Jr. and Agnes F. Hoover, Photographic Section, U.S. Naval Historical Center; John Vajda, U.S. Navy Library; Alexandria, Virginia—Kenneth Dillon; Commander Timothy Goetz, R.N., and Commander T. H. S. Haigh, R.N., Office of the British Naval Attaché; Arlington, Virginia—Dana Bell, Archives Technician, U.S. Air Force Still Photographic Section; Half Moon Bay, California—Janet Zich.

A particularly valuable source of information and quotations was From the Dreadnought to Scapa Flow by Arthur J. Marder, Oxford University Press, 1961-1970, © Arthur J. Marder, 1961. Charts of the Battle of Jutland, © Oxford University Press, 1966, redrawn by permission of the publisher. Other valuable sources for quotations were The Fighting at Jutland by H. W. Fawcett and G. W. W. Hooper, Macmillan, 1921, and Kiel and Jutland by Georg von Hase, E. P. Dutton, 1922.

Index

Printed in U.S.A.

THE DREADNOUGHTS

SHETLAND ISLANDS

ORKNEY ISLANDS

Hoxa Sound — Scapa Flow

Moray Firth

Cromarty

Kinnairds Head

HEBRIDES

SCOTLAND

LONG FORTIES

NORTH ATLANTIC OCEAN

Clydebank
Glasgow
Rosyth
Firth of Forth
Leith
Edinburgh

54° N.

Lough Swilly

Alnwick

GREAT BRITAIN

Hartlepool

DOGGER BA

IRELAND

IRISH SEA

Whitby

Scarborough

BATTLE OF
THE DOGGER BA
January 24, 191

52° N.

NORT

ENGLAND

WALES

Great Yarmouth
Lowestoft

Shotley Barracks
Harwich

London
Greenwich

Thames Estuary

Hook
Holla

50° N.

Dover

Strait of Dover

Ostend

BELGIU

Dartmouth

Portland
Harbor

Osborne
Portsmouth

Plymouth

Isle of
Wight
Spithead

FLANDERS

ENGLISH CHANNEL

FRANCE

NAVAL REVIEW, June 26, 1897

8° W.   6° W.   4° W.   2° W.   0°   2° E.   4° E.